Women and Human Rights

Women and Human Rights

Bharti Satsangi

RANDOM PUBLICATIONS
NEW DELHI (INDIA)

Women and Human Rights

ISBN 978-93-5111-511-3

Published in 2015 in India by

RANDOM PUBLICATIONS

4376-A/4B, Gali Murari Lal, Ansari Road
New Delhi-110 002
Phone : +9111-43580356, 011-23289044, 011-43142548
e-mail: sales@randompublications.com,
info@randompublications.com, randomexports@gmail.com

Reprinted 2025

Type Setting by : Friends Media, Delhi-110089
Printed at : Replika Press Pvt. Ltd.

Preface

Women's rights are the rights and entitlements claimed for women and girls of many societies worldwide. In some places these rights are institutionalized or supported by law, local custom, and behaviour, whereas in others they may be ignored or suppressed. They differ from broader notions of human rights through claims of an inherent historical and traditional bias against the exercise of rights by women and girls in favour of men and boys.

Issues commonly associated with notions of women's rights include, though are not limited to, the right: to bodily integrity and autonomy; to vote (suffrage); to hold public office; to work; to fair wages or equal pay; to own property; to education; to serve in the military or be conscripted; to enter into legal contracts; and to have marital, parental and religious rights.

Numerous international and regional instruments have drawn attention to gender-related dimensions of human rights issues, the most important being the UN Convention on the Elimination of All Forms of Discrimination against Women (CEDAW), adopted in 1979. In 1993, 45 years after the Universal Declaration of Human Rights was adopted, and eight years after CEDAW entered into force, the UN World Conference on Human Rights in Vienna confirmed that women's rights were human rights. That this statement was even necessary is striking – women's status as human beings entitled to rights should have never been in doubt.

Women and Human Rights is a comprehensive book which provides detailed information and insight into the complex issues of international human rights and the laws and customs that specifically impact women in countries all over the world. The book examines women's civil, political, social, economic, and cultural rights, their right to be free from slavery and sex trafficking; the rights of women with disabilities; and the right of women to be free from female infanticide, violence and torture. It will be a useful book for courses in international human rights and women and the law.

Author

Contents

1

Women's Human Rights: An Overview

The term "women's human rights" and the set of practices that accompanies its use are the continuously evolving product of an international movement to improve the status of women. In the 1980s and 1990s, women's movements around the world formed networks and coalitions to give greater visibility both to the problems that women face every day and to the centrality of women's experiences in economic, social, political and environmental issues. In the evolution of what is becoming a global women's movement, the term "women's human rights" has served as a locus for praxis, that is, for the development of political strategies shaped by the interaction between analytical insights and concrete political practices. Further, the critical tools, the concerted activism, and the broad-based international networks that have grown up around movements for women's human rights have become a vehicle for women to develop the political skills necessary for the twenty-first century.

The concept of women's human rights owes its success and the proliferation of its use to the fact that it is simultaneously prosaic and revolutionary. On the one hand, the idea of women's human rights makes common sense. It declares, quite simply, that as human beings women have human rights. Anyone would find her or himself hard-pressed to publicly make and defend the contrary argument that women are not human. So in many ways, the claim that women have human rights seems quite ordinary. On the other hand, "women's human rights" is a revolutionary notion. This radical reclamation of humanity and the corollary insistence that women's rights are human rights have profound transformative potential. The incorporation of women's perspectives and lives into human rights standards and practice forces recognition of the dismal failure of countries worldwide to accord women the human dignity and respect that they deserve-simply as human beings. A woman's human rights framework equips women with a way to define, analyze, and articulate their experiences of violence, degradation, and marginality. Finally, and very importantly, the idea of women's human rights provides a common framework for developing a vast array of visions and concrete strategies for change.

Women's rights are the rights and entitlements claimed for women and girls of many societies worldwide. In some places these rights are institutionalized or supported by law, local custom, and behaviour, whereas in others they may be ignored or suppressed. They differ from broader notions of human rights through claims of an inherent historical and traditional bias against the exercise of rights by women and girls in favour of men and boys.Issues commonly associated with notions of women's rights include, though are not limited to, the right: to bodily integrity and autonomy; to vote (suffrage); to hold public office; to work; to fair wages or equal pay; to own property; to education; to serve in the military or be conscripted; to enter into legal contracts; and to have marital, parental and religious rights.

A Short History of Human Rights

The *Universal Declaration of Human Rights* adopted by the United Nations General Assembly in 1948 outlines what is considered in this century to be the fundamental consensus on the human rights of all people in relation to such matters as security of person, slavery, torture, protection of the law, freedom of movement & speech, religion, and assembly, and rights to social security, work, health, education, culture, & citizenship. It clearly stipulates that these human rights apply to all equally "without distinction of any kind such as race, color, sex, language... or other status" (Art.2). Obviously, then, the human rights delineated by the Universal Declaration are to be understood as applying to women. However, tradition, prejudice, social, economic and political interests have combined to exclude women from prevailing definitions of "general" human rights and to relegate women to secondary and/or "special interest" status within human rights considerations. This marginalisation of women in the world of human rights has been a reflection of gender inequity in the world at large and has also had a formidable impact on women's lives. It has contributed to the perpetuation, and indeed the condoning, of women's subordinate status. It has limited the scope of what was seen as governmental responsibility, and thus has made the process of seeking redress for human rights violations disproportionately difficult for women and in many cases outright impossible.

The division between the so-called "public" has compounded the difficulties posed by women's peripheral status within international human rights mechanisms and organizations and "private" spheres prevalent in so many societies. The pervasive division of life into "public" and "private" spheres has its roots in the desire to limit the jurisdiction of the government. In many countries, this has meant that what individuals do in the "public" sphere is subject to regulation, while activities taking place in the "private" sphere are thought to be exempt from governmental scrutiny. Since this "public" sphere is seen as the focus of interaction between state actors and citizens, abuses of that relationship have been the focus of international human rights advocacy. Of course, the status of citizen has often been exclusionary, formally or informally entailing gender, racial and socio-economic bias and privileges. Thus, for those citizens-primarily men-who predominate in public and governmental realms and who enjoy gender, racial and economic privilege, the issues of primary concern have tended to be those abuses to which they are most vulnerable-abuses of civil and political aspects of human rights such as the violation of the right to speech, arbitrary detention, torture during imprisonment, and summary execution.

While women have been able to invoke international human rights machinery when they have found themselves in such situations, some of their specifically gender experiences of such human rights abuse-for example, rape in detention-have not been visible within the prevailing definitions of abuse. This is because women have traditionally been relegated to the "private" sphere of the home and family; the typical citizen has been portrayed as male, and thus the dominant notions of human rights abuse have implicitly had a man as their archetype. A major effect of the gender nature of the public/private split is that human rights violations of women that occur between "private" individuals have been made invisible and deemed to be beyond the purview of the state. It is particularly important to note that gender is a significant factor in the decisions of governments to intervene in the so-called private sphere to prosecute human rights violations. For example, many activities that take place in the private sphere, such as murder between siblings or the systematic enslavement African peoples in the Americas, are subject to government censure internationally. However, governments overlook much of what happens to women at the hands of men and male family members, for example domestic violence or confinement, even when there are laws against such abuse. Thus, abuses done to women in the name of family, religion, and culture have been hidden by the sanctity of the so-called private sphere, and perpetrators of such human rights violations have enjoyed immunity from accountability for their actions.

The historical emphasis on human rights abuses in the public sphere and the concomitant neglect of the human rights of women were exacerbated by the politics of the Cold War. The United Nations' human rights treaties and mechanisms developed after the horrors of World War II and consolidated during the Cold War. The purpose of many human rights organizations that developed along with them was to monitor the treatment of citizens by their governments and to ensure respect for citizens' human rights as they worked for democratic governance. As positions polarized during the Cold War, western governments attributed priority to civil and political rights, which they believed were integral to a prosperous free market economy. Meanwhile, the socio-economic rights to work, shelter, and health, for example, became identified with the socialist bloc and were thus suspect to many in the West. Thus, human rights bodies dominated by western conceptions of human rights priorities, focused on violations within the civil and political realm-the "public" sphere. So, in addition to the obstacles for women posed by the split between so-called public and private spheres, the predominance of civil and political rights within human rights organizations eclipsed the ways in which women often do not enjoy the social and economic conditions that make possible the exercise of civil and political rights and participation in public life.

The Concept of Women's Human Rights

During the United Nations Decade for Women (1976-1985), women from many geographical, racial, religious, cultural, and class backgrounds took up organizing to improve the status of women. The United Nations-sponsored women's conferences, which took place in Mexico City in 1975, Copenhagen in 1980, and Nairobi in 1985, were convened to evaluate the status of women and to formulate strategies for women's advancement.

These conferences were critical venues at which women came together, debated their differences and discovered their commonalties, and gradually began learning to bridge differences to create a global movement. In the late eighties and early nineties, women in diverse countries took up the human rights framework and began developing the analytic and political tools that together constitute the ideas and practices of women's human rights.

Taking up the human rights framework has involved a double shift in thinking about human rights and talking about women's lives. Put quite simply, it has entailed examining the human rights framework through a gender lens, and describing women's lives through a human rights framework. In looking at the human rights framework from women's perspectives, women have shown how current human rights definitions and practices fail to account for the ways in which already recognized human rights abuses often affect women differently because of their gender. This approach acknowledges the importance of the existing concepts and activities, but also points out that there are dimensions within these received definitions that are gender-specific and that need to be addressed if the mechanisms, programs, and the human rights framework itself are to include and reflect the experiences of the female half of the world's population.

When people utilize the human rights framework to articulate the vast array of human rights abuses that women face, they bring clarifying analyses and powerful tools to bear on women's experiences. This strategy has been pivotal in efforts to draw attention to human rights that are specific to women that heretofore have been seen as women's rights but not recognized as "human" rights. Take, for example, the issue of violence against women. The Universal Declaration states: "No one shall be subject to torture or to cruel, inhuman or degrading treatment or punishment." This formulation provides a vocabulary for women to define and articulate experiences of violence such as rape, sexual terrorism and domestic violence as violations of the human right not to be subject to torture or to cruel, inhuman or degrading treatment or punishment. The recognition of such issues as human rights abuses raises the level of expectation about what can and should be done about them. This definition of violence against women in terms of human rights establishes unequivocally that states are responsible for such abuse. It also raises questions about how to hold governments accountable for their indifference in such situations and what sorts of mechanisms are needed to expedite the process of redress.

History of Women's Rights

According to Dr. Jamal A. Badawin "the status which women reached during the present era was not achieved due to the kindness of men or due to natural progress. It was rather achieved through a long struggle and sacrifice on woman's part and only when society needed her contribution and work, more especial!; during the two world wars, and due to the escalation of technological change."

Ancient Civilisations

In ancient India, women are believed to have enjoyed equal status with men in all fields of life. Ancient Hindu scriptures describe a good wife as follows "a woman whose mind, speech and body are kept in subjection, acquires high renown in this world, and, in the next, the same abode with her husband." In ancient Athens women were always minors and subject to a male, such as their father, brother or some other male kin. A women's consent in marriage was not generally thought to be necessary and women were obliged to submit to the wishes of her parents or husband. Ancient Rome subject all legitimate children, regardless of age or sex to the authority of their Pater Familias while he lived, and they would only acquire any legal independence when he died. The Pater Familias could grant any of his children or slaves a Peculium, but that belonged to him and they were merely allowed to use it. All transactions made by a child in power regardless of age or sex had to be directly approved of by their Pater Familias. All children inherited equally from their Pater Familias regardless of age or sex, by the Imperial Period of Roman history even bastards were included as intestate heirs. Early in the Republic women were subject to Manus Marriage, but the custom died out by the Late Republic in favor of marriage without Manus which did not grant the husband any rights over his wife. When married without Manus a woman was not only free of her husbands legal authority, but could divorce him as she pleased without any reason required. Women in Ancient Rome when no longer under the control of their Pater Familias could and did contract, work for wages (usually without many other options), own property, and perform some (but not all) legal functions.

Under Islamic Rule

Efforts to improve the status of women in Islam occurred during the early reforms under Islam between 610 and 661, when Arab women were given greater rights in marriage, divorce and inheritance. In 622 the Constitution of Medina was drafted by the Islamic prophet Muhammad, outlining many of Muhammad's early reforms under Islam, including an improved legal status for women in Islam, who were generally given greater rights than women in pre-Islamic Arabia and medieval Europe. Women were not accorded with such legal status in other cultures until centuries later. Indeed according to Professor William Montgomery Watt, when seen in such historical context, Muhammad "can be seen as a figure who testified on behalf of women's rights."

The general improvement of the status of Arab women included prohibition of female infanticide and recognizing women's full personhood. "The dowry, previously regarded as a bride-price paid to the father, became a nuptial gift retained by the wife as part of her personal property." Under Islamic law, marriage was no longer viewed as a "status" but rather as a "contract", in which the woman's consent was imperative. "Women were given inheritance rights in a patriarchal society that had previously restricted inheritance to male relatives." Annemarie Schimmel states that "compared to the pre-Islamic position of women, Islamic legislation meant an enormous progress; the woman has the right, at least according to the letter of the law, to administer the wealth she has brought into the family or has earned by her own work."

The Middle Ages

According to English Common Law, which developed from the 12th Century onward all property which a wife held at the time of a marriage became a possession of her husband. Eventually English courts forbid a husband's transferring property without the consent of his wife, but he still retained the right to manage it and to receive the money which it produced. "French married women suffered from restrictions on their legal capacity which were removed only in 1965." In the 16th century, the Reformation in Europe allowed more women to add their voices, including the English writers Jane Anger, Aemilia Lanyer, and the prophetess Anna Trapnell. Despite relatively greater freedom for Anglo-Saxon women, until the mid-nineteenth century, writers largely assumed that a patriarchal order was a natural order that had existed. This perception was not seriously challenged until the eighteenth century when Jesuit missionaries found matrilineality in native North American peoples.

The Enlightenment Period

In the late 18th Century the question of women's rights became central to political debates in both France and Britain. At the time some of the greatest thinkers of the Enlightenment, who defended democratic principles of equality and challenged notions that a privileged few should rule over the vast majority of the population, believed that these principles should be applied only to their own gender and their own race. The philosopher Jean Jacques Rousseau for example thought that it was the order of nature for woman to obey men. He wrote "Women do wrong to complain of the inequality of man-made laws" and claimed that "when she tries to usurp our rights, she is our inferior".

In 1791 the French playwright and political activist Olympe de Gouges published the *Declaration of the Rights of Woman and the Female Citizen*, modelled on the Declaration of the Rights of Man and of the Citizen of 1789. The Declaration is ironic in formulation and exposes the failure of the French Revolution, which had been devoted to equality. It states that: "This revolution will only take effect when all women become fully aware of their deplorable condition, and of the rights they have lost in society". The Declaration of the Rights of Woman and the Female Citizen follows the seventeen articles of the Declaration of the Rights of Man and of the Citizen point for point and has been described by Camille Naish as "almost a parody... of the original document". The first article of the Declaration of the Rights of Man and of the Citizen proclaims that "Men are born and remain free and equal in rights. Social distinctions may be based only on common utility." The first article of Declaration of the Rights of Woman and the Female Citizen replied: "Woman is born free and remains equal to man in rights. Social distinctions may only be based on common utility". De Gouges expands the sixth article of the Declaration of the Rights of Man and of the Citizen, which declared the rights of citizens to take part in the formation of law, to:

"All citizens including women are equally admissible to all public dignities, offices and employments, according to their capacity, and with no other distinction than that of their virtues and talents".

De Gouges also draws attention to the fact that under French law women were fully punishable, yet denied equal rights.

Mary Wollstonecraft, a British writer and philosopher, published *A Vindication of the Rights of Woman* in 1792, arguing that it was the education and upbringing of women that created limited expectations. Wollstonecraft attacked gender oppression, pressing for equal educational opportunities, and demanded "justice!" and "rights to humanity" for all.

The 19th Century

In his 1869 essay The Subjection of Women the English philosopher and political theorist John Stuart Mill described the situation for women in Britain as follows:

> "We are continually told that civilization and Christianity have restored to the woman her just rights. Meanwhile the wife is the actual bondservant of her husband; no less so, as far as the legal obligation goes, than slaves commonly so called."

During the 1800s women in the United States and Britain began to challenge laws that denied them the right to their property once they married. Under the common law doctrine of *coverture* husbands gained control of their wives' real estate and wages. Beginning in the 1840s, state legislatures in the United States and the British Parliament began passing statutes that protected women's property from their husbands and their husbands' creditors. These laws were known as the Married Women's Property Acts. Courts in the nineteenth-century United States also continued to require privy examinations of married women who sold their property. A privy examination was a practice in which a married woman who wished to sell her property had to be separately examined by a judge or justice of the peace outside of the presence of her husband and asked if her husband was pressuring her into signing the document.

Suffrage and Rright to Vote

During the 19th Century women began to agitate for the right to vote and participate in government and law making. The ideals of women's suffrage developed alongside that of universal suffrage and today women's suffrage is considered a right (under the Convention on the Elimination of All Forms of Discrimination Against Women). During the 19th Century the right to vote was gradually extended in many countries and women started to campaign for their right to vote. In 1893 New Zealand became the first country to give women the right to vote on a national level. Australia gave women the right to vote in 1902, while the USA, Britain and Canada gave women the vote after the First World War. Sweden would also be a contestant as the first independent nation to grant women the right to vote. Conditional female suffrage was granted in Sweden during the age of liberty (1718–1771)

In Britain women's suffrage gained attention when John Stuart Mill called for the inclusion of women's suffrage in the Reform Act of 1867 in a petition that he presented to Parliament. Initially only one of several women's rights campaign, suffrage became the primary cause of the British women's movement at the beginning of the 20th Century. At the time the ability to vote was restricted to wealthy property owners within British jurisdictions. This arrangement implicitly excluded women as property law and marriage law gave men ownership rights at marriage or inheritance until the 19th century. Although male suffrage broadened during the century, women were explicitly prohibited from voting nationally and locally in the 1830s by a Reform Act and the Municipal Corporations Act. Throughout the 19th century women had organised through various groups until, by 1903, the National Union of Women's Suffrage Societies and the Women's Social and Political Union had emerged. Leaders in the struggle were Millicent Fawcett and Emmeline Pankhurst with her daughter Christabel. In 1918 the British Parliament passed a bill allowing women over the age of 30 to vote, and the voting age for women was lowered to 21 in 1928.

The Seneca Falls Convention of 1848 formulated the demand for women's suffrage in the United States of America and after the American Civil War (1861–1865) agitation for the cause became more prominent. In 1869 the proposed Fourteenth Amendment to the United States Constitution, which gave the vote to black men, caused controversy as women's suffrage campaigners such as Susan B. Anthony and Elizabeth Cady Stanton refused to endorse the amendment, as it did not give the vote to women. Others, such as Lucy Stone and Julia Ward Howe however argued that black men were enfranchised, women would achieve their goal. The conflict caused two organisations to emerge, the National Woman Suffrage Association, which campaigned for women's suffrage at a federal level as well as for married women to be given property rights, and the American Woman Suffrage Association, which aimed to secure women's suffrage through state legislation. In 1920 the Nineteenth Amendment to the United States Constitution gave women the right to vote.

Nordic countries gave women the right to vote in the early 20th Century – Finland (1906), Norway (1913), Denmark and Iceland (1915). With the end of the First World War many other countries followed - the Union of Soviet Socialist Republics and the Netherlands (1917), Austria, Czechoslovakia, Poland and Sweden (1918), Germany and Lunenburg (1919). Spain gave women the right to vote in 1931, France in 1944, Belgium, Italy, Romania and Yugoslavia in 1946. Switzerland gave women the right to vote in 1971, and Liechtenstein in 1984.

In Canada women's suffrage was achieved first on a provincial level in Alberta, Manitoba and Saskatchewan on 1916, with federal suffrage being granted in 1918. In Latin America some countries gave women the right to vote in the first half of the 20th Century – Ecuador (1929), Brazil (1932), El Salvador (1939), Dominican Republic (1942), Guatemala (1956) and Argentina (1946). In India, under colonial rule, universal suffrage was granted in 1935. Other Asian countries gave women the right to vote in mid of the Century – Japan (1945), China (1947) and Indonesia (1955). In Africa women generally got the right to vote along with men through universal suffrage – Liberia (1947), Uganda (1958) and Nigeria (1960). In many countries in the Middle East universal suffrage was acquired after the Second World War, although in others, such as Kuwait, suffrage is very limited. On 16 May 2005, the Parliament of Kuwait extended suffrage to women by a 35-23 vote, and women have been elected to Parliament.

Modern Movement

In the subsequent decades women's rights again became an important issue in the English speaking world. By the 1960s the movement was called "feminism" or "women's liberation." Reformers wanted the same pay as men, equal rights in law, and the freedom to plan their families or not have children at all. Their efforts were met with mixed results.

In the UK, a public groundswell of opinion in favour of legal equality had gained pace, partly through the extensive employment of women in what were traditional male roles during both world wars. By the 1960s the legislative process was being readied, tracing through MP Willie Hamilton's select committee report, his Equal Pay For Equal Work Bill, the creation of a Sex Discrimination Board, Lady Sear's draft sex anti-discrimination bill, a government Green Paper of 1973, until 1975 when the first British Sex Discrimination Act, an Equal Pay Act, and an Equal Opportunities Commission came into force. With encouragement from the UK government, the other countries of the EEC soon followed suit with an agreement to ensure that discrimination laws would be phased out across the European Community.

In the USA, the National Organization for Women (NOW) was created in 1966 with the purpose of bringing about equality for all women. NOW was one important group that fought for the Equal Rights Amendment (ERA). This amendment stated that "equality of rights under the law shall not be denied or abridged by the United States or any state on account of sex." But there was disagreement on how the proposed amendment would be understood. Supporters believed it would guarantee women equal treatment. But critics feared it might deny women the right be financially supported by their husbands. The amendment died in 1982 because not enough states had ratified it. ERAs have been included in subsequent Congresses, but have still failed to be ratified.

In the last three decades of the 20th century, Western women knew a new freedom through birth control, which enabled women to plan their adult lives, often making way for both career and family. The movement had been started in the 1910s by US pioneering social reformer Margaret Sanger and in the UK and internationally by Marie Stopes.

Over the course of the 20th century women took on greater roles in society such as serving in government. In the United States some served as U.S. Senators and others as members of the U.S. Cabinet. Many women took advantage of opportunities in higher education. In the United States at the beginning of the 20th century less than 20% of all college degrees were earned by women. By the end of the century this figure had risen to about 50%.

Progress was made in professional opportunities. Fields such as medicine, law, and science opened to include more women. At the beginning of the 20th century about 5% of the doctors in the United States were women. As of 2006, over 38% of all doctors in the United States were women, and today, women make almost 50% of the medical student population. While the numbers of women in these fields increased, many women still continued to hold clerical, factory, retail, or service jobs. For example, they worked as office assistants, on assembly lines, or as cooks.

The United Nations and Womens' Rights

In 1946 the United Nations established a Commission on the Status of Women. Originally as the Section on the Status of Women, Human Rights

Division, Department of Social Affairs, and now part of the Economic and Social Council (ECOSOC). Since 1975 the UN has held a series of world conferences on women's issues, starting with the World Conference of the International Women's Year in Mexico City. These conferences created an international forum for women's rights, but also illustrated divisions between women of different cultures and the difficulties of attempting to apply principles universally

Four World Conferences have been held, the first in Mexico City (International Women's Year, 1975), the second in Copenhagen (1980) and the third in Nairobi (1985). At the Fourth World Conference on Women in Beijing (1995), *The Platform for Action* was signed. This included a commitment to achieve "gender equality and the empowerment of women".

The Universal Declaration of Human Rights, adopted in 1948, enshrines "the equal rights of men and women", and addressed both the equality and equity issues. In 1979 the United Nations General Assembly adopted the Convention on the Elimination of All Forms of Discrimination against Women (CEDAW). Described as an international bill of rights for women, it came into force on 3 September 1981. The seven UN member states that have not ratified the convention are Iran, Nauru, Palau, Somalia, Sudan, Tonga, and the United States. Niue and the Vatican City have also not signed it. The United States has signed, but not yet ratified.

The Convention defines discrimination against women in the following terms:

> Any distinction, exclusion or restriction made on the basis of sex which has the effect or purpose of impairing or nullifying the recognition, enjoyment or exercise by women, irrespective of their marital status, on a basis of equality of men and women, of human rights and fundamental freedoms in the political, economic, social, cultural, civil or any other field.

It also establishes an agenda of action for putting an end to sex-based discrimination for which states ratifying the Convention are required to enshrine gender equality into their domestic legislation, repeal all discriminatory provisions in their laws, and enact new provisions to guard against discrimination against women. They must also establish tribunals and public institutions to guarantee women effective protection against discrimination, and take steps to eliminate all forms of discrimination practiced against women by individuals, organizations, and enterprises.

The Protocol to the African Charter on Human and Peoples' Rights on the Rights of Women in Africa, better known as the Maputo Protocol, was adopted by the African Union on 11 July 2003 at its second summit in Maputo, Mozambique. On 25 November 2005, having been ratified by the required 15 member nations of the African Union, the protocol entered into force. The protocol guarantees comprehensive rights to women including the right to take part in the political process, to social and political equality with men, and to control of their reproductive health, and an end to female genital mutilation.

International and Regional Instruments

Numerous international and regional instruments have drawn attention to gender-related dimensions of human rights issues, the most important being the UN Convention on the Elimination of All Forms of Discrimination against Women (CEDAW), adopted in 1979.

CEDAW defines the right of women to be free from discrimination and sets the core principles to protect this right. It establishes an agenda for national action to end discrimination, and provides the basis for achieving equality between men and women through ensuring women's equal access to, and equal opportunities in, political and public life as well as education, health and employment. CEDAW is the only human rights treaty that affirms the reproductive rights of women.

The Convention has been ratified by 180 states, making it one of the most ratified international treaties. State parties to the Convention must submit periodic reports on women's status in their respective countries. CEDAW's Optional Protocol establishes procedures for individual complaints on alleged violations of the Convention by State parties, as well as an inquiry procedure that allows the Committee to conduct inquiries into serious and systematic abuses of women's human rights in countries. So far the Protocol has been ratified by 71 States.

In 1993, 45 years after the Universal Declaration of Human Rights was adopted, and eight years after CEDAW entered into force, the UN World Conference on Human Rights in Vienna confirmed that women's rights were human rights. That this statement was even necessary is striking – women's status as human beings entitled to rights should have never been in doubt. And yet this was a step forward in recognizing the rightful claims of one half of humanity, in identifying neglect of women's rights as a human rights violation and in drawing attention to the relationship between gender and human rights violations.

In 1994, the International Conference on Population and Development in Cairo (ICPD) articulated and affirmed the relationship between advancement and fulfilment of rights and gender equality and equity. It also clarified the concepts of women's empowerment, gender equity, and reproductive health and rights. The Programme of Action of ICPD asserted that the empowerment and autonomy of women and the improvement of their political, social, economic and health status was a highly important end in itself as well as essential for the achievement of sustainable development. In 1995, the Fourth World Conference on Women in Beijing generated global commitments to advance a wider range of women's rights. The inclusion of gender equality and women's empowerment as one of the eight Millennium Development Goals was a reminder that many of those promises have yet to be kept. It also represents a critical opportunity to implement those promises.

In spite of these international agreements, the denial of women's basic human rights is persistent and widespread. For instance:

- Over half a million women continue to die each year from pregnancy and childbirth-related causes.
- Rates of HIV infection among women are rapidly increasing. Among those 15-24 years of age, young women now constitute the majority of those newly infected, in part because of their economic and social vulnerability.
- Gender-based violence kills and disables as many women between the ages of 15 and 44 as cancer. More often than not, perpetrators go unpunished.
- Worldwide, women are twice as likely as men to be illiterate.
- As a consequence of their working conditions and characteristics, a disproportionate number of women are impoverished in both developing and developed countries. Despite some progress in women's wages in the 1990s, women still earn less than men, even for similar kinds of work.
- Many of the countries that have ratified CEDAW still have discriminatory laws governing marriage, land, property and inheritance.

While progress has been made in some areas, many of the challenges and obstacles identified in 1995 still remain. In addition, the new challenges for women's empowerment and gender equality that have emerged over the past decade, such as the feminization of the AIDS epidemic, feminization of migration, and increasing of trafficking on women need to be more effectively addressed.

In every region of the world, UNFPA is working to promote women's rights and end discrimination against them. The Fund is increasingly involved in protecting the rights of women affected by conflict, and ensuring that women can have an active role in peacebuilding and reconstruction efforts. The Fund's programming also addresses all 12 of the critical areas of concern identified at Beijing.

In many cases, UNFPA is able to multiply its effectiveness by supporting legislation that protects the rights of women, such as groundbreaking laws in Ecuador and Guatemala granting women the right to reproductive health care. In some cases, the Fund gets results by partnering with men as in Uganda. The Fund also supports services for women who are victimized by various forms of gender-based violence. For instance, it supports help for women who are abused by their husbands in the Gaza Strip. It has helped establish a shelter for women who have been trafficked in Moldova and funds a safe haven for girls running away from female genital mutilation or forced marriage in Kenya.

Applying the Human Rights Framework

The *Universal Declaration of Human Rights* defines human rights as universal, inalienable, and indivisible. In unison, these defining characteristics are tremendously important for women's human rights. The universality of human rights means that human rights apply to every single person by virtue of their humanity; this also means that human rights apply to everyone equally, for everyone is equal in simply being human. In many ways, this universality theme may seem patently obvious, but its egalitarian premise has a radical edge. By invoking the universality of human rights, women have demanded that their very humanity be acknowledged. That acknowledgement and the concomitant recognition of women as bearers of human rights-mandates the incorporation of women and gender perspectives into all of the ideas and institutions that are already committed to the promotion and protection of human rights. The idea that human rights are universal also challenges the contention that the human rights of women can be limited by culturally specific definitions of what count as human rights and of women's role in society.

The idea of human rights as inalienable means that it is impossible for anyone to abdicate her human rights, even if she wanted to, since every person is accorded those rights by virtue of being human. It also means that no person or group of persons can deprive another individual of her or his human rights. Thus, for example, debts incurred by migrant workers or by women caught up in sex trafficking can never justify indentured servitude (slavery), or the deprivation of food, of freedom of movement, or of compensation. The idea of inalienable rights means that human rights cannot be sold, ransomed, or forfeited for any reason. The idea of inalienability has also been important in negotiations over the priority given to social, religious and cultural practices in relation to human rights. For decades, work to transform practices which are physically or psychologically damaging to women and that have often been "protected" under the rubric of religion, tradition or culture has been particularly difficult, given both the integrity of culture guaranteed by the*Universal Declaration* and the history of Northern domination in much of the world. Thus it was important that both the *Vienna Declaration and Programs of Action* from the World Conference on Human Rights held in Vienna in 1993, and the United Nations *Declaration Against Violence Against Women* passed by the General Assembly the same year, affirmed that in cases of conflict between women's human rights and cultural or religious practices, the human rights of women must prevail.

The indivisibility of human rights means that none of the rights that are considered to be fundamental human rights is more important than any of the others more specifically, that they are inter-related. Human rights encompass civil, political, social, economic and cultural facets of human existence; the indivisibility premise highlights that the ability of people to live their lives in dignity and to exercise their human rights fully depends upon the recognition that these aspects are all interdependent. The fact that human rights are indivisible is important for women, since their civil and political rights historically have been compromised by their economic status, by social and cultural limitations placed on their activities, and by the ever-present threat of violence that often constitutes an insurmountable obstacle to women's participation in public and political life. The idea of indivisibility has provided women with a common framework through which to emphasize the complexity of the challenges they face, and to highlight the necessity of including women and gender conscious perspectives in the development and implementation of policy. By calling upon the indivisibility of women's human rights, women have rejected a human rights hierarchy, which places either political or civil rights or socio-economic rights as primary. Instead, women have charged that political stability cannot be realized unless women's social and economic rights are also addressed; that sustainable development is impossible without the simultaneous respect for, and incorporation into the policy process of women's cultural and social roles in the daily reproduction of life; and that social equity cannot be generated without economic justice and women's participation in all levels of political decision-making.

Movement for Women's Rights

The concept of women's human rights has opened the way for women around the world to ask hard questions about the official inattention and general indifference to the widespread discrimination and violence that women experience everyday. Whether used in political lobbying, in legal cases, in grassroots mobilization, or in broad-based educational efforts, the idea of women's human rights has been a rallying point for women across many boundaries and has facilitated the creation of collaborative strategies for promoting and protecting the human rights of women.

While women have raised questions for a long time about why their rights are seen as ancillary to human rights, a coordinated effort to change this attitude using a human rights framework gained particular momentum in the early part of the 1990s. The opening of space for new debates afforded by the end of the Cold War facilitated the exchange of ideas and experiences among women around the world that led to strategizing about how to make women's human rights perspectives more visible. As women's activities developed globally during and following the United Nations' Decade for Women, more and more women raised the question of why "women's rights" and women's lives have been deemed secondary to the "human rights" and lives of men. Over the past decade, a movement around women's human rights has emerged to challenge limited notions of human rights, and it has focused particularly on violence against women as a prime example of the bias against women in human rights practice and theory.

The United Nations World Conference on Human Rights held in Vienna in 1993 was the first such meeting since 1968, and it became a natural vehicle to highlight the new visions of human rights thinking and practice being developed by women. Its initial call did not mention women nor did it recognize any gender-specific aspects of human rights in its proposed agenda. Since the conference represented an historic reassessment of the status of human rights, it became the unifying public focus of a worldwide Global Campaign for Women's Human Rights-a broad and loose international collaborative effort to advance women's human rights. The campaign launched a petition calling upon the World Conference "to comprehensively address women's human rights at every level of its proceedings" and to recognize "gender violence, a universal phenomenon which takes many forms across culture, race, and class... as a violation of human rights requiring immediate action." The petition was eventually translated into 23 languages, and was used by over 1,000 sponsoring groups who gathered a half million signatures from 124 countries. The petition and its demands instigated discussions about why women's rights, and gender-based violence in particular, were left out of human rights considerations, and served to mobilize women around the World Conference. Women acted to inject issues of women's human rights into the entire pre-conference preparatory process: Women from all regions demanded that women's human rights be discussed at the preparatory meetings held in Tunis, San Jose, and Bangkok, as well as at other non-governmental and national preparatory events. The idea of women's human rights was a framework for women to articulate and collaborate around broad and similar concerns about the status of women; it also provided women with a way to elaborate on the most pressing human rights issues specific to particular political, geographic, economic, and cultural contexts.

By the time the World Conference convened, the idea that "women's rights are human rights" had become the rallying call of thousands of people all over the world and one of the most discussed "new" human rights debates. The *Vienna Declaration and Program of Action*, which is the product of the conference and is meant to signal the agreement of the international community on the status of human rights, states unequivocally that:

The human rights of women and of the girl-child are an inalienable, integral and indivisible part of universal human rights. *Vienna Declaration* (I,18,1993).

Women continued to lobby for and gain wider recognition of women's human rights at subsequent United Nations Conferences. So, for example, at the International Conference on Population and Development in Cairo in 1994, women's reproductive rights were explicitly recognized as human rights. A particularly significant development was the way in which the Platform for Action at the IV World Conference on Women in Beijing in 1995 became virtually an agenda about the human rights of women. This signaled the successful mainstreaming of women's rights as human rights.

The agreements that are produced by such conferences are not legally binding; however, they do have ethical and political weight and can be used to pursue regional, national, or local objectives. Conference documents can also be used to reinforce and interpret international treaties such as the *Covenant on Civil and Political Rights*, or the *Covenant of Social, Economic and Cultural Rights*. These covenants, when signed by a country, do have the status of international law and have been used in courts by lawyers seeking redress for human rights violations. The most important international treaty specifically addressing women's human rights is the *Convention on the Elimination of All Forms of Discrimination Against Women (CEDAW)*which was initiated during the UN Decade for Women and has been ratified by over 130 countries. Further, local women's groups have integrated the women's human rights framework into their legal literacy programs and legal strategies.

Although the framework of women's human rights has been tremendously useful in efforts to lobby for legislative and policy changes at local, national and international levels, it has been an equally as important tool for grassroots organizing. Women's human rights not only teaches women about the range of rights that their governments must honor; it also functions as a kind of gestalt by which to organize analyses of their experiences and plan action for change. The human rights framework creates a space in which the possibility for a different account of women's lives can be developed. What is so useful about this framework is that it provides women with principles by which to develop alternative visions of their lives without suggesting the substance of those visions. The fundamental principles of human rights that accord to each and every person the entitlement to human dignity give women a vocabulary for describing both violations and impediments to the exercise of their human rights. The large body of international covenants, agreements and commitments about human rights gives women political leverage and a tenable point of reference. And finally, the idea of women's human rights enables women to define and articulate the specificity of the experiences in their lives at the same time that it provides a vocabulary for women to share the experiences of other women around the world and work collaboratively for change.

References

Blundell, Sue (1995). *Women in ancient Greece*, Volume 2.. Harvard University Press. p. 224.

Pomeroy, Sarah B. (2002). *Spartan Women*. Oxford: Oxford University Press.

Gerhard, Ute (2001). *Debating women's equality: toward a feminist theory of law from a European perspective*. Rutgers University Press. p. 33.

Lauren, Paul Gordon (2003). *The evolution of international human rights: visions seen*. University of Pennsylvania Press. pp. 29 & 30.

United Nations *Convention on the Elimination of All Forms of Discrimination against Women*: Introduction

Walters, Margaret, (2005). *Feminism: A very short introduction*. Oxford.

2

Women's Suffrage

Women's suffrage is the right of women to vote and to run for office. Limited voting rights were gained by women in Sweden, Britain, Finland and some western U.S. states in the late 19th century. International organizations were formed to coordinate efforts, especially the International Council of Women (1888) and the International Woman Suffrage Alliance (1904). In 1893, New Zealand became the first nation to extend the right to vote to all adult women. The women in South Australia achieved the same right in 1894 but became the first to obtain the right to stand (run) for Parliament. The first European country to introduce women's suffrage was the Grand Duchy of Finland—then a part of the Russian Empire with autonomous powers—which also produced the world's first female members of parliament as a result of the 1907 parliamentary elections. In most Western nations, women's suffrage came at the end of World War I, with some important late adopters such as France in 1944 and Switzerland in 1971.

Women's suffrage has generally been recognized after political campaigns to obtain it were waged. In many countries it was granted before universal suffrage. Women's suffrage is explicitly stated as a right under the Convention on the Elimination of All Forms of Discrimination Against Women, adopted by the United Nations in 1979.

Historical Background

In ancient Athenian Democracy, often cited as the birthplace of democracy, only men were permitted to vote. Through subsequent centuries, Europe was generally ruled by monarchs, though various forms of Parliament arose at different times. The high rank ascribed to abbesses within the Catholic Church permitted some women the right to sit and vote at national assemblies - as with various high ranking abbesses in Medieval Germany, who were ranked among the independent princes of the empire and could therefore sit and vote in the Diet. Their Protestant successors enjoyed the same privilege almost into modern times. Generally speaking however, the emergence of modern democracy began with male citizens obtaining the right to vote in advance of female citizens.

A movement for women's suffrage originated in France in the 1780s and 1790s, where Antoine Condorcet and Olympe de Gouges advocated women's suffrage in national elections.Various countries, colonies and states granted restricted women's suffrage in the latter half of the 19th century.

In Sweden, conditional women's suffrage was in effect during the Age of Liberty (1718–1771). Other possible contenders for first "country" to grant female suffrage include the Corsican Republic (1755), the Pitcairn Islands (1838), the Isle of Man (1881), and Franceville (1889), but some of these had brief existences as independent states and others were not clearly independent.

In 1756, Lydia Taft became the first legal woman voter in colonial America. This occurred under British rule in the Massachusetts Colony. This was in a New England town meeting and she voted on at least three occasions in Uxbridge, Massachusetts. Unmarried women who owned property could vote in New Jersey from 1776 to 1807.

In the 1792 elections in Sierra Leone, all heads of household—one-third of whom were African women—could vote.

The female descendants of the Bounty mutineers who lived on Pitcairn Islands could vote from 1838, and this right transferred with their resettlement to Norfolk Island (now an Australian external territory) in 1856.

The seed for the first Woman's Rights Convention was planted in 1840, when Elizabeth Cady Stanton met Lucretia Mott at the World Anti-Slavery Convention in London, the conference that refused to seat Mott and other women delegates from America because of their sex. In 1851, Stanton met temperance worker Susan B. Anthony, and shortly the two would be joined in the long struggle to secure the vote for women. In 1868 Anthony encouraged working women from the printing and sewing trades in New

York, who were excluded from men's trade unions, to form Workingwomen's Associations. As a delegate to the National Labor Congress in 1868 Anthony persuaded the committee on female labor to call for votes for women and equal pay for equal work, although the men at the conference deleted the reference to the vote.

The 1871 Paris Commune recognized women's right to vote, but with its fall women were again deprived of the right, which would only be recognized again in July 1944 by Charles de Gaulle (at that time most of France—including Paris—was under Nazi occupation; Paris was liberated the following month).

In 1881 the Isle of Man, an internally self-governing dependent territory of the British Crown, enfranchised women property owners and delivered the first installment of women's right to vote in parliamentary elections within the British Isles.

The Pacific colony of Franceville, declaring independence in 1889, became the first self-governing nation to adopt universal suffrage without distinction of sex or color; however, it soon came back under French and British colonial rule.

Of currently existing independent countries, New Zealand was the first to acknowledge women's right to vote in 1893 when it was a self-governing British colony. Unrestricted women's suffrage in terms of voting rights (women were not initially permitted to stand for election) was adopted in New Zealand in 1893. Following a successful movement led by Kate Sheppard, the women's suffrage bill was adopted mere weeks before the general election of that year. The women of the British protectorate of Cook Islands obtained the same right soon after and beat New Zealand's women to the polls in 1893.

The self-governing British colony of South Australia enacted universal suffrage and, furthermore, enabled women to stand for the colonial parliament in 1894. The Commonwealth of Australia federated in 1901, with women voting and standing for office in some states. The Australian Federal Parliament extended voting rights to all adult women for Federal elections from 1902 (with the exception of Aboriginal women in some states).

The first European country to introduce women's suffrage was the Grand Duchy of Finland. Amidst administrative reforms following the 1905 uprising, Finnish women's demand for both the right to vote (universal and equal suffrage) and the right to stand for election were met in 1906. The world's first female members of parliament were also Finnish, when on 1907, 19 women took up their places in the Parliament of Finland as a result of the 1907 parliamentary elections.

In the years before World War I, women in Norway (1913) and Denmark (1915) also won the right to vote, as did women in the remaining Australian states. Near the end of the war, Canada, Soviet Russia, Germany, and Poland also recognized women's right to participate in the elective franchise. British women over 30 had the vote in 1918, Dutch women in 1919, and American women won the vote August 26, 1920 with the passage of the 19th Amendment. Women in Turkey won voting rights in 1926. In 1928, British women won suffrage on the same terms as men, that is, for persons 21 years old and older. One of the most recent jurisdictions to acknowledge women's full right to vote was Bhutan in 2008 (its first national elections).

Voting rights for women were introduced into international law by the United Nations' Human Rights Commission, whose elected chair was Eleanor Roosevelt. In 1948 the United Nations adopted the Universal Declaration of Human Rights; Article 21 stated: "(1) Everyone has the right to take part in the government of his country, directly or through freely chosen representatives. (3) The will of the people shall be the basis of the authority of government; this will shall be expressed in periodic and genuine elections which shall be by universal and equal suffrage and shall be held by secret vote or by equivalent free voting procedures."

The United Nations General Assembly adopted the Convention on the Political Rights of Women, which went into force in 1954, enshrining the equal rights of women to vote, hold office, and access public services as set out by national laws.

Suffrage Movements

The suffrage movement was a very broad one which encompassed women and men with a very broad range of views. One major division, especially in Britain, was between suffragists, who sought to create change constitutionally, and suffragettes, led by iconic English political activist Emmeline Pankhurst, who in 1903 formed the more militant Women's Social and Political Union. Pankhurst would not be satisfied with anything but action on the question of women's enfranchisement, with "deeds, not words" the organisation's motto. There was also a diversity of views on a "woman's place". Some who campaigned for women's suffrage felt that women were naturally kinder, gentler, and more concerned about weaker members of society, especially children. It was often assumed that women voters would have a civilizing effect on politics and would tend to support controls on alcohol, for example. Societies believed that although a woman's place was in the home, she should be able to influence laws which impacted upon that home. Other campaigners felt that men and women should be equal in every way and that there was no such thing as a woman's "natural role". There were also differences in opinion about other voters. Some campaigners felt that all adults were entitled to a vote, whether rich or poor, male or female, and regardless of race. Others saw women's suffrage as a way of canceling out the votes of lower class or non-white men.

Asia

India

Basu shows that the Women's Indian Association (WIA) was founded in 1917. It sought votes for women and the right to hold legislative office on the same basis as men. These positions were endorsed by the main political groupings, the Indian National Congress and the All-India Muslim League. British and Indian feminists combined in 1918 to publish a magazine Stri Dharma that featured international news from a feminist perspective. In 1919 in the Montagu–Chelmsford Reforms, the British set up provincial legislatures which had the power to grant women's suffrage. Madras in 1921 granted votes to wealthy and educated women, under the same terms that applied to men. The other provinces followed, but not the princely states (which did not have votes for men either). In Bengal province, the provincial assembly rejected it in 1921 but Southard shows an intense campaign produced victory in 1921. The original idea came from British suffragettes. Success in Bengal depended on middle class Indian women, who emerged from a fast-growing urban elite that favoured European fashions and ideas. The women leaders in Bengal linked their crusade to a moderate nationalist agenda, by showing how they could participate more fully in nation-building by having voting power. They carefully avoided attacking traditional gender roles by arguing that traditions could coexist with political modernization.

In the Government of India Act 1935 the British Raj set up a system of separate electorates and separate seats for women. Most women's leaders opposed segregated electorates and demanded adult franchise. In 1931 the Congress promised universal adult franchise when it came to power. It enacted equal voting rights for both men and women in 1947.

Pakistan

Pakistan was part of India until 1947, when it became independent. Women received full suffrage in 1947. Ali points out that Muslim women leaders from all classes actively supported the Pakistan movement in the mid-1940s. Their movement was led by wives and other relatives of leading politicians. Women were sometimes organized into large-scale public demonstrations. Before 1947 there was a tendency for the Muslim women in Punjab to vote for the Muslim League while their menfolk supported the Unionist Party.

Bangladesh

Bangladesh was (mostly) the province of Bengal in India until 1947, then it became part of Pakistan. It became an independent nation in 1971. Women have had equal suffrage since 1947, and they have reserved seats in parliament. Bangladesh is notable in that since 1991, two women, namely Sheikh Hasina and Begum Khaleda Zia, have served terms as the country's Prime Minister continuously. Women have traditionally played a minimal role in politics beyond the anomaly of the two leaders; few used to run against men; few have been ministers. Recently, however, women have become more active in politics, with several prominent ministerial posts given to women and women participating in national, district and municipal elections against men and winning on several occasions. Choudhury and Hasanuzzaman argue that the strong patriarchal traditions of Bangladesh explain why women are so reluctant to stand up in politics.

Indonesia

In the first half of the 20th century, Indonesia (pre-independence era as Dutch East Indies) was one of the slowest moving countries to gain women's suffrage. They began their fight in 1905 by introducing municipal councils that included some members elected by a restricted district. Voting rights only went to males that could read and write, which excluded many non-European males. At the time, the literacy rate for males was 11% and for females 2%. The main group who pressured the Indonesian government for women's suffrage was the Dutch Vereeninging voor Vrouwenkiesrecht (VVV-Women's Suffrage Association) which was founded in the

Netherlands in 1894. They tried to attract Indonesian membership, but had very limited success because the leaders of the organization had little skill in relating to even the educated class of the Indonesians. When they eventually did connect somewhat with women, they failed to sympathize with them and thus ended up alienating many well-educated Indonesians. In 1918 the colony gained its first national representative body called the Volksraad, which still excluded women in voting. In 1935, the colonial administration used its power of nomination to appoint a European woman to the Volksraad. In 1938, the administration introduced the right of women to be elected to urban representative institution, which resulted in some Indonesian and European women entering municipal councils. Eventually, the law became that only European women and municipal councils could vote, which excluded all other women and local councils. September 1941 was when this law was amended and the law extended to women of all races by the Volksraad. Finally, in November 1941, the right to vote for municipal councils was granted to all women on a similar basis to men (with property and educational qualifications). There are a lot of women that supports the rights for women. The famous one is Raden Ajeng Kartini. She is also famous for her quote, "Habis Gelap, Terbitlah Terang" or in English, "After Dark, Comes the Light". It means that after bad days or dark days, there will always be hope everything including the success of the Women's Suffrage. Raden Ajeng Kartini did succeed. The other women that also fights for women's right also succeed. Raden Ajeng Kartini is so famous, Indonesians made a special date just for her, Hari Kartini, or Kartini's Day on 21 April, which is Kartini's birthday.

Iran

In 1963, a referendum overwhelmingly approved by voters gave women the right to vote, a right previously denied to them under the Iranian Constitution of 1906 pursuant to Chapter 2, Article 3.

Japan

lthough women were allowed to vote in some counties in 1880, women's suffrage was enacted at a national level in 1945.

Kuwait

Women's suffrage in Kuwait was recognized in an amendment to electoral law on May 17, 2005.

Saudi Arabia

In late September 2011, King Abdullah bin Abdulaziz al-Saud declared that women would be able to vote and run for office starting in 2015. The franchise will apply to the only (semi-)elected bodies in the kingdom, the municipal councils. Half of the seats on municipal councils are elective, and the councils have few powers. The council elections have been held since 2005 (the first time they were held before that was the 1960s). The King also declared that women would be eligible to be appointed to the Shura Council, an unelected body that issues advisory opinions on national policy. '"This is great news," said Saudi writer and women's rights activist Wajeha al-Huwaider. "Women's voices will finally be heard. Now it is time to remove other barriers like not allowing women to drive cars and not being able to function, to live a normal life without male guardians."' Robert Lacey, author of two books about the kingdom, said, "This is the first positive, progressive speech out of the government since the Arab Spring.... First the warnings, then the payments, now the beginnings of solid reform." The king made the announcement in a five-minute speech to the Shura Council.

Sri Lanka

Sri Lanka (at that time Ceylon) was one of the first Asian countries to allow voting rights to women over the age of 21 without any restrictions. Since then, women have enjoyed a significant presence in the Sri Lankan political arena. The zenith of this favourable condition to women has been the 1960 July General Elections, in which Ceylon elected the world's first woman Prime Minister, Mrs. Sirimavo Bandaranaike. Her daughter, Mrs. Chandrika Kumaratunga also became the Prime Minister later in 1994, and the same year she was elected as the Executive President of Sri Lanka, making her the fourth woman in the world to hold the portfolio.

Africa

South Africa

The franchise was extended to white women 21 years or older by the Women's Enfranchisement Act, 1930. The first general election at which women could vote was the 1933 election. At that election Leila Reitz (wife of Deneys Reitz) was elected as the first female MP, representing Parktown for the South African Party. The limited voting rights available to non-white men in the Cape Province and Natal (Transvaal and the Orange Free State practically denied all non-whites the right to vote, and had also done so to non-Afrikaner uitlanders when independent in the 1800s) were not extended to women, and were themselves progressively eliminated between 1936 and 1968.

The right to vote for the Transkei Legislative Assembly, established in 1963 for the Transkei bantustan, was granted to all adult citizens of the Transkei, including women. Similar provision was made for the Legislative Assemblies created for other bantustans. All adult coloured citizens were eligible to vote for the Coloured Persons Representative Council, which was established in 1968 with limited legislative powers; the council was however abolished in 1980. Similarly, all adult Indian citizens were eligible to vote for the South African Indian Council in 1981. In 1984 the Tricameral Parliament was established, and the right to vote for the House of Representatives and House of Delegates was granted to all adult Coloured and Indian citizens, respectively.

In 1994 the bantustans and the Tricameral Parliament were abolished and the right to vote for the National Assembly was granted to all adult citizens.

Southern Rhodesia

Southern Rhodesian women won the vote in 1919 and Ethel Tawse Jollie (1875–1950) was elected to the Southern Rhodesia legislature 1920-1928, the first woman to sit in any national Commonwealth Parliament outwith Westminster. The influx of women settlers from the United Kingdom and the British Dominions proved a decisive factor in the 1922 referendum that rejected annexation by a South Africa increasingly under the sway of traditionalist Afrikaner Nationalists in favor of Rhodesian Home Rule or "responsible government". Only 51 black Rhodesians qualified for the vote in 1923 (based upon property, assets, income, and literacy). It is unclear when the first black woman qualified for the vote.

Europe

Austria

After the 1848 revolutions, the right to vote was bound to the ownership of property and thus paying of taxes. While it was also bound to being male, a small number of privileged women who owned property were actually allowed to vote as a result. In 1889 this "loophole" was closed in Lower Austria, which led some to mobilise for the struggle for political rights and the right to vote for women.

It was only after the breakdown of the Habsburg Monarchy, that the new Austria would grant the general, equal, direct and secret right to vote to all citizens, regardless of sex, in 1919.

Belgium

After a revision of the constitution in 1921 the general right to vote was introduced according to the "one man, one vote" principle. Women obtained voting rights at the municipal level. As an exception, widows of World War I were allowed to vote at the national level as well. The introduction of women's suffrage was already put onto the agenda at the time, by means of including an article in the constitution that allowed approval of women's suffrage by special law. This happened no sooner than after World War II, in 1948. In Belgium, voting is compulsory but not enforced.

Czech Republic

In the former Bohemia, taxpaying women and women in "learned profession" were allowed to vote by proxy and made eligible to the legislative body in 1864. The general public obtained the right to vote and be elected, based on age but regardless of sex, when Czechoslovakia was established in 1918.

Denmark

In Denmark, women were given the right to vote in municipal elections on April 20, 1909. However it was not until June 5, 1915 that they were allowed to vote in Rigsdag elections.

Finland

The area that in 1809 became Finland was a group of integral provinces of the Kingdom of Sweden for over 600 years, signifying that also women in Finland were allowed to vote during the Swedish Age of Liberty (1718–1771), when suffrage was granted to tax-paying female members of guilds

The predecessor state of modern Finland, the Grand Principality of Finland was part of the Russian Empire from 1809 to 1917 and enjoyed a high degree of autonomy. In 1863 taxpaying women were granted municipal suffrage in the country side, and in 1872, the same reform was given to the cities The Parliament Act in 1906 established the unicameral parliament of Finland and both women and men were given the right to vote and stand for election. Thus Finnish women became the first in the world to have unrestricted rights both to vote and to stand for parliament. In elections the next year, 19 female MPs, first ones in the world, were elected and women have continued to play a central role in the nation's politics ever since. Miina Sillanpää, a key figure in the worker's movement, became the first female minister in 1926.

Finland's first female President Tarja Halonen was voted into office in 2000 and for a second term in 2006. Since the 2011 parliamentary election, women's representation stands at 42,5%. In 2003 Anneli Jäätteenmäki became the first female Prime Minister of Finland, and in 2007 Matti Vanhanen's second cabinet made history as for the first time there were more women than men in the cabinet of Finland (12 vs. 8).

France

The 21 April 1944 ordinance of the French provisional government extended suffrage to French women. The first elections with female participation were the municipal elections of 29 April 1945 and the parliamentary elections of 21 October 1945. "Indigenous Muslim" women in French Algeria had to wait until a 3 July 1958 decree.

Germany

In Germany, women's suffrage was granted by decree by the revolutionary Council of People's Deputies (Rat der Volksbeauftragten) on November 12, 1918. Women were subsequently eligible to participate in elections in January 1919 for the National Assembly that drafted what became the constitution of the Weimar Republic, ratified in August 1919.

Italy

In Italy, women's suffrage was not introduced following the World War I, but upheld by Socialist and Fascist activists and partly introduced by Benito Mussolini's government in 1925. Following the war, in the 1946 election, all Italians simultaneously voted for the Constituent Assembly and for a referendum about keeping Italy a monarchy or creating a republic instead. Elections were not held in the Julian March and South Tyrol because they were under UN occupation.

Liechtenstein

In Liechtenstein, women's suffrage was granted via referendum in 1984. Previously, referendums on the issue of women's suffrage had been held in 1968, 1971 and 1973.

Netherlands

The group working for women's suffrage in the Netherlands was the Dutch Vereeniging voor Vrouwenkiesrecht (Women's Suffrage Association), founded in 1894. In 1917 Dutch women became electable in national elections, which led to the election of Suze Groeneweg of the SDAP party in the general elections of 1918. On 15 May 1919 a new law was drafted to allow women's suffrage without any limitations. The law was passed and the right to vote could be exercised for the first time in the general elections of 1922. Voting was made mandatory from 1918, which was not lifted until 1970.

Norway

Middle class women could vote for the first time in 1907 (i.e., women coming from families with a certain level of prosperity). Women in general were allowed to vote in local elections from 1910 on, and in 1913 a motion on general suffrage for women was carried unanimously in the Norwegian parliament (Stortinget).

Poland

Poland in its first days after regaining independence (1918) following the 123 year period of the Partition of Poland (before 1795 tax-paying females were allowed to take part in political life), allowed voting rights to women, as well as rights to be elected, without any restrictions. The first women elected to the Sejm in 1919 were: Gabriela Balicka, Jadwiga Dziubinska, Irena Kosmowska, Maria Moczydlowska, Zofia Moraczewska, Anna Piasecka, Zofia Sokolnicka, Franciszka Wilczkowiakowa.,

Portugal

Carolina Beatriz Ângelo was the first Portuguese woman to vote, in 1911, for the Republican Constitutional Parliament. She argued that she was entitled to do so as she was the head of a household. The law was changed some time later, stating that only male heads of households could vote. In 1931 during the Estado Novo regime, women were allowed to vote for the first time, but only if they had a high school or university degree, while men had only to be able to read and write. In 1946 a new electoral law enlarged the possibility of female vote, but still with some differences regarding men. A law from 1968 claimed to establish “equality of political rights for men and women”, but a few electoral rights were reserved for men. After the Carnation Revolution, in 1974, women were granted full and equal electoral rights.

Spain

In the Basque provinces of Biscay and Gipuzkoa women who paid a special election tax were allowed to vote and get elected to office till the abolition of the Basque fueros. Nonetheless the possibility of being elected without the right to vote persisted, hence María Isabel de Ayala was elected mayor in Ikastegieta in 1865. Women’s suffrage was officially adopted in 1931 not without the opposition of Margarita Nelken and Victoria Kent, two female MPs (both members of the Republican Radical-Socialist Party), who argued that women in Spain and at that time, were far too immature and ignorant to vote responsibly, thus putting at risk the existence of the Second Republic. During the Franco regime only women who were considered heads of household were allowed to vote; in the “organic democracy” type of elections called “referendums” (Franco’s regime was dictatorial) women were allowed to vote. From 1976, during the Spanish transition to democracy women fully exercised the right to vote and be elected to office.

Sweden

During the Age of Liberty (1718–1771), tax-paying female members of guilds (most often widows), had been allowed to vote. Furthermore, new tax regulations made the participation of women in the elections even more extensive from 1743 onward.

The vote was sometimes given through a male representative, which was one of the most prominent reasons cited by those in opposition to female suffrage. In 1758 women were excluded from mayoral and local elections, but continued to vote in national elections. In 1771 women’s suffrage was abolished through the new constitution.

In 1862 tax-paying women of legal majority (unmarried women and widows) were again allowed to vote in municipal elections, making Sweden the first country in the world to grant women the right to vote. The right to vote in municipal elections applied only to people of legal majority, which excluded married women, as they were juridically under the guardianship of their husbands. In 1884 the suggestion to grant women the right to vote in national elections was initially voted down in Parliament. In 1902 the Swedish Society for Woman Suffrage was founded. In 1906 the suggestion of women's suffrage was voted down in parliament again. However, the same year, also married women were granted municipal suffrage. In 1909 women were granted eligibility to municipal councils, and in the following 1910–11 municipal elections, forty women were elected to different municipal councils, Gertrud Månsson being the first. In 1914 Emilia Broomé became the first woman in the legislative assembly.

The right to vote in national elections was not returned to women until 1919, and was practised again in the election of 1921, for the first time in 150 years. In the election of 1921 more women than men had the right to vote because women got the right just by turning 21 years old while men had to undergo military service for the right to vote. In a decision 1921 men received the same right as women and this was practised in the election of 1924.

After the 1921 election, the first women were elected to Swedish Parliament after the suffrage: Kerstin Hesselgren in the Upper chamber and Nelly Thüring (Social Democrat), Agda Östlund (Social Democrat) Elisabeth Tamm (liberal) and Bertha Wellin (Conservative) in the Lower chamber. Karin Kock-Lindberg became the first female government minister, and in 1958, Ulla Lindström became the first acting Prime Minister.

Switzerland

A referendum on women's suffrage was held on 1 February 1959. The majority of Switzerland's men voted against it, but in some cantons women obtained the vote. The first Swiss woman to hold political office, Trudy Späth-Schweizer, was elected to the municipal government of Riehen in 1958. Switzerland was the last Western republic to grant women's suffrage; they gained the right to vote in federal elections in 1971 after a second referendum that year. In 1991 following a decision by the Federal Supreme Court of Switzerland, Appenzell Innerrhoden became the last Swiss canton to grant women the vote on local issues.

Turkey

In Turkey women were given the right to vote in municipal elections on March 20, 1930. Women's suffrage was achieved for parliament elections on December 5, 1934 by the constitutional amendment. Turkish women who participated for the parliament elections as a first time on February 8, 1935 obtained 18 seats. Latife Ussaki (wife of the founder of the Republic of Turkey) is known for being in the Emancipation of Women.

United Kingdom

The campaign for women's suffrage gained momentum throughout the early part of the 19th century as women became increasingly politically active, particularly during the campaigns to reform suffrage in the United Kingdom. John Stuart Mill, elected to Parliament in 1865 and an open advocate of female suffrage (about to publish The Subjection of Women), campaigned for an amendment to the Reform Act to include female suffrage. Roundly defeated in an all male parliament under a Conservative government, the issue of women's suffrage came to the fore.

During the later half of the 19th century, a number of campaign groups were formed in an attempt to lobby Members of Parliament and gain support. In 1897, seventeen of these groups came together to form the National Union of Women's Suffrage Societies (NUWSS), who held public meetings, wrote letters to politicians and published various texts. In 1907 the NUWSS organized its first large procession. This march became known as the Mud March as over 3,000 women trudged through the streets of London from Hyde Park to Exeter Hall to advocate for women's suffrage.

In 1903 a number of members of the NUWSS broke away and, led by Emmeline Pankhurst, formed the Women's Social and Political Union (WSPU). As the national media lost interest in the suffrage campaign, the WSPU decided it would use other methods to create publicity. This began in 1905 at a meeting where Edward Grey, 1st Viscount Grey of Fallodon, a member of the newly elected Liberal government, was speaking. As he was talking, two members of the WSPU constantly shouted out, 'Will the Liberal Government give votes to women?'. When they refused to cease calling out, police were called to evict them and the two suffragettes (as members of the WSPU became known after this incident) were involved in a struggle which ended with them being arrested and charged for assault. When they refused to pay their fine, they were sent to prison for one week, and three days. The British public were shocked and took notice at this use of violence to win the vote for women.

After this media success, the WSPU's tactics became increasingly violent. This included an attempt in 1908 to storm the House of Commons, the arson of David Lloyd George's country home (despite his support for women's suffrage). In 1909 Lady Constance Lytton was imprisoned, but immediately released when her identity was discovered, so in 1910 she disguised herself as a working class seamstress called Jane Warton and endured inhumane treatment which included force-feeding. In 1913, suffragette Emily Davison protested by interfering with a horse owned by King George V during the running of the Epsom Derby; she was trampled and died four days later. The WSPU ceased their militant activities during World War I and agreed to assist with the war effort.

The National Union of Women's Suffrage Societies, which had always employed 'constitutional' methods, continued to lobby during the war years, and compromises were worked out between the NUWSS and the coalition government. On 6 February, the Representation of the People Act 1918 was passed, enfranchising women over the age of 30 who met minimum property qualifications. About 8.4 million women gained the vote. In November 1918, the Eligibility of Women Act was passed, allowing women to be elected into Parliament. The Representation of the People Act 1928 extended the voting franchise to all women over the age of 21, granting women the vote on the same terms as men.

In 1999 Time magazine in naming Emmeline Pankhurst as one of the 100 Most Important People of the 20th Century, states..”she shaped an idea of women for our time; she shook society into a new pattern from which there could be no going back”.

The Americas

Brazil

The first Brazilian women enrolled as a voter was Celina Guimarães Viana, who was able to vote based on a state electoral law, after being authorized by a local judge in 1927. After this precedent, women from at least nine Brazilians states could be enrolled via judicial decisions. The female lawyer Mietta Santiago filed a writ of security alleging that the prohibition of women's suffrage was unconstitutional. She also managed a judicial decision to vote in 1928. All restrictions to women's suffrage in Brazil were removed on February 24, 1932, when President Getúlio Vargas issued the Brazilian Electoral Code (Decrete 21076), whose Article 2 stated that the right to vote was granted to all Brazilian citizens with at least 21 years old, without distinction of sex. The first occasion on which all Brazilian women could finally vote was the 1934 election for the National Constituent Assembly.

Canada

In the 19th century, female property holders could demand municipal voting rights on the principle of "no taxation without representation". Propertied women in Québec voted unchallenged between 1809 and 1849, when the word "male" was inserted into Québec's franchise act. What women in Québec lost, women in Ontario soon gained; from 1850, women with property, married or single, could vote for school trustees. By the 1900s municipal voting privileges for propertied women were general throughout Canada. Bills to enfranchise women in provincial elections failed to pass in any province until Manitoba finally succeeded in 1916. At the federal level it was a two step process. On September 20, 1917, women gained a limited right to vote: According to the Parliament of Canada website, the Military Voters Act established that "women who are British subjects and have close relatives in the armed forces can vote on behalf of their male relatives, in federal elections." In 1919, the right to vote was extended to all women in the Act to confer the Electoral Franchise upon Women. The remaining provinces quickly followed suit, except for Quebec, which did not do so until 1940. Agnes Macphail became the first woman elected to Parliament in 1921.

United States

Lydia Taft was an early forerunner in Colonial America who was allowed to vote in three New England town meetings, beginning in 1756, at Uxbridge, Massachusetts. Following the American Revolution, women were allowed to vote in New Jersey, but no other state, from 1790 until 1807, provided they met property requirements then in place. In 1807 all women were taken off the voters' roll as universal male suffrage was instated.

In June 1848, Gerrit Smith made women's suffrage a plank in the Liberty Party platform. In July, at the Seneca Falls Convention in upstate New York, activists including Elizabeth Cady Stanton and Lucretia Mott began a seventy-year struggle by women to secure the right to vote. Attendees signed a document known as the Declaration of Rights and Sentiments, of which Stanton was the primary author. Equal rights became the rallying cry of the early movement for women's rights, and equal rights meant claiming access to all the prevailing definitions of freedom. In 1850 Lucy Stone organized a larger assembly with a wider focus, the National Women's Rights Convention in Worcester, Massachusetts. Susan B. Anthony, a native of Rochester, New York, joined the cause in 1852 after reading Stone's 1850 speech. Women's suffrage activists pointed out that blacks had been granted the franchise and had not been included in the language of the United States Constitution's Fourteenth and Fifteenth amendments (which gave people equal protection under the law and the right to vote regardless of their race, respectively). This, they contended, had been unjust. Early victories were won in the territories of Wyoming (1869) and Utah (1870).

John Allen Campbell, the first Governor of the Wyoming Territory, approved the first law in United States history explicitly granting women the right to vote. The law was approved on December 10, 1869. This day was later commemorated as Wyoming Day.

Utah women were disenfranchised by provisions of the federal Edmunds–Tucker Act enacted by the U.S. Congress in 1887.

The push to grant Utah women's suffrage was at least partially fueled by the belief that, given the right to vote, Utah women would dispose of polygamy. It was only after Utah women exercised their suffrage rights in favor of polygamy that the U.S. Congress disenfranchised Utah women.

By the end of the 19th century, Idaho, Colorado, Utah, and Wyoming had enfranchised women after effort by the suffrage associations at the state level.

During the beginning of the 20th century, as women's suffrage faced several important federal votes, a portion of the suffrage movement known as the National Women's Party led by suffragist Alice Paul became the first "cause" to picket outside the White House. Paul and Lucy Burns led a series of protests against the Wilson Administration in Washington. Wilson ignored the protests for six months, but on June 20, 1917, as a Russian delegation drove up to the White House, suffragists unfurled a banner which stated: "We women of America tell you that America is not a democracy. Twenty million women are denied the right to vote. President Wilson is the chief opponent of their national enfranchisement". Another banner on August 14, 1917, referred to "Kaiser Wilson" and compared the plight of the German people with that of American women. With this manner of protest, the women were subject to arrests and many were jailed. On October 17, Alice Paul was sentenced to seven months and on October 30 began a hunger strike, but after a few days prison authorities began to force feed her. After years of opposition, Wilson changed his position in 1918 to advocate women's suffrage as a war measure.

The key vote came on June 4, 1919, when the Senate approved the amendment by 56 to 25 after four hours of debate, during which Democratic Senators opposed to the amendment filibustered to prevent a roll call until their absent Senators could be protected by pairs. The Ayes included 36 (82%) Republicans and 20 (54%) Democrats. The Nays comprised 8 (18%) Republicans and 17 (46%) Democrats. It was ratified by sufficient states in 1920, the Nineteenth Amendment, which prohibited state or federal sex-based restrictions on voting.

Mexico

Women gained the right to vote in 1947 for local elections and for national elections in 1953 (article 34 of the constitution).

Oceania

Australia

The female descendants of the Bounty mutineers who lived on Pitcairn Islands could vote from 1838, and this right transferred with their resettlement to Norfolk Island (now an Australian external territory) in 1856.

Propertied women in the colony of South Australia were granted the vote in local elections (but not parliamentary elections) in 1861. Henrietta Dugdale formed the first Australian women's suffrage society in Melbourne, Victoria in 1884. Women became eligible to vote for the Parliament of South Australia in 1894 and in 1897, Catherine Helen Spence became the first female political candidate for political office, unsuccessfully standing for election as a delegate to Federal Convention on Australian Federation. Western Australia granted voting rights to women in 1899.

The first election for the Parliament of the newly formed Commonwealth of Australia in 1901 was based on the electoral provisions of the six pre-existing colonies, so that women who had the vote and the right to stand for Parliament at state level had the same rights for the 1901 Australian Federal election. In 1902, the Commonwealth Parliament passed the Commonwealth Franchise Act, which enabled all women to vote and stand for election for the Federal Parliament. Four women stood for election in 1903. The Act did, however, specifically exclude 'natives' from Commonwealth franchise unless already enrolled in a state. In 1949, The right to vote in federal elections was extended to all Indigenous people who had served in the armed forces, or were enrolled to vote in state elections (Queensland, Western Australia, and the Northern Territory still excluded indigenous women from voting rights). Remaining restrictions were abolished in 1962 by the Commonwealth Electoral Act.

Edith Cowan was elected to the West Australian Legislative Assembly in 1921, the first woman elected to any Australian Parliament. Dame Enid Lyons, in the Australian House of Representatives and Senator Dorothy Tangney became the first women in the Federal Parliament in 1943. Lyons went on to be the first woman to hold a Cabinet post in the 1949 ministry of Robert Menzies. Rosemary Follett was elected Chief Minister of the Australian Capital Territory in 1989, becoming the first woman elected to lead a state or territory. By 2010, the people of Australia's oldest city, Sydney had female leaders occupying every major political office above them, with Clover Moore as Lord Mayor, Kristina Keneally as Premier of New South Wales, Marie Bashir as Governor of New South Wales, Julia Gillard as Prime Minister, Quentin Bryce as Governor-General of Australia and Elizabeth II as Queen of Australia.

Cook Islands

Women in Rarotonga were given the right to vote in 1893, shortly after New Zealand.

New Zealand

New Zealand's Electoral Act of 19 September 1893 made this country of the British Empire the first in the world to grant women the right to vote in parliamentary elections.

Women who owned property and paid rates—usually widows or "spinsters"—had been allowed to vote in local elections in Otago and Nelson since 1867; women in other provinces were granted suffrage in 1876. Women in New Zealand were inspired to fight for universal voting rights by the equal-rights philosopher John Stuart Mill and the British feminists' aggression. In addition, the missionary efforts of the American-based Woman's Christian Temperance Union gave them the motivation to fight—and their efforts were supported by a number of important male politicians including John Hall, Robert Stout, Julius Vogel, and William Fox. In 1878, 1879, and 1887 amendments extending the vote to women failed by a hair each time. In 1893 the reformers at last succeeded in extending the franchise to women.

Although the Liberal government which passed the bill generally advocated social and political reform, the electoral bill was only passed because of a combination of personality issues and political accident. The bill granted the vote to women of all races. New Zealand women were not given the right to stand for parliament, however, until 1919. In 2005 almost a third of the Members of Parliament elected were female. Women recently have also occupied powerful and symbolic offices such as those of Prime Minister, Governor-General, Speaker of the House of Representatives, and between 2005, and 2006, all three of these posts were held by women. New Zealand's first chief justice, Sian Elias is also a woman.

Women's Suffrage in Religions

Catholicism

The Pope is only elected by the College of Cardinals. Women are not appointed as cardinals, so women cannot vote for the Pope. The female offices of Abbess or Mother Superior are elective, the choice being made by the secret votes of the nuns belonging to the community.

Islam

Although Women were included in the process of electing the Caliph during the Rashidun Caliphate (632-661), Women's rights vary in Islamic countries in the modern era. The question of women's right to become imams (a religious leader) is disputed by many.

Judaism

Women are denied the vote and the ability to be elected to positions of authority in many Orthodox Jewish synagogues and religious organizations. This is not true of the non-Orthodox branches of Judaism, especially in the United States.

References

DuBois, Ellen Carol. (1997). *Harriot Stanton Blatch and the Winning of Woman Suffrage* (New Haven and London: Yale University Press.

Lloyd, Trevor, (1971). *Suffragettes International: The Worldwide Campaign for Women's Rights* New York: American Heritage Press,

Lowry, D. (1997) 'White woman's' country: Ethel Tawse Jollie and the Making of White Rhodesia, Journal of Southern African Studies, 23(2), pp. 259–281.

Mackenzie, Midge, (1975), *Shoulder to Shoulder: A Documentary*. New York: Alfred A. Knopf,

Raeburn, Antonia. (1973). *Militant Suffragettes*. London: New English Library.

Stevens, Doris, edited by Carol O'Hare, (1920). *Jailed for Freedom: American Women Win the Vote* Troutdale, OR: NewSage Press.

Wheeler, Marjorie Spruill, ed., (1995). *One Woman, One Vote: Rediscovering the Woman Suffrage Movement*, Troutdale, OR: NewSage Press.

3

Women's Right to Property

There are numerous cultural, racial, political, and legal factors that influence women's lack of property and inheritance rights, and specific patterns of ownership and disenfranchisement that vary widely. The lack of control over both productive and non-productive resources that is apparent in both rural and urban settings places women at a reduced level of advantage in areas of security of home, maintaining a basis for survival, and accessing economic opportunities. Development-related problems faced across the globe have been increasingly linked to women's lack of property and inheritance rights, especially in regards to land and property ownership, encompassing areas such as low levels of education, hunger, and poor health. Thus land property rights, through their impact on patterns of production, distribution of wealth, as well as market development, has evolved as one of the prerequisites of economic growth and poverty reduction.

Defining Land Rights

Rights, in any form of property, are claims that are legally and socially recognized and enforceable by external legitimized authority. Broadly defined, land rights can be understood as a variety of legitimate claims to land and the benefits and products produced on that land. Inheritance, transfers from the State, tenancy arrangements, and land purchase are all constructs of land rights. These rights can be in the form of actual ownership or usufruct, the rights of use.

Global Overview

Women play an integral part in the production of food and goods, from work in fields, factories, and home-based business across the globe. There is a critical relationship in the role that women play and the sustenance provided for families, communities, and nations. Globally, an estimated 41% of women headed households live below the locally defined poverty line, with one-third of the world's women either homeless or living in inadequate housing facilities. The additional exclusion of women from access to land pushes them towards cities, where they often join the ranks of increasing number of women-headed households in slum areas. However, through the processes of globalization and industrialization, there has been a noted increase in the numbers of women entering in the waged labor sectors. Rural women are solely responsible for half of the world's food production, and in developing countries, as much as 80% of food crops. More recent estimates claim that half of the world's food and in developing countries, between 60-80% of food crops are the results of growth from seeds that have been planted by a woman's hand. This persistence of traditional divisions of labor, in which women hold primary responsibility for producing food, as well as other labor intensive tasks such as gather water and fuel, contributes to the large percentage of women informally working in rural areas. The roles that women play differ significantly by region, with an average of 43% of the agricultural labor force in developing countries, ranging from 20% in Latin America to 50% in Eastern Asia and sub-Saharan Africa. Thus, in addition to increasing vulnerability and reducing status, exclusion of women from the decision making process and the control and transfer of land has also led to a decrease in food security and sustainable development.

Shifting System

Though women's lack of formal control over land and resources has long persisting historical roots, economies and societies undergoing extensive change have created deep implications for ownership rights. In subsistence production systems, access to land was determined by status within the family rather than actual ownership rights; resulting in both men and women having "user rights" to produce food for their families. The combined processes of industrialization and globalization have disrupted longstanding livelihoods and systems of production, forcing many families to focus more on income-generating activities than on subsistence practices.

Impact of Gender Bias

The typical process of agrarian transformation under which labor shifts from agriculture to nonagricultural has occurred slowly and with heavy gender-bias. Because women's property rights are often assumed through the security of the oftentimes, male, household head, some inheritance laws allocate less property to female heirs than male heirs. Ongoing adherence to male-dominated traditions of property ownership has generally meant that women cannot take advantage of the wide range of benefits associated with ownership and control of property According to the Land Tenure Service at FAO, poverty is inversely correlated with household land ownership and direct access to land minimizes women's risk of impoverishment and improvements the physical well-being and prospects for children.

The process of titling has been administered with strong gender bias, with women usually denied equal ownership rights. It is estimated that women own less than 2% of all titled land. Furthermore, property and inheritance claims are generally processed through loosely organized administrative bodies consisting of local leaders and clerks with limited legal training. Closer inspection of the decision makers, notes a body of mostly males.

Patriarchal Property Rights

Women who are potentially able to meet their subsistence needs on their own may threaten to leave the household if they are not given a large share of the surplus. However, due to patriarchal property rights, husbands control over the allocation of wives' labor time, husbands can make decisions that reduce the value of their wives' alternatives to marriage. Both the right to manage land and control the income from production, encompassing secure rights to land access, have much deeper implications than mere access. For many women, access to land and property are essential to the production of food as well as sustainable livelihoods, but are dependent on natal and marital affiliations. In many countries, women can lose rights to land when there is a change in marital status, including marriage, divorce, or even death of a spouse.

Because of the worldwide prevalence of patrilineal inheritance customs, both productive resources and property such as household goods have ended up in the hands of men and not women. When only men have rights of inheritance or family succession, women have little opportunity to improve their status or living conditions within the family and community. Consequently, they are rendered dependent on male relatives for survival and have little say over how property is used to generate income or to support families. Additionally, within patrilineal communities, there is a strong resistance by men towards endowing women, especially daughters, with rights to land access.

Barriers to Change in Status

In many cities of developing countries, more than half of the urban population lives in slums and informal settlements, in sub-standard housing, without basic services and without the enjoyment of their human rights to land and adequate housing. Women headed households form a high proportion of the population in many of such settlements.

While lack of security of tenure affects millions of people across the world, women face added risks and deprivations: in Africa and South-Asia especially, women are systematically denied their human rights to access, own, control or inherit land and property. The vast majority of women cannot afford to buy land, and usually can only access land and housing through male relatives, which makes their security of tenure dependent on good marital and family relations. At the same time, millions of women in Asia, Africa and Latin America depend critically on land for a livelihood.

Globally, an estimated 41% of women headed households live below the locally defined poverty line and close to one third of the world's women is homeless or lives in inadequate housing. Exclusion of women from access to land pushes them towards the cities, where they often join the ranks of the increasing number of women headed households in slum areas. In Kenya, for example, where women head 70% of all squatter households, over 25% of women slum dwellers migrated from their rural homes because of land dispossession.

Forced Evictions and Exclusion

Alarming numbers of cases are reported of in-laws having evicted widows upon the death of their husband. A widow is not considered to be part of the clan and is expected to return to her parents and/or fend for herself. The HIV/AIDS pandemic has contributed to an increase in such evictions. In many Sub-Saharan African countries, married women also face eviction from the marital home, when their husband takes a second (or third) wife and cannot afford to support both his wives. Very rarely can a woman in such cases return to her parent's land. When a man sells the family land and leaves for the city, women and children are often also left landless. All these cases show that the household relationship is not equal to start with. The commercialized tradition of dowry is contributing to this inequality: asked about co-ownership of land between him and his wife, a Ugandan farmer compared his wife with a tractor, that he had paid for. How could she (co-) own property if she herself was (seen as) his property? In addition to increasing vulnerability to evictions, exclusion of women from decisions on the use, control and transfer of land has also led to a decrease in food security and sustainable development.

While too many women face forced evictions by their in-laws and domestic violence within the marital home, they are also affected disproportionately by forced evictions, resettlement schemes, slum clearance and development projects carried out by or through state actors. Armed conflicts and resulting displacement, destruction of homes, family structure and communities often leave women more vulnerable. The lack of documentation combined with legal or customary discrimination often block women from accessing their land rights. In cases such as Rwanda, the deprivation of widows after the 1994 genocide led to fierce lobbying for the reform of Rwanda's civil code, which now allows widows to inherit property.

Women headed households and single women have little access to credit and other resources, often because of lack of collateral and/or the assumption that they will be unable to meet financial obligations in the absence of a male partner. In various countries, married women still need the consent of their husband before taking a loan, a requirement that violates international human rights law.

The UN Special Rapporteur on Adequate Housing confirms the dire situation of millions of women across the world: "In almost all countries, whether 'developed' or 'developing', legal security of tenure for women is almost entirely dependent on the men they are associated with. Women headed households and women in general are far less secure than men. Very few women own land. A separated or divorced woman with no land and a family to care for often ends up in an urban slum, where her security of tenure is at best questionable".

Underlying Causes

Women's equal rights to access, own and control land, adequate housing and property are firmly recognized under international law. However, at country level, the persistence of discriminatory laws, policies, patriarchal customs, traditions and attitudes in various countries are still blocking women from enjoying their rights.

Eroded customary laws and practices

Due to colonial influences, individualization of land tenure, land market pressure and other factors, many customary laws and practices have eroded over time; the forms of solidarity that used to exist and that protected women from exclusion, have now disappeared in many areas. Even where statutory national laws recognize women's rights to land, housing and property, "traditional" values prevail amongst judges, police officers, local councilors and land officials. They often interpret statutory laws in what at present are understood to be "customary ways", as a result of which women are deprived of the rights they should enjoy under statutory law.

Registration of land in name of husband

While in communal land tenure systems, women had significant indirect access and rights to use communal resources through their roles as household managers, they were further excluded when land tenure was individualized and invariably adjudicated and registered in the name of "heads of households" or men. Without legal protection, women are at risk of suddenly becoming landless, as has happened in the many cases where the husband sells the family land. Upon divorce, women still have to prove their contribution to the marital home in court. Upon the death of the husband, the marital home is included in the deceased husband's estate and is divided among his heirs. Many succession laws only entitle widows to a temporary use right of the marital home. If the marital home had been registered jointly, it would not become part of the estate upon the death of any spouse, and instead the widow would remain registered right holder of the land and house with the authority to sell, mortgage or carry out any other transaction. Unequal land distribution and widening gaps between rich and poor have further excluded women. Overemphasis on privatisation, individual freehold tenure and rigid planning and registration procedures that are costly, lengthy and often inaccessible to the (urban) poor deepens the gap between those who can and those who cannot afford.

Discriminatory laws and policies

An increasing number of countries has now recognized women's equal rights in their Constitution, thus complying with international human rights standards and obligations. However, there still are countries, such as Zimbabwe, Zambia, Lesotho and Kenya, where discrimination in customary and personal law matters (such as inheritance) is still permitted in their current Constitution. The notorious Magaya case in Zimbabwe, in which the Supreme Court ruled that Ms. Magaya could not inherit land, because customary law does not permit women to inherit and the Constitution still allowed for discrimination in such matters, shows the disastrous consequences that can follow from such legal provisions. The necessity of a constitutional provision that prohibits discrimination, including in customary law and practice (as laid down in the Constitutions of Uganda, South Africa and Mozambique) cannot be overemphasized.

Even today, laws and policies related to land and housing that explicitly discriminate against women still exist, as in the case of Swaziland, where married women are specifically excluded from registration of title to land in their name. In most countries, such laws and policies are gender neutral, but do not address existing discrimination. For example, many land laws allow for co-ownership of land, but spouses have to mutually agree on this and take active steps to register as co-owners. In practice, it is only a small proportion of, usually well educated, urban-based and relatively wealthy people who do so. And even among this group, many women face cultural attitudes that favor registration of land and housing in the name of men. Innovative approaches, such as in Tanzania's Land Act of 1999, where land occupied by both spouses is now presumed to be co-registered unless otherwise indicated by the spouses, are much more protective of women's interests and needs and actually implement women's rights. In Latin-America, most civil codes now include joint titling of spouses. However, in practice, these provisions are widely misunderstood and misused: cases of brothers or fathers and sons registering land jointly are widespread, and defeating the purpose for which this provision was formulated. Cultural attitudes and lack of clarity about implementation of such provisions go hand in hand to prevent the implementation of joint titling for spouses.

Laws related to marital property and inheritance rights remain discriminatory in most Sub-Saharan African and various other countries. In countries like Lesotho and Swaziland, married women are seen as legal minors, who cannot enter into contracts without consent of their husband. While laws increasingly recognize equal inheritance rights of daughters, this is often not the case regarding widows. In the few countries where the laws recognize women's equal marital property and inheritance rights (for example in Latin America), cultural attitudes in many areas in Latin America expect a daughter to relinquish her right to inherit land to her brother. In many sub-Saharan African countries, the idea of women inheriting land is seen as a threat to the continuity of clan land. Even in various matrilineal societies, such as in Malawi, Zambia, Mozambique and Tanzania, land market pressure and individual registration processes are threatening the continuity of inheritance systems that so far have protected women more. Religious laws usually entitle women to inherit, but the share of inheritance is invariably smaller, and there is an emphasis on access rather than ownership rights.

Limited implementation

Laws and policies, even if recognizing women's equal rights to land and property, are still very difficult to implement. Regulations and guidelines for implementation of laws and policies are often very technical and in many cases have not yet been written from a gender perspective. As a result, forms for registration of land for example, often simply lack the space to indicate joint registration of both spouses. And the land officials having to work with these forms often lack any gender awareness. Persistent cultural and customary attitudes also work against implementation of women's rights.

Lack of representation on decision-making bodies

Without gender aware officials on bodies dealing with land allocation, inheritance and dispute settlement, a male bias among these officials will continue to stand in the way to women's enjoyment of their rights. Moreover, inclusion of women in decision-making and policy formulation processes, especially among vulnerable groups such as slum dwellers, ethnic minorities etc. is crucial.

Lack of Awareness of Existing Laws

Levels of education, oftentimes products of restrictions on women's interaction with institutions which are primarily composed of men, create a mystique and illusion about legal actions. Additionally, ideologies about the conduct that a woman displays, normally taking the form of docility, can bring shame to the idea of challenging persisting gender inequalities in law, policy and land rights.

Prevalence of Traditional Attitudes and Practices

Gender ideologies, or beliefs and stereotypes of the expected characteristics of a particular gender, provide a barrier for women to gain property rights and enhance status These ideologies may take the form of assumptions of the role that a woman plays in society, her needs or capabilities, which thus affect the way that an issue is framed and implemented.

Women's Rights to Land and Property in South Asia

Land is a critical asset in most developing countries, especially for the poor. Most of the rural poor rely on subsistence agriculture for their survival. Furthermore, customary and formal rights to land act both as a form of economic access to key markets and as a form of social access to nonmarket institutions, such as the household and community-level governance structures. Land ownership confers economic benefits as an input into agricultural production, as a source of income from rental or sale, and as collateral for credit that can be used for either consumption or investment purposes.

Women may not fully share these benefits if they do not share formal or customary property rights. In addition to the short- and medium-term economic gains generated by greater access to land, capital, and product markets, women with stronger property rights to land are also less likely to become economically vulnerable in their old age, or in the event of the death of or divorce or abandonment from a spouse. Land is a particularly critical resource for a woman in the event that she becomes a de facto household head as a result of male migration, abandonment, divorce, or death. In both urban and rural settings, independent land property rights under these circumstances can mean the difference between dependence on natal family support and the ability to form a viable, self-reliant, female-headed household.

Land in South Asia.

In South Asia, land is the most valued form of property, conveying economic, political and symbolic significance. While there are significant differences in history, politics, terrain and culture in the six countries addressed here, they share a number of common features. Most countries in this survey suffer from population pressure and landlessness, where a large portion of the population owns little to no land. In these cases, the rural landless typically work as agricultural laborers or as tenants on the land of others to survive. In addition, each of the countries studied have high levels of poverty, with the majority of the poor being rural, and with close poverty-landlessness links. Many of the countries studied have experienced some form of conflict in the recent past, and while they each claim nationhood, each country is composed of significant and determinative regional, ethnic, tribal, religious, class, and caste differences. While the legal framework for each country reflects its own particular political, social, and economic history, all countries are characterized by some degree of legal pluralism, especially when it comes to women's land rights.

In South Asia, inheritance is often the vehicle that grants women property rights. Women's inheritance rights are mostly governed by formal and customary laws, and the primary formal laws are personal laws which tend to be heavily influenced by custom and religion. Personal laws are those laws that deal with matters pertaining to a person and his or

her family. While women often gain property rights through personal laws that govern inheritance, the right to inherit is impacted by other personal laws and practices such as polygamy, marital property rules, bride price or dowry and inter vivos gift or partition. To a lesser extent women's inheritance rights can be impacted by laws that govern transfer of property as well, such as government allocation, purchase, or lease.

The personal laws which govern inheritance for women may be statutory, religious, or customary. However, it is often difficult to precisely identify a given personal law as either one of those types; rather, personal laws evolve from the interplay of statute, religion, and custom, and, how those bodies of laws are interpreted by judicial or other official decisions.

For example, in Afghanistan Islamic law has been codified making it the statutory law for all matters that it covers, yet in practice tribal law determines inheritance. Likewise, Islamic law has been codified in Sri Lanka, as has the customs of two historically important ethnic groups, and all three form part of the body of statutory law for the country.

Defining the types of personal law is perhaps less important than recognizing that most South Asian countries have pluralistic legal systems. Legal pluralism generally means that there is more than one body of law which operates in a given area or for a given people. The bodies of law may be formal, or they may be the unwritten rules and practices that become an intrinsic part of the accepted conduct in a community.

The remainder of this document discusses the personal laws that govern women's inheritance rights in more detail. Section Two provides a table of the formal personal laws governing the inheritance rights of women, as daughters or wives for each country. Section Three discusses the other formal laws and customary laws impacting women's inheritance rights. Section Four provides examples of the types of interventions which might be considered to address women's property rights in South Asia. Following the conclusion, the annexes contain background studies on each of the countries studied.

Inheritance Laws

If a woman acquires land rights, it is most often via inheritance. Like many other laws governing property rights for women, inheritance laws fall within the class of personal laws, and it is in the realm of personal laws that the legally pluralistic nature of most South Asian countries is evident. The following chart briefly describes the formal inheritance laws in the six countries studied.

Laws and Customs which Impact Women's Inheritance

Reviewing the formal personal laws only tells part of the story of women's inheritance rights in South Asia, and most of the world. There are many other factors that impact a woman's right to inherit. On the one hand, there may be issues with the formal laws themselves. On the other hand, despite what might otherwise be classified as legal pluralism, customary practices are often overwhelmingly more important to women's land rights than formal laws. In addition, whatever rights women may have to inherit are significantly impacted by other laws and customs that govern family and social relationships. Following is a description of the key issues influencing women's and girl's inheritance in the six countries studied, with examples from those countries.

Formal laws discriminate based on sex by deferring to customary or religious law

Women's property rights are often at the intersection of formal, customary and/or religious laws because they are most often granted via a personal relationship.

Formal laws may be prima facie discriminatory. For example in 2008 Nepal had 137 provisions, two rules and 121 schedules in 85 laws which were discriminatory in favor of men. The rules on inheritance are an example of this type of discrimination: under the Eleventh Amendment of the Muluki Ain (Nepalese Civil Code), daughters and sons inherit equally, yet after marriage, daughters are expected to return their share of family property to the heir, who can only be a male.

Likewise, formal laws of inheritance may recognize or codify customary or religious law that is discriminatory. Until very recently in India, if a Hindu father died intestate, his ancestral property devolved equally to members of the coparceny, a traditional unit of property ownership under Hindu Mitakshara law, which conferred rights of co-ownership to male family members upon their birth. This provision essentially prevented Hindu females from succeeding to their father's ancestral estate.

Formal law may defer to customary or religious law that is discriminatory in practice. In Afghanistan, the civil code states that statutory law prevails, but where statutory law is silent, religious law applies, and where religious law is silent, customary law applies. Islamic law is codified in Afghanistan, so it is unclear which religious law applies if this formal religious law is silent. In practice, however, tribal or customary law, which is not codified, is applied first and is not only influential at the local level, but also in formal courts, where judges attempt to apply tribal law to appease local authorities and maintain peace.

In some cases, more than one law may apply to the same set of facts leaving a decision maker with a choice of which law to apply to an inheritance issue. This is the case in Sri Lanka, where inheritance questions may be answered by the body of case law, Roman-Dutch law, Shari 'a law, or, depending on the ethnic group, one of two recognized customary legal systems. Likewise, family law in Bangladesh covering marriage, division of property, and inheritance is not uniform but is determined by personal laws applicable to the religion of the deceased, which may be Christian, Hindu, Buddhist, Muslim or tribal.

In other cases, one law may trump all others. For instance, in Afghanistan, the civil code, which is mostly a codification of Hanafi school Islamic law, governs property rights generally, but when it comes to women's property rights, the statute recognizes customary law.

The fact that multiple laws intersect on the question of women's property rights can be problematic. If formal laws grant rights to women that they may not have in custom, and if those same formal laws recognize customary laws as valid, then potentially progressive provisions for women may not be implemented in practice. Also, since women tend to occupy the less powerful positions in society, if a decision-maker has a choice between which laws he can follow, it is likely that he would choose that law which is most favorable to the property rights of males rather than females.

Inheritance may be restricted to certain categories of land

Women's right to inherit may be influenced by the origin of the property in question. For instance, tribal or family land may be treated differently than purchased land. In Nepal, the rights of the kin group or family take precedence over the rights of women; by law male and female descendants have an equal right to inherit ancestral land, provided that the female is not married. If she is married she is not entitled to inherit ancestral land, and if she marries subsequent to the inheritance she must return the land to the male heir. These same restrictions do not apply to land which was jointly purchased by the married couple.

Likewise, under Kandyan law, which applies to certain people in Sri Lanka, women's inheritance rights differ depending on whether the property in question is acquired during the marriage or if it was inherited ancestral land; and within the category of ancestral land, paternal and maternal land is treated differently.

Polygamy/marriage practices may impact inheritance

The practice of and justification for polygamy can impact women's inheritance rights. Polygamy is the practice of a person having more than one spouse, and can be either polygyny or polyandry. Polygyny is the practice of a man having more than one wife, and is permitted by all Muslim societies, whether the Shari'a has been codified or not. Polygyny specifically impacts the property rights of women, which are already unequal from those of male heirs under Shari' a law: with each additional wife and child the possible share that each potential heir can take from the deceased's estate is reduced.

In some areas of Nepal where polyandry (more than one man marries the same woman) is practiced, it is justified on the grounds of not dividing family land between sons. The practice is fraternal polyandry, where brothers marry the same woman. Family land in this case is not divided among sons, rather they remain in a communal type living arrangement, and the woman moves to the brothers' land. This practice has significant economic advantages for the family by retaining male labor for the family land. The practice is often justified as a means to prevent fragmentation of family land by attaching all males to the ancestral land and restricting the addition of non-family members (wives). However, since a woman's right to inherit ancestral land in Nepal is already circumscribed, the practice also becomes a further impediment to her having exclusive rights over any property, and her options outside of the home are severely constrained.

The practice of levirate can also impact a woman's property rights. Levirate, sometimes known as bride inheritance, is the custom where the brother of the deceased marries his brother's widow. Like polyandry, levirate is justified as a means to prevent family land from fragmenting, and ensures that the family retains control over family land. It also means that the widow forgoes whatever rights she might have to her deceased spouse's property. Levirate is practiced in parts of Pakistan to prevent land rights going to an outsider.

Bride price and/or dowry often seen as equivalent for inheritance

The payment of dowry or bride price is often considered the daughter's share of the family assets and is the accepted justification for why daughters should not inherit equally with sons. The practice has very strong roots. In many countries, the common perception is that payment of dowry or bride price ensures the security of the daughter and that without such payment a daughter may not get married and will remain a burden on her family. This is the case in India, where families may be happy to pay dowry in hopes that their daughters will be well cared for. Payment of a large dowry is also intended to ensure that the new husband is from a well-established family, is educated, does not have bad habits (e.g., drinking, gambling), and has a good character.

For Hindus, typically the daughter's family gives dowry to her new husband and his family. If the daughter comes from a family with land, the payment of dowry and the cost of the wedding incurred by her family can impact a daughter's entitlement to a share of her family's In India, although prohibited by law, land, in practice. Any formal right the custom of dowry is common. the daughter may have to inherit a portion of the family land is trumped by the cultural understanding that the dowry and wedding costs represent the daughter's share of the family assets. Yet, during the term of the marriage, the daughter (now wife) has no right to the dowry paid by her family. Thus, while dowry is understood as the daughter's share of the family inheritance, in practice it does not benefit her or provide her economic security.

Likewise, women in Afghanistan do not benefit from the dowry, although the practice was initially justified as providing for her security in the event of marital difficulties. Under the Afghan civil code and Islamic law, a wife is entitled to inherit and to receive mahr, or dowry, on marriage. Mahr is exclusively the wife's property and is intended to give her financial security in the event of divorce. However, by custom a woman does not inherit, and walwar is paid in place of mahr. Walwar is a sum of money or property paid by the groom to the head of the bride's household. The value for walwar can be quite high and it is prohibited by formal law. This leaves the woman in the marriage without the right to inherit from her family or the financial security envisioned in Shari 'a and the Afghan civil code. Moreover, the value of a daughter to the family materializes at her marriage, after that she is of little value to them. This gives her family an incentive to marry her early and makes it less likely she can successfully return to her family if her marriage fails.

On the other hand, in Pakistan, when dowry is paid, the wife often does obtain access to the property although the value of dowry is rarely equivalent to what she would have received as inheritance of the family estate. Women are paid a dowry in small gifts of moveable property, often jewelry or household items, rather than immovable property. In Pakistan as in other South Asian countries, the practice of dowry was originally intended to compensate a woman for family property that she does not inherit. Yet the value, power and respect that land ownership brings is not comparable to the gifts of movable property typically given as dowry.

Moreover, even if her family provides dowry, the daughter often does not have exclusive ownership or control over it. In Nepal, dayo or dowry is property – usually but not exclusively movable – that is given to the woman at the time of marriage. Things that are part of the dayo are not considered ancestral property for the purpose of inheritance; however, neither are they considered the woman's separate property. Rather, it is considered joint property of the husband and wife and is ordinarily inherited by the wives' sons.

Other social factors that impact inheritance rights

There are a number of other factors, mostly related to women's social position, that make it less likely that a woman will gain land and property rights via inheritance, or will seek to enforce her rights even when given the chance.

Most women, in the six countries studied here, have less social mobility than men and are thus less capable, willing, or able to enforce the land rights they do have. This is partially explained by the fact that women have less access to information and thus may not be aware of their property rights. Also, in South Asia, most women's interactions are limited to the homestead, and sometimes the village. Any property-related claims a woman may have are more likely to be handled within the family rather than by outsiders. Few women would appear in a formal court against their family. This is especially the case in places where purdah is strictly adhered to. Purdah, literally meaning "curtain," is a cultural practice that restricts women's movement outside the home, and obliges women to be veiled in public. For instance, in Pakistan, most women practice purdah, which prevents them from learning new agricultural skills, or learning how to negotiate in the market. Many men in Pakistan believe that a woman should not own or manage family land because of her lack of social mobility and skills.

Beyond this, women often face social pressures not to claim her property rights, and making such a claim may come at a significant personal cost for her. For example, if she speaks up in defense of her rights, a woman may be ostracized by her kin group, on whom she relies to ensure her own survival and her place in the community. Or, even if she inherits property, a woman may gift the property to her male kin because good relations with male kin are regarded as an important safety net in the case of future financial difficulties. In Afghanistan, it is culturally inappropriate for women to inherit any property and women may refuse an inheritance and give it instead to her brothers out of "respect" and love for them even when such women have a formal legal right to inherit the property. Similarly, in Bangladesh it is customary for women not to claim their share of family property unless it is given willingly and with the support of the entire family. It is customary for a woman to surrender her legal right to family property in exchange for the right to visit her parental home and the right to seek support from her brothers in the case of marital conflict.

Women may resist enforcing legal inheritance rights for other reasons. In Pakistan, women often believe themselves not to be part of either their birth family or their spouse's family, and thus do not believe themselves entitled to property rights from either. In India, women may not believe that daughters should have the right to inherit land because they did not inherit from their parents, or because a daughter will leave the family village and cannot take the land with them.

In many cases in South Asia, families do not have land for a woman to inherit. In situations of pre-existing landlessness, women's land rights may take second place to general land rights for tenant farmer, sharecropper, or laborer households. In these cases, the issue of land rights for women is colored by the socio-economic status of her family, whereby women from land owning classes are interested in gaining inheritance rights and women from landless classes are more interested in just gaining access to land. The significance of this point cannot be understated given the prevalence of landlessness among the very poor in Nepal, Bangladesh, India, Afghanistan, and Pakistan. In Pakistan, for example, less than 50% of rural households own agricultural land and 40% of agricultural land is owned by 2.5% of households. And, in India, landlessness is the best predictor of poverty; an even better predictor of illiteracy or membership in a scheduled caste or tribe.

Women's Rights to Land and Property in Afghanistan

Afghanistan is a mountainous landlocked country located approximately in the center of Asia. The country has a total land area of 647,500 square kilometers, 12 percent of which is arable, 46 percent is used as permanent pastures, 3 percent of which is forests and woodland, and the remaining 39 percent of which is put to other uses. Approximately 80 percent of the country's estimated 32.7 million people live in rural areas.

Afghanistan has suffered from chronic instability and conflict in recent years and its economy and infrastructure have failed. Many Afghan people are refugees. After the fall of the Taliban administration in 2001, Afghanistan became an Islamic republic and is currently comprised of 34 provinces. The new constitution was ratified in January of 2004. President Hamid Karzai became the first democratically elected President of Afghanistan on December 7, 2004. The legal system is based on statutory, customary, and Shari'a laws. Under Afghanistan's Constitution, land issues are matters for legislation and control by both the central and provincial governments. Yet women's land rights are governed by personal laws.

Afghanistan is extremely poor, and remains highly dependent on foreign aid, agriculture, and trade with neighboring countries. Much of the population continues to suffer from shortages of housing, clean water, electricity, medical care, and jobs. Expanding poppy cultivation and a growing opium trade have boomed since the fall of the Taliban and Afghanistan supplies about 93 percent of the world's opium. Approximately eighty percent of Afghanistan's population is rural and eighty percent of the total workforce still works primarily in agriculture.

Rural land ownership is highly skewed. Five percent of the farms in the country are located on 40% of the arable land. Seventy-three percent of farms are less than five hectares. Average farm size is 1.6 hectares.

Afghanistan has a largely rural population with a high number of landless peoples. A significant percentage of Afghanistan's rural people are landless or near-landless (owning farms too small for survival), contributing to agricultural production, as sharecroppers, laborers, or tenants. Farm laborers generally receive 1/5 of the crop as payment and sharecroppers up to 1/3, insufficient to live on. Well over half the rural population is below the poverty line. A large number of rural families are homeless as well as landless, depending upon landlords or relatives for shelter, generation to generation.

Disadvantaged Groups

Nationally, 21% of rural households are landless. The poorest households are those headed by women and the landless. Almost five million refugees have returned to Afghanistan from Pakistan and Iran since 2002, a majority of whom are landless or who returned to find that their land had been taken in their absence. They are often forced to join the growing population inhabiting squatter settlements in urban areas. Two million more refugees wait in Pakistan, 90% of whom reportedly have no access to land or housing in Afghanistan.

Local Land Related Challenges

Afghanistan's farmland, pastures, forests, and water resources have suffered from successive years of extreme drought and extended conflict. The population's traditional methods of coping have been undermined by soil degradation, deforestation, and flooding caused by unsustainable land use practices, military action, and chronic insecurity of livelihoods. Land ownership is concentrated in the hands of a few. An elite minority has traditionally owned disproportionate areas of the total land, with surveys indicating that 2.2 percent of the population owned 19 percent of the total land area in 2002.

Yet, uncertainty over land tenure in Afghanistan is high. This is partially due to high regional variation also because of the highly intertwined markets for sharecropping and land mortgaging. Sharecropping and land mortgaging in particular involve a web of relationships in which it is difficult to distinguish creditors/debtors from owners/sharecroppers, or to know precisely who the legal or accepted right-holder of the property is. Further complicating matters is the fact the country lacks a clear regime for managing land rights and with the increased instability and coercion by warlords in the last decade, land rights management and dispute resolution has lost credibility in many rural areas, resulting in rural Afghans' tend to rely on customary methods to regulate their land tenure relations, which favors wealthier elites, men, and dominant ethnicities.

Women's Property Ownership, Activities and Employment

Women's lives in Afghanistan are highly proscribed. Since most of them don't work, women usually want to marry to have a better life and believe that marriage is the only option to have financial security and an opportunity to live with less stress from their family. Women hardly have a say in their marital life and most people are unaware of women's rights under the formal or religious law.

There is strong opposition from men to allowing women more liberties or granting them their Islamic marital rights and this causes serious problems for Afghan women who are deprived of their basic rights and education, and suffer many social and personal restrictions in their daily life, such as house detention and abuse.

Land Policy and Reform

Land reform efforts in 1970s were intended to limit the size of land holdings and distribute the surplus to landless and near-landless households. The reforms were largely unsuccessful because they lacked support in the rural areas, were technically flawed, and spawned violent reactions among landowners that deterred implementation.

Legal and Customary Land Rights for Women

Afghanistan has a pluralist legal system. Land rights are governed by customary law, religious law and state law. Customary law (rawaj) governs how land is owned and transacted as established through community practice and adherence by members to group norms. They also govern women's rights to land. Customary rules are rarely codified and appropriately change with time. Pashtunwali (Pashtun customary law) is one of the more elaborated operating laws, and dominates the norms in many areas. Shariat and custom often conjoin on land matters, except with respect to usury, women's land rights and common property rights. The former is more liberal — and generally less adhered to because of this.

State law includes the civil code, statutory law and supreme or constitutional law. The Civil Code is a written expression of mainly Islamic law principles and includes more than 1,000 directives relating to property. The Code was compiled in the 1970s building in large part on historical treatments of the Hanafi school of Islamic jurisprudence.

Religious law (Shariat or Shar'ia) in its original rules as laid down in the Koran and expressed in many scholarly treatises, may be directly applied when the issue is not covered in the Civil Code. Similarly, the Civil Code is only applied if the issue is not covered in state law. Land cases are officially dealt with in civil courts, which rule on the basis of state, civil and religious law, in uncertain mix and measure.

Despite the pluralism, customary law dominates in Afghanistan. While the Constitution is silent on the authority of customary law it prohibits adoption of laws that are inconsistent with the tenets of Islam and the Civil Code recognizes the application of customary law with regard to land rights. Customary law is in large measure consistent with Shari'a, and Shari'a permits the practice of customary law so long as it does not interfere with tenets of Islam. Customary law systems vary between regions and tribes. It is generally understood that those refuse the application of customary law will be condemned by their families and have no real choice to refuse its application. However, even when the decisions of the jirgas (local dispute resolution actors) are not in accordance with Islamic law, the participation of religious figures in the decision-making of the jirga makes people believe that the decision complies with Islamic law.

Marriage

The Afghan Civil Code governs all marriages in Afghanistan. However, in practice, all marriage practices are almost entirely governed by custom. Some customs related to marriage are outlined below.

In Afghanistan, a man and a woman rarely meet before their wedding. This is especially the case in tribal and rural areas where women are considered personal property of the men and part of their honor. The seclusion of women and segregation of gender prevent any contact between eligible men and women before marriage. There are some variations in this belief amongst urban, educated, or wealthy elites.

An Afghan woman has the right to dower, or mahr, which is derived from Islamic law and enshrined in the Afghan Civil Code. However, women often don't know about their right to mahr and its importance or they may undervalue the mahr because of it association with divorce which is culturally unacceptable. Though illegal, walwar is common in Afghanistan especially among the poorer rural families, and is understood as a compensation for the family of the bride for having nursed the girl. The amount of walwar is not fixed and may vary according to the economic background of the bride's family. Generally, if the bride's family is rich, they will not ask for walwar; but if the bride's family is poor, walwar will be the single most important issue during marriage negotiations as it is important income for the bride's family.

Marriages of minors and forced marriages are also prevalent in Afghanistan, even though they may contradict Islamic principles. They emanate from such traditions as: badal, or the exchange of girls between two families as additional wives; marriage promise, where an unborn girl is promised to an unborn boy; badd, where girls are given into marriage for compensation for a crime, marrying a member of the victim's family to ensure future peace between the two families; and the negotiation of marriages simply so the brides' family can receive the walwar. It is primarily weak economic conditions that encourage families to marry their minor girls. This tendency has grown with the growing influences of warlords, who can pay great amounts of money to the parents of the girl. In these cases, the parents will agree even if their girls are still minors.

According to Islamic law and the Afghan Civil Code, polygamy is a legal institution whereby a man can marry up to four wives simultaneously. However, the conditions set for multiple marriages, such as the equal treatment of all wives, are not observed in practice by the bride's parents or the polygamous husband. In urban areas, polygamy is hardly practiced. Only exceptionally, particularly in issues revolving around succession, polygamy also occurs in urban areas (e.g. if the first wife has had no sons).

Divorce, Separation and Abandonment

The incidence of divorce is very low in Afghanistan. Divorce is seen as a bad thing, the social prestige of a divorcee is very, very low, and for the majority of women, living alone is not an option. As mentioned above, although Islamic law provides for property rights for women after a divorce, which are to be stipulated during marriage negotiations, the social stigma against divorce is so great that those negotiations do not take place very often.

Inheritance and Division of Property

In Afghanistan as a whole, customs and Islamic rules predominate in questions of inheritance. Despite their intimate relationship with agriculture and the land, in practice Afghan women are typically denied of their legal rights to inheritance and ownership over land or any other immoveable property by culture, traditional, and tremendous societal pressure.

While civil law grants women the right to inherit land, few women, especially daughters, inherit in practice. Under Shari'a law women have rights to inherit both as daughters and as widows, however, divorced women enjoy no rights to their husbands' property. Widows are to receive one-eighth of the property or one-fourth if they have no children. Where the marriage was polygamous, this proportion is shared among all the wives. The provision for widows is the priority.

Widows, particularly those living in separate households (i.e. not with other related families), more readily receive their share of the land. Still, these widows often transfer the land into their sons' names to avoid any confusion later on, although they do retain some control over the land. Sons may still consider the land to belong to their mother. In contrast, widows, living in joint households, often do not receive their inheritance share of land because the land has not beendivided and all land is in the family.

While daughters are their brothers' share of the parental property, under Shari' a law, in practice daughters rarely receive or accept their share of land. This is because it is culturally inappropriate for a woman to own land outright since the expectation is that she is cared for by her husband. Also, they may refuse their share and give it to their brothers out of respect for their brothers and also so that they maintain peaceful relations with brothers who are their social protection in the case of divorce or widowhood.

Key NGOs Working on Women's Land Rights

Afghanistan Research and Evaluation Unit (AREU)

AREU is an independent research organization based in Kabul whose mission is to conduct high-quality research that informs and influences policy and practice.

Afghan Women Council (AWC)

AWC is a non-profit founded in Peshawar, Pakistan in 1986 to support the Afghan refugees, which aims to assist Afghan women and children. Working in Afghanistan since 1992, AWC's predominant objective is to empower women by building their capacity, improving their health, education, and living conditions, and by strengthening their socio-economic status in society by multi-lateral involvement in development activities.

Afghan Women's Network (AWN)

AWN is a network of 72 NGOs and over 3,000 individuals working for the promotion of Afghan women's empowerment, rights and equal participation in society. AWN is considered the only umbrella entity for women/gender-based organizations in Afghanistan. Most of the member NGOs focus on training women skills – education, literacy, productive products (e.g., tomato paste), shoemaking, sewing, carpentry, handicraft, cheese making, IT and website, finances – as well as women rights – rights, available social services, violence against women

Women's Rights to Land and Property in Bangladesh

Bangladesh has a complicated legal foundation based largely on its political history. Europeans began setting up trading posts in the area of Bangladesh in the 16th century. Eventually, the British came to dominate the region and it became part of British India. In 1947, West Pakistan and East Bengal (both primarily Muslim) separated from India (largely Hindu) and jointly became the new country of Pakistan. In 1955, East Bengal became East Pakistan, but the awkward arrangement of a country consisting of two disconnected geographies left the Bengalis marginalized and distanced from the central government. In 1971, East Pakistan seceded from its union with West Pakistan and was renamed Bangladesh.

After nationhood, Bangladesh has experienced many political upheavals with short periods of relative peace which rendered many legal, social and political institutions very weak. Elections were held in 2008 after one year of the military-backed caretaker government, and Sheikh Hasina Wajed was reappointed prime minister.

Most Bangladeshis are rural. Three-quarters of the country's total population and 85 percent of the total number of the poor live and earn their livelihood in the rural areas. Agriculture makes up around 25% of the GDP, and the rural non-farm sector makes up an additional 30%. Agriculture generates two-thirds of total employment, contributes a quarter of total export earnings and provides food security to the increasing population. The current labor force is estimated at around 50 million.

Many Bangladeshis are poor. While incidence of poverty was in decline by official estimates, from a high of 57% of the population in the 1990s to 40% in 2005, the Gini coefficient of consumption has remained stable in that time. However, recent shocks from natural disasters and a sharp rise in food prices have dampened economic growth.

Poverty in Bangladesh is mainly rural. Seventy-seven percent of rural households say they are at break-even or deficit status. Within this bracket, 18% comprise the hardcore poor who are always in deficit. The rural poor are traditionally the most natural resource dependent and landless communities whose lives are totally dependent on natural capital.

Land and Natural Resources

Seventy-percent of Bangladeshis depend on natural resources for their livelihoods. Degradation of natural capital and biodiversity has a serious and direct impact on the food security, nutrition and income of the poor. This is especially the case for water and fish resources. The people of Bangladesh have a historical dependency on the floodplain system as a source of income and food security. An estimated 70 million rural households rely on the wetlands to survive. These resources are estimated to supply between 60% and 80% of the animal protein needs of the country. Between 1995 and 2000, freshwater fish consumption fell by 38% among poor wetlands inhabitants. Open water fish that once supplied 80% of the animal protein consumed by the rural poor, now supply less than 60%.

Disadvantaged Groups

In Bangladesh, there are small groups of extremely disadvantaged poor people. Among these are the refugees, the disabled and certain groups who are associated with a particular occupation. In regard to the latter, although in Bangladesh there is no caste system per se, these groups have the same social status as the lower castes in a caste system. Some of these communities are Bawalies (those who live of the resources of the Sunderban forest areas) and mawalies (honey collectors in Sunderban areas); Bede or river gypsy (engaged in snake charming and small trade in the rural areas); Methor, Dalich (sweepers, sewerage cleaners and scavengers); Mymal (fisherman on the big water bodies); Muchis (cobblers and shoe makers); Nagarchi (traditional folk singers); Kulies (tea garden worker originally brought to Bangladesh from various parts of India). These communities have been living a segregated life, parallel with the mainstream population, for many years. They are spread all over the country and constitute a portion of those who are classified as the extreme poor and often live in very challenging conditions.

Local Land-Related Challenges

Land as a resource is under enormous pressure in Bangladesh. On the one hand, Bangladesh loses around one percent of arable land annually to degradation and natural disaster, and on the other hand, it is under the pressure of a rapidly growing population and the competing needs of subsistence farming, the agricultural sector, industry, housing, and urbanization.

In addition, unequal land distribution is a major source of rural income inequality. The number of effectively landless households is increasing. In 1995, the number of rural landless households, defined as those with less than 0.2 hectares of land, was estimated to be 49.6%. Most of landless in rural areas are poor and work as agricultural wage laborers.

Women's Property Ownership, Activities and Employment

Access to property for women is still a distant goal in Bangladesh. Although equality is enshrined in the legal system, in 1996, only 3.5 percent (0.62 million) out of 17.8 million agricultural holdings were female owned. Women's ownership of homesteads is only slightly higher than their ownership of agricultural land and women are more likely to own the homestead if it is not attached to cultivable land.

Most Bangladeshi women are employed in the informal sector. According to official estimates as of 2003, only 26 percent of women ages 15-59 were employed in the formal sector, and only 10 percent of employed women and 22 percent of employed men, aged 20-55, receive any cash wages. In addition, women who are employed year-round earn 60-65% of what their male counterparts do in the agricultural sector. Just a little over 4 percent of all women and 13 percent of employed women are casual workers in Bangladesh.

Women in Bangladesh are mostly involved in homestead based activities contributing to the household nutrition intake. Women are customarily involved in the post-harvest processing of crops, rearing of livestock animals and poultry birds, and home-gardening of fruits and vegetables. To the extent that they sell the products themselves, they do contribute to household savings, expenditures, and investment, and there are some poor rural women who earn from lending their small savings to various productive rural enterprises. Women are also formally and informally engaged in the fishing industry, which is the second most important occupation for them in the non-farm sector.

Land Policy and Reform

Land administration in Bangladesh today is firmly rooted in colonial era practices. The British gave high priority to the organization of a centrally controlled management system that was designed to maintain political control and secure a steady source of state finance. Relatively little has changed in the post-independence era.

Attempts at reform through land ceilings and redistribution have been a feature of both the Pakistan and Bangladesh periods. In 1984, in a populist move by the Ershad regime, a new Land Reforms Ordinance was promulgated. The ordinance set a new land ceiling at 20 acres (8.1 hectares) per family, and stipulated that baragadars (sharecroppers) had the right to cultivate five acres of land. This was to be explicit in a legally binding contract between the landowner and the baragadar, thus doing away with the tradition of oral contracts, which proved to be increasingly precarious. The contract set up the terms and conditions of cultivation and was valid for five years, and could be renewed if the conditions were satisfactorily met by the sharecropper. Furthermore, the ordinance included a clause giving the sharecropper the option of purchasing the land. It obliged the landowner to give notice of intent to sell, and the sharecropper had a period of 15 days to make an offer. With the provision of rural credit facilities, it was hoped that tenants would be able to secure loans and gain title to land in this way.

But these have largely been circumvented by the wealthy and powerful and, while tenants' rights are enshrined in law, they are largely ignored in practice. The Land Reforms Ordinance of 1984 has remained virtually unimplemented. This is partially because of weak protections in the law, for instance, legally binding contracts aimed to guarantee security of tenure for the sharecropper permit a significant number of escape clauses for the landowner; land can be repossessed if the landowner believes that it is not being personally cultivated by the bargadar. Furthermore, the owner can simply decide to take back the land for personal cultivation. The vagueness of the terms could lead not only to land repossession, but potentially to eviction of sharecroppers. Land purchase by a sharecropper may also be circumvented by landowners who sell or give land to their relatives.

Legal and Customary Land Rights for Women

The original Constitution of Bangladesh, effective in 1972, guaranteed equal rights to all citizens, regardless of gender, religion, and other social divisions. The constitution includes provisions granting equal protection under the law, forbidding negative discrimination of women, providing equal rights for men and women in all spheres, and allowing positive discrimination, or making special provisions in favor of women for their advancement.

No uniform civil law exists in Bangladesh to govern family law matters, such as marriage, divorce, division of property, or inheritance. Family law in Bangladesh is governed by the personal laws applicable to each community – Muslim, Hindu, Christian, Buddhist, and tribal communities have separate laws.

Much of the Muslim personal law is unlegislated, the basis for the law being classical Hanafi fiqh except where this has been amended by legislation. The Muslim Marriages and Divorces (Registration) Act requires civil registration of marriages. Although there is no law to this effect, there is a custom in Bangladesh of inserting stipulations relating to property rights on divorce in the marriage contract.

The Family Courts Ordinance provides that the application of the personal laws of all Bangladesh is through Family Court of the state judiciary. Family Courts have exclusive jurisdiction to try and dispose of suits relating to the dissolution of marriage, including those matters that pertain to property such as dower and maintenance.

The Child Marriage Restraint Act sets the minimum age of marriage as 21 for men and 18 for women. Penal sanctions apply to those who contract an under-age marriage; however an under-age marriage is not invalidated by contravening the law.

The Bangladeshi Muslim Family Laws Ordinance governs, in part, the application process for contracting polygamous marriages (i.e., requiring the reasons for wanting to contract a polygamous marriage and certification attesting to the existing wife's or wives' consent). The Ordinance also establishes penalties for contracting polygamous marriages which contravene the law; but again, such marriages are not invalidated. In addition, there is no penalty for failing to obtain the existing wife's consent.

The Dissolution of Muslim Marriages Act remains in force in Bangladesh, with amendments initiated in Pakistan by the Muslim Family Laws Ordinance 1961 and governs Muslim divorce.

Marriage

The majority of Bangladeshi marriages are arranged by parentsalthough men frequently exercise some influence over the choice of spouse. In middle-class urban families men negotiate their own marriages. Only in the most sophisticated elite class does a woman participate in her own marriage arrangements. Marriage generally is made between families of similar social standing.

Marriage practices are generally determined by cultural or religious norms. However, a few facts cross those lines: early marriage is common; and the average age at marriage is about 16 years. Polygamy, divorce, and cross-cousin marriages are uncommon, although abandonment of women is quite common. While the Dowry Prohibition Act prohibits it, the payment of dowry is widespread in Bangladesh. One study from the University of Bath claims that dowry payments can be more than 200 times the daily wage. It is customary for Bangladeshi women to leave their family home at marriage and take up residence with her in-laws. She is then expected to seek permission to visit her own home. The Muslim Family Law Ordinance permits polygamy of up to four wives for a Muslim man.

Marriage of the Buddhist is mostly arranged through consent of parents and the wedding is solemnized in the bridegroom's house by pronouncing some religious and social mantras. The various tribal communities of Bangladesh are guided by their respective customs and traditions in respect of their marriage systems.

Divorce, Separation and Abandonment

Women suffer when they become widowed, divorced or abandoned by their husbands. At present, widowed, divorced and abandoned women constitute about 11 percent of total married women.

Divorce is permitted in Muslim law. A Muslim husband may declare talaq, a separation which would lead to divorce without cause. A wife may divorce her husband for a few narrow reasons, and only when such power of divorce is delegated to her by her husband, this is known as talaq-i-tafweez. Rural Bangladeshi women suffer a high incidence of irrevocable divorce, giving rise to numerous hardships for both parties. The practice, known as hila is largely a result of illiteracy and inadequate grasp of Islamic concepts.

Divorce is not legally possible for Hindus in Bangladesh as it is unknown in Hindu law. In Hindu law, marriage is regarded as an indissoluble union between husband and wife. Neither party to a marriage can divorce the other. Divorce is allowed in the Christian community according to the provisions of Divorce Act, 1869.

Inheritance and Division of Property

As in marriage, in Bangladesh, inheritance is governed by Muslim personal law or the law of the religion of the person to which it applies. The Muslim law of Inheritance is also a Quranic law prescribing specific shares for each individual's nearest relations including female heirs in the property left by a deceased person. The distribution of property of a deceased Muslim person is made according to the principle that within the limits of each class of heirs, the nearer in degree excludes the more remote. While Muslim women have the right to inherit in Bangladesh, many women forgo that right in exchange for naior, a right to visit her parents once or twice year.

The Dayabhaga school governs the system of inheritance for Hindus in Bangladesh. A Hindu woman's inheritance rights in Bangladesh are virtually non-existent. Under the Dayabhaga law, the right to inherit arises on the heirs capacity to confer salvation to the souls of the paternal and maternal ancestors through those who live. A widowed, sonless, or childless daughter cannot inherit, but unmarried daughters and daughters with sons can inherit. A widow is only given a life estate to the deceased's property, and this is believed to be her inheritance.

The Succession Act of 1925 governs inheritance in the case of the Christians. Under this act, a wife will inherit one third of the intestate deceased's estate and the remaining two thirds are divided equally among lineal descendants regardless of sex.

Generally, son preference prevails in Bangladesh. For the most part, property is inherited along the male line. The basis for this norm is that daughters only "belong" to their natal family until they are married and parents should not live with their married daughters or accept financial help from them.

Key NGOs Working on Women's Land Rights

Centre for Development Services (CDS)

CDS aims to conduct an interactive, informative media campaigns on women's property and inheritance rights; and to mobilize and train women to redress violations through advocacy. CDS has conducted research to identify discriminatory laws and customary practices that inhibit women from claiming property. Community-based "mobilizers" trained by CDS have conducted awareness-raising sessions that integrate messages on property and inheritance rights with street theater and folk songs. The mobilizers also provide information on changes made in personal laws in 1961 to mediation committees and local leaders to improve the resolution of local land disputes.

CDS took a human rights-based approach in its project, emphasizing how virtually every aspect of inheritance traditions in Bangladesh affords girls and women half of what boys and men receive. CDS aims to ensure that the next generation of women is more aware of their rights, and can in turn address violations and, ultimately, live as equals with full protection of the law.

Aga Khan Foundation Project

The Aga Khan Foundation seeks to increase the knowledge and abilities of locally elected women to advocate on property and inheritance issues. It recently provided information and skills training to 400 locally elected women so that they would be able to help promote awareness and action on issues and laws pertaining to property and inheritance rights. Participants were also introduced to the Women's Lawyers Network, which is funded by the Khan Foundation and can serve as a free legal resource at the local level. The Aga Khan Foundation also produced useful materials for participants to use and distribute in their local communities.

Madaripur Legal Aid Association (MLAA)

MLAA aims to create a network of informed Muslim women leaders who can address gender equity issues and property inheritance rights. MLAA has developed a unified network of women leaders from grassroots women's groups, with which it provides information and logistical support for the promotion of women's rights. MLAA conducted a field survey to assess awareness of property and inheritance rights and Muslim inheritance law among local women. The survey results were used to develop informational materials. To date, about 300 leaders have been trained and 10,000 women informed of their rights. MLAA takes socioeconomic factors into account, such as when it had to take low literacy rates in target areas into account in its work to build networks of women leaders in local villages. According to MLAA, only about 32% of rural women in Bangladesh are literate, making the distribution of written materials difficult.

Women's Rights to Land and Property in India

The British came to India as traders in the 17th century and gradually conquered the entire sub-continent. They established their own courts and judges. The law administered was British law as extended to India, however, in matters of personal law, the British applied the personal laws of the subject. A substantial portion of the Hindu Law has been codified by the Indian parliament after independence.

Land is the most important asset to the majority of Indians who live in rural areas. Moreover, land is a basis for status within the family and community and can be the foundation for political power.

The composition of India's GDP in 2006 was 18% agriculture, 28% industry and 55% services. Approximately 70% of India's rural population is engaged in agriculture. Women provide more than half of all agricultural labor.

Slightly less than 23% of India's territory is forested. India has over 200 million acres of community property land resources, of which more than 80 million hectares is forest land. Community waste land (degraded grazing land, barren land, roadside strips, etc) and forestland constitute the greatest proportion of community property land.

Disadvantaged Groups

Among those considered disadvantaged in India are the tribal populations and the scheduled castes. Scheduled Castes and Scheduled Tribes are Indian population groupings that are explicitly recognized by the Constitution of India as disadvantaged. They are otherwise known as untouchables.

Tribal livelihoods are highly dependent on land for sustenance and their culture is closely linked to their ancestral lands. India's indigenous groups are referred to as adivasis or original inhabitants; they number 75-80 million, and comprise nearly 8% of India's population. Adivasis are an extremely diverse group of peoples, speaking over one hundred languages and divided into 635 communities with 414 main tribal affiliations. Ninety-four percent of adivasis are rural and 80% live as hunter-gatherers or engage in subsistence agriculture.

Local Land Related Challenges

Approximately 17 million rural families in India are completely landless. While the net annual forest loss is reported to be zero, forest cover is declining in the northeastern states. Soil erosion is an ongoing problem in India due to cyclones, flooding, environmentally unfriendly agricultural practices, increasing consumption, industrialization and other factors. Protected areas make up 5.3% of India's land area.

Women's Property Ownership, Activities and Employment

India was one of the first countries in the world to give women the right to vote, and it has a long history of female scholars and leaders. Yet, there are very real differences between men and women in Indian society. For instance, men outnumber women in India; in 1991 there were 927 women for every 1000 men. The majority of women go through life under nutritional stress, and face nutritional discrimination within the family and only 50% of Indian women are literate as compared with 65.5% of men. There are fewer women in paid employment than men, and if they are employed they earn far lower than their male counterparts.

Women have the same right to own land as men in India, yet privately owned land is overwhelmingly held in the name of men. In India, 86% of rural women depend on agriculture for their livelihoods yet one survey revealed that less than 10% of privately held land nationwide was in the name of women. The extensive land reforms adopted throughout India since

Independence in 1947 have resulted in community land to which women traditionally had usufruct rights being formally titled in the name of men. Also, women face opposition from male relatives or community members who are far more economically, socially and physically powerful than they are.

Land Policy and Reform

More than 14 million hectares of agricultural land have been converted to non-agricultural land since Independence. The poor have been negatively affected by this conversion as the cumbersome, expensive and corruption-prone process of conversion has meant that poor landowners have not shared in the increase in value that generally accompanies conversion of private land.

The other major land reform adopted by all states imposes ceilings on the amount of land that can be owned by one person or family. The intent of the ceiling laws is to redistribute land above the ceiling amount to the poor. More than 5 million acres of land has been redistributed, 20% of which has been in the state of West Bengal. The ceiling amount ranges from 9 to 54 acres. In some states, beneficiaries receive the land free of charge; in others they must make payments that may equal the amount paid by the state. Generally, the beneficiary may not sell the land for a lengthy period of time (10-20 years in Karnataka, for example) or, as in West Bengal, are permanently prohibited from selling. With the exception of the states of West Bengal, Jammu & Kashmir and Assam, the ceiling laws have not resulted in a significant redistribution of agricultural land in India as it has been relatively easy for owners to evade the laws.

Other land reform measures include the allocation of government-owned barren or mostly barren "wasteland" to the rural poor families, allocation of house sites and the distribution of Bhoodan (land gift) land.

Legal and Customary Land Rights for Women

The Constitution of India provides that all citizens are entitled to equal treatment under the law and prohibits the government from discriminating against any person because of her sex. The Constitution expressly permits the government to make special provisions for women and children.

In India, land is controlled largely by state law, each state has its own land legislation. Different personal laws apply to different groups of people based on religion in India; these laws exist on a national and regional level, though the regional laws are largely unimplemented. Thus, Hindus are governed by the Hindu Marriage Act and the Hindu

Succession Law. The Muslim Personal Law Application Act and the Dissolution of Muslim Marriages Act cover the Muslim community, while Christians are covered by the Indian Christian Marriage Act and portions of the Indian Succession Act. The Parsi community is governed by the Parsi Marriage and Divorce Act and portions of the Indian Succession Act. Finally, in addition to national statutes, the other principal source of personal laws is customary law, as practiced and sometimes applied in judicial decisions.

It is possible for members of any religious group to choose to avail themselves of the secular family law, though this is rare in practice.

Marriage

The formal laws governing women's land rights during marriage depend on which state the family resides in and the family's religion.

Both the Hindu Marriage Act and the Indian Christian Marriage Act provide that the minimum age of marriage for men is 21 years and for women is 18 years. Under the Muslim Personal Law (Shariat) Application Act, 1937, the permissible age of marriage is at puberty.

Whether joint ownership of marital property is permissible, depends on the state law. As an example, in Andra Pradesh, married women uniformly enjoy all the rights and privileges of ownership, however, the joint titling of land is prohibited in Andrah Pradesh under the Splitting Up of Joint Pattas Act. The only exception is for titling of family land held by Hindu families. As a result of the Act, land cannot be titled in the name of both the husband and wife but only in the name of either the husband or wife.

The Dowry Prohibition Act prohibits both the taking and giving of dowry regardless of whether it is given on behalf of the bride or groom. However it does not apply to people in the states of Jamma or Kashmir, and does not apply to the payment of dower or mahr by the Islamic population. Despite this prohibition of dowry, it is widely practiced.

Personal laws for Hindus and Christians prohibit polygamy and it is criminalized by the penal code for non-Muslims, it is permissible for those who are covered by the Muslim Personal law.

Divorce, Separation and Abandonment

Divorce laws, like other personal laws in India, differ depending on the religion of the parties. For Hindus (including Sikhs, Jains and Buddists) the Hindu Marriage Act, 1955 applies, for Muslims the Dissolution of Muslim Marriages Act, 1939, Christians are governed by the Indian Divorce Act, 1869, Parsis by The Parsi Marriage and Divorce Act, 1936 and Inter-Cast or Inter-Religion divorces are governed by Special Marriage Act, 1954. Divorce rates, however, are quite low as there is a social stigma associated with it.

Inheritance and Division of Property

The law governing inheritance in India is varied and complex. As with marriage, the law governing inheritance varies based on the religion of the deceased.

Hindu personal law divides property into two classes: separate property, usually self- or ancestral land owned by coparceners, a traditional unit of property under Hindu Mitakshara law which confers rights of co-ownership on male family members upon their birth. In the case of intestate succession of separate property, the Act provides for devolution in equal shares to the male and female children and widow of the deceased, and if the deceased is male, his mother.

In contrast, for ancestral property, when a coparcener dies, his share is divided among the others, increasing the size of each ancestral property. With passage of the 2005 Succession Amendment Act, however, daughters are considered coparceners entitled to shares of ancestral land. A widow is not a coparcener.

Under the Muslim Personal Law widows and daughters of an intestate deceased have the right to inherit family land. However, widows and daughters receive half the share of property received by their male heir counterpart. The Act prohibits Muslim men and women from bequeathing by will more than one-third of his property, so he cannot completely disinherit his spouse and daughters. The Muslim personal law does not extend to agricultural land, leaving it to devolve by state law or, if state law is silent, custom.

Under the Indian Succession Act, no matter the origin of the land, when a Christian dies intestate, his widow receives one-third of the estate and his sons and daughters receive equal shares of the remainder. If there are no children, but there are other more distant heirs, the widow receives half of the estate; otherwise, she inherits the entire estate.

Key NGOs Working on Women's Land Rights

IFAD's Women's Resource Access Program (WRAP)

The overall goal of WRAP is to raise international understanding of the need to improve women's access to land and other productive resources. WRAP draws directly on the views, experiences and knowledge of rural poor women in order to demonstrate the importance of land and other productive resources to their livelihoods and food security. It also ensures that the views of these women contribute directly to national and international decision-making and policy formulation on these issues.

WRAP objectives are to:

- Provide opportunities for the views and perceptions of rural poor women on the importance of resource-access to be heard at local, national and regional levels in order to contribute to, and influence, policy-making debates;
- Train and strengthen the capacity of civil-society organizations to listen, document and share rural poor women's views and perceptions on the importance of resource access in order to increase their ability to influence local, national and international decision-making processes;
- Develop a rapid low-cost methodology to facilitate up-take and up-scaling of the WRAP approach by international organizations and governments.

National Commission for Women, India

The National Commission for Women was set up as statutory body in January 1992 to review the Constitutional and Legal safeguards for women; recommend remedial legislative measures; facilitate redress of grievances and, advise the Government on all policy matters affecting women. In keeping with its mandate, the Commission initiated various steps to improve the status of women and worked for their economic empowerment during the year under report.

The Commission visits all the States except Lakshdweep and prepares Gender Profiles to assess the status of women and their empowerment. It also undertakes impact litigation

Rural Development Institute (RDI)

RDI is securing women's land rights through "micro-ownership" of land titled in women's names, and holds state level policy workshops on woman's land rights.

Working Group on Women and Land Ownership (WGWLO)

A network of 23 non-governmental organizations (NGOs) based in Gujarat, India. The goal of WGWLO is to bring visibility to the issue of women and agricultural land ownership, and to advocate changing aspects in laws and policies of the Government of Gujarat which inhibit women from owning land in their name. Strategies used include organizing workshops at the grassroots level to raise awareness of the issues, conducting research, reaching out to the media, carrying out capacity building and advocacy at the national level -for example advocating for incentives to be incorporated into government schemes so that men are motivated to transfer land in the name of women from their household - and trying to integrate the issue of women's land ownership within ongoing NGO programs.

Women's Rights to Land and Property in Nepal

An isolated, agrarian society until the mid-20th century, Nepal entered the modern era in 1951 without schools, hospitals, roads, telecommunications, electric power, industry, or a civil service. The country has, however, made progress toward sustainable economic growth since the 1950s and is committed to a program of economic liberalization.

Nepal is a country at cross-roads, an "open moment" in its history. Nepal's decade-long conflict between the Maoists and the constitutional monarchy formally ended in November 2006. The last vestiges of the centuries-old monarchy were officially decommissioned with the adoption of the Interim Constitution in 2007. In 2008, the country voted in a Constituent Assembly, named a President, elected a Prime Minister, formed a coalition government, and set about the task of writing a new Constitution by 2010, with a new round of elections planned for 2011. The new Nepal that is to emerge is expected to take on a federal character, vastly altering administrative and decision-making powers. The next few years are critical as Nepal faces transition to the new State and confronts long-standing development challenges at a time of global economic downturn. The key challenge facing the new government, at this juncture, will be to rebuild the legitimacy of the state, maintain law and order, and deliver benefits to those excluded and to society at large.

Nepal ranks among the world's poorest countries, with a per capita income of around $470 in 2009. Based on national calorie/GNP criteria, an estimated 31% of the population is below the poverty line. In terms of human and social development, Nepal ranks 136 out of 177 countries in the Human Development Index. Nepal has a population of 27.6 million people 84% of which are rural. There is a wide disparity in infrastructure and markets between the urban and rural areas. The GDP of US$8.9 billion is mostly derived from the service industry, at 49%. Agriculture makes up 34% of the GDP, while industry makes up 16%.

Agriculture is the main source of livelihood for most Nepalese. Nearly four fifths of all Nepalese households are farm households, who derive nearly half of their income from agricultural sources consisting of farm income and agricultural wage income. Agriculture engages two-thirds of the labor force. Poverty is highest among agricultural wage earners, small agricultural households, Dalits, Janjaits, Muslem and illiterate households. In Nepal, food insecurity is a major challenge. Rural areas have particularly high levels of poverty with 44% of the rural population living below the poverty line and 56% of rural children under-five-year-olds considered to be chronically malnourished.

Disadvantaged Groups

Although discrimination on the basis of caste is illegal according to the Country Code of 1963, it is still common across Nepal, particularly in the more orthodox communities. Nepalese society is rigidly hierarchical; pervasive social inequality based on caste, ethnicity, and gender is deeply rooted in culture, religion, and centuries of feudal rule. Social inequality is comprehensive, including disparity of access to livelihood resources, government services, and economic opportunity. Women, Madhesis, Janajatis, and others are regarded as discriminated groups.

Local Land Related Challenges

Nepal's pattern of agricultural land distribution has become more concentrated over time. At current estimates, 5% of the population control around 27% of the land and own three or more hectares. Forty-four percent of hectare or less and occupy 14% of cultivatable area; this figure includes the 22 to 31% of the rural population that are either completely landlessor own less than 0.2 hectares of land.

Smallholder farms dominate, with the average holding size 0.8 hectares. About 2% of total farm holdings are worked by landless tenant farmers while the many farmers operate under mixed tenure arrangements and rent in land in addition to land they own. In terms of area, land under some form of tenancy officially constitutes around 10% of all farmland in Nepal; though, the actual incidence of tenancy is likely higher due to the presence of informal unregistered tenants. The land tenure picture is further complicated by the presence of illegal cultivators from India.

Women's Property Ownership, Activities and Employment

Women constitute 51% of the Nepali population and represent 66% of the agricultural labor, yet only own an estimated 8% of the land. The family and kin group are of great importance to Nepalese. Sociologically, the family gives the individual a caste, an identity, a religion, and a home. Economically, the extended family provides all that an individual needs for survival, by access to resources and the pooling of labor. There is a gendered division of labor, with women, especially married women, doing the bulk of the work for the extended family, in addition to their own domestic chores.

Land Policy and Reform

Land rights can be acquired by inheritance, purchase, or tenancy in Nepal. The Land Act of 1964 imposed ceilings on household land holdings. Under that law, land held above the ceiling was to be redistributed to the landless and small holders. The Act also set ceilings for tenant holdings that were significantly lower than those for landowners. The Act granted tenants heritable occupancy rights, limited rents to 50% of gross annual produce, instituted a compulsory savings scheme for tenants, and limited the grounds for eviction. The Act did not grant tenants ownership rights.

In 1997, the Land Act was amended and tenants were to be given 50% of land he/she had hitherto cultivated to create the opportunity for tenants to eventually become land-owners. This amendment has been largely unimplemented in practice partially because of a lack of political will. Also, even if implemented, it would have had minimal impact on the many informal (unregistered) tenants in Nepal. In 2001 the Land Act was amended again to lower ceilings, introduce incentives to cooperative farming, and control land fragmentation; however this amendment too, has been largely unimplemented. The Land Act's objective to redistribute land among the landless and small holder peasants had only a small impact on land distribution in the country and only redistributed 1.5% of land.

Legal and Customary Land Rights for Women

The status of the Nepali Constitution is uncertain. Currently the country operates under the Interim Constitution, adopted on January 15, 2007, which expressed, inter alia, full commitment to democratic ideals and norms, civil liberties, fundamental human rights, and the rule of law. It also recognizes equality before the law and no discrimination based on class, caste, sex, tribe, origin, language or religion.

The legal code, or Muluki Ain, was introduced in 1854 and revised in 1963 (the "Naya Muluki Ain" or "New Civil Code"). The Muluki Ain, derived from Hindu caste law and custom, has served as a general code of civil and criminal law and procedure, applicable to all Nepalese regardless of religion or ethnicity. It covers property, inheritance, adoption, marriage, divorce, homicide, rape, incest, and many other subjects. The Muluki Ain in its current form, combines Hindu laws and sanctions, British and Indian codes, and traditional rules of behavior among the Newars in the Kathmandu Valley. Issues not covered by the code are generally dealt with according to customs of local communities.

One review of Nepalese law in 2003 identified 137 provisions, two rules in their entirety, and 121 schedules in 85 laws that were discriminatory. The government has constituted a high-level commission to review all existing discriminatory laws, and its work is ongoing. In 2006, Nepal had about 150 special measures for women spread across 56 laws. However, a number of these 'special measures' were mixed blessings, often resulting in less freedom and reduced rights for women. In 2002 the Eleventh Amendment to the Muluki Ain was enacted and contained a number of positive provisions for women's property rights, yet women's and men's property rights are still not equitable.

Marriage

In the Muluki Ain, in case of bigamy, the first wife, son and daughter must share their property with the second wife and her children. Arranged marriages are the norm in the mainstream culture of Nepal. Because marriages forge important social bonds between families, when a child reaches marriageable age, the family elders are responsible for finding a suitable mate of the appropriate caste, education level, and social stratum. Also, fraternal polyandry, where two or more brothers marry the same woman, is not an uncommon practice.

Daijo, or dowry, consists of property usually moveable proeprty, given to a woman at the time of marriage by relatives from her parents' side (maiti), her mother's parents' side (mamulipatti), or by neighbors and friends (istamitraheru). It usually consists of items that the bride can take to her new home. Things that are part of the daijo, and which can be proved to be part of the daijo, are not included in the ancestral property of the husband, and thus need not be shared among the husband and his brothers at the time that ancestral property is divided. However, neither is daijo a separate form of "female property." It is considered part of the joint conjugal property of the husband and wife, and it is ordinarily inherited by a woman's sons after her death.

Divorce, Separation and Abandonment

Under the Muluki Ain, only men may divorce if his wife is childless. However, divorce itself is discouraged, and the local government is authorized and instructed to attempt to reconcile the parties should a divorce action commence. Unilateral divorce is permitted only under certain circumstances."

Inheritance and Division of Property

Under the Muluki Ain (Eleventh Amendment) widows have the right to inherit her husband's property. Daughters may inherit equally with sons, however, if she is married after inheriting, she must return her share to the other heirs. Also, the Muluki Ain discriminates among daughters on the basis of marital status or between married and unmarried daughters in partition, intestate property and in transaction of property.

While the code does grant women some important property rights, it also contains biases against women's property rights by emphasizing the rights of the kin group (husband's linage, including ancestors) to land over that of women who are considered peripheral and dependant on the kin group.

Under custom, the family unit is most important to Nepalese. While the family shares the same hearth, the senior members (mother and father) and the permanent junior members (sons) make all decisions about production, consumption and labor. These joint extended families usually co-reside for two generations and are broken up at the time of the marriageof the youngest son or after the senior male has died. After that point the heirs come together and divide their assets and their liabilities into even shares. Generally heirs to ancestral property are male.

Key NGOs Working on Women's Land Rights

Community Self Reliance Center (CSRC)

CSRC advocates for women's property rights as equal as to the men. It reviews property rights laws and state policies in collaboration with other human rights organizations and launches advocacy campaigns to create pressure on the state. CSRC has further engaged with political actors and government officials in the form of consultations, dialogues, debates and policy formulation processes in advocating for women's property rights especially land rights. CSRC carries out similar process at the community to educate ordinary people on the subject matter, build public opinion and create pressure to the policy makers from the ground. Since its creation, the CSRC has helped 15,000 farmers acquire land.

CSRC has had lasting impact on policy and political discussion on land rights as a 'development issue' as well as on 'poverty' discourse. It intends to direct more focus specifically on women's land rights, by

- Conducting gender-sensitive land tenure context mapping at community, district and national levels
- Campaigning for joint land entitlement between men and women
- Advocating for sole land ownership to women in case she is a single woman
- Advocating for collective rights for managing lands by group of women at community level. However, there is a need for critical scrutiny in the cases of so-called 'fallow' land, as the collective in the authority.
- Promoting women's stake in managing communal and other public lands, management committee not less than 50%
- Campaigning for women's land right as an integral component of human rights to be recognized by the government, international community and other concerned.
- Advocating theset up special mechanism and procedures for ensuring women's land rights

- Linking Nepal's women's land rights movement to other countries in the region and beyond, and share good practices and learning.

Rural Women Development Centre (RWDC), Nepal

Rural Women Development Centre (RWDC) has been championing the prime cause of land rights for the landless people (ex-Kamaiyas, tenants) in Dang since 2004. This land rights movement initiated from Dang has evolved into a national movement at the central level that has highlighted the land rights issues before the major political parties.

All Nepalese Women's Assocation (ANWA)

ANWA is strongly committed and dedicated to create awareness and to organize women to fight inequality, injustice, all forms of feudal, capitalist and imperial exploitation, superstitious beliefs and social evils. It has played a very important role in the restoration of democracy in the country in 1950 and 1990 respectively. Since the beginning, it has launched an awareness building campaign on literacy, women's education, and has raised voices against polygamy, child marriage, and equal rights in all sectors of society.

Women's Rights to Land and Property in Pakistan

Pakistan, a country just less than twice the size of California, is located in south central Asia and is bordered by Iran, Afghanistan, China and India. It is divided into four provinces: Balochistan, North-West Frontier Province, Punjab, and Sindh; and two territories: Islamabad Capital Territory and the Federally Administered Tribal Areas. Pakistan also has two administrative entities (Azad Kashmir and Northern Areas) in the Jammu and Kashmir region which have been the subject neighboring India.

In Pakistan the livelihoods of rural people revolve around arable land; it a basic resource which provides food, shelter, and place to grow and tend to livestock. It is also a determinant of social status and non-ownership of land is considered a key factor in poverty.

Seventy-three percent of the population lives on less than $2 a day, 17% on less than $1 a day. Total GDP in 2007 was $143 billion, with 53% attributed to services, 27% to industry, and 21% to agriculture. Livestock accounts for half of agricultural GDP.

Pakistan's economy has improved since the '90s, a decade plagued with instability resulting from an increase in poverty, the devaluation of Pakistani currency, and increase in foreign and domestic debt. Since then, due to drastic measures taken to arrest the economic decline, and agreement with the US to oppose the Taliban, the growth rate has increased, foreign reserves have crossed the $12 billion mark, and the number of Pakistanis living in poverty has reduced. However, the estimated number living under the poverty line currently is somewhere around 28%.

Disadvantaged Groups

Pakistan is a class and casted based society. The most disadvantaged groups are the poor landless and sharecroppers, as well as the some of the occupational groups – like cobblers and potters – who are lower end of the social ladder. Other marginal groups are the gypsies who move around in construction sites begging and the brick kiln and mine works. The majority of these people live in bondage against loans taken from their employers.

Pakistan is divided into four Provinces: Punjab, Sindh, North West Frontier Territory (NWFT), and Balochistan. Pakistan's Tribal Areas stretch along the eastern border of Afghanistan and are administratively divided into the Provincially Administered Tribal Areas (PATA) and the Federally Administered Tribal Area (FATA). The inhabitants of the Tribal Areas are ethnically and linguistically distinct from the rest of the country, with most belonging to the Pukhtun-Afghan race. The Tribal Areas contain Pakistan's poorest and most remote populations, with most dependent on livestock rearing and subsistence farming for their livelihoods. Ninety-seven percent of the women in FATA are illiterate.

Local Land Related Challenges

Pakistan's land suffers from heavy soil erosion and steady degradation. Deforestation, livestock grazing, and improper land cultivation techniques have caused reservoirs to silt up, reducing the capacity to generate power and the availability of water for irrigation. Countrywide, livestock populations exceed the carrying capacity of the rangeland, destroy natural vegetation, overwhelm water sources, and cause soil erosion. Much of the country's irrigated land suffers from various levels of salinity, and the coastal strips and mangrove areas are stressed by reduced fresh water flow, sewage, and industrial pollution.

Uneven land distribution has been a major cause of income inequality in rural Pakistan since well before Independence and stretching to present day. In 2000, only 37% of rural households owned agricultural land; 63%

were landless. Rural poverty is highest among landless households (55%), followed by non-agricultural households (39%). The incidence of poverty declines with increases in landholdings and vanishes in households with land holdings of 1-2 hectares and above.

Women's Property Ownership, Activities and Employment

The status of women across Pakistan is not uniform as there are socio-cultural, regional, tribal, and other factors which come into play. There is considerable diversity in the status of women across classes, regions, and the rural/urban divide due to uneven socioeconomic development and the impact of tribal, feudal, and capitalist social formations on women's lives. However, women's situation vis-à-vis men is one of systemic subordination, determined by the forces of patriarchy across classes, regions, and the rural/ urban divide. However, as in other orthodox Muslim societies, most Pakistani women are charged with the responsibility of maintaining the honor of their families. This responsibility manifests itself through limitations upon a woman's freedom of mobility, association, dress; these constraints are known as Purdah, (Persian for curtain), which is practiced to different extents in different regions of the country. Women in more rural communities in Punjab and Sindh are allowed greater freedom as they have many agricultural responsibilities.

Women have a secondary status in Pakistan. Pakistan women's labor force participation is low at just under 16% and they also suffer a poor literacy rate as compared with men, 40% and 65% respectively. Women have little access to or control over productive resources.

In the household, Pakistani women are generally expected to cook, clean, and care for the young and the elderly while the men are expected to earn a livelihood and support their families financially. This division in labor, however, which was once clear-cut, is slowly changing as women are given more opportunities to become involved in their communities, and to seek education or outside employment. Women are even beginning to comprise a significant part of Pakistan's uniformed services with representatives in the police force, airport security force, and army medial corps.

Land Policy and Reform

Pakistan has engaged in three land reform efforts under three different governments. The Land Reform Act of 1977, Pakistan's third effort at addressing inequality of land access and insecurity of land tenure since Independence, attempted to plug gaps in prior land reform legislation and implement tenancy, land ceilings (limits of size of holdings), and land distribution reforms. The passage of the Act was followed by the imposition of martial law and much of the momentum fueling reforms dissipated. In the years that followed, the courts ruled various provisions of the Act un-Islamic and political will to address land issues waned. A resurgence of interest in land reform and attendant revisions to the Act (mostly to pave the way for expansion of commercial farming interests) took place in the 1980s. To date, however, in most of Pakistan issues of land distribution and insecure tenure remain unaddressed.

Legal and Customary Land Rights for Women

The structure of Pakistan's legislation is fluid and in a near constant state of amendment as it continues to conform and adjust to Islamic jurisprudence, which is itself evolving. Statutory law specific to land rights in Pakistan is dated, fragmented, and incomplete. More than two dozen laws govern a variety of land matters at national and provincial levels. The tribal population of FATA is subject to a separate legal framework.

Article 23 of the Constitution of Pakistan states that, "every citizen shall have the right to acquire, hold, and dispose of property in any part of Pakistan." It also guarantees equal rights to property and calls for bringing all laws in conformity with the Holy Quran and Sunnah and to strike down any custom having the force of law as far as it is inconsistent with fundamental rights. Women's property rights derive from Muslim personal law, and tribal and regional custom.

Marriage

Under the Muslim Family Law, women have unequal rights to inheritance, termination of marriage, minimum age of marriage, and natural guardianship of children; polygamy has not been banned or even sufficiently restricted by law; and there are grossly inadequate provisions for women's financial security after termination of marriage. Muslim law recognizes the payment of dower in marriage, however, by application of custom dower is generally deferred (not paid at the time of entering into the marriage contract) and later waived by the wife.

Pakistani law does not recognize the rights of women to property which may have been acquired during the marriage. Currently the law does not have the concept of co-ownership of marital property. About 23 percent of females between the ages of 15 and 19 are married, compared with 5 percent of the male population in the same age group. A majority of women are married to their close relatives, i.e., first and second cousins and only 37 percent of married women are not related to their spouses before marriage.

Divorce, Separation and Abandonment

The divorce rate in Pakistan is extremely low due to the social stigma attached to it. While Islamic law provides for maintenance a woman cannot claim a share in her husband's property and she is not entitled to maintenance in the long term. Her claim to dower also has to be forfeited if she has asked for the divorce. In the agricultural context a divorced woman would lose her right to work on the household land or access any common land which perhaps was being used by her husband's family as tenant farmers or share croppers.

Inheritance and Division of Property

Inheritance in Pakistan is governed by Islamic Shariah as codified in the Family Laws Ordinance 1961, and the West Pakistan Muslim Personal Law (Shariat) Application Act (Vof 1962) which consolidated and amended the various Muslim laws. Pursuant to the West Pakistan Muslim Personal Law (Shariat Application) Act 1962 the issue of inheritance is to be dealt with under the personal law of each citizen residing within the State. Moreover, the Courts have decided that every Muslim is presumed to be Hanafi unless proved otherwise.

The general rule for inheritance is that women inherit half as much as the men in the same class of heirs, though the proportion of shares varies not only according to the relationship to the deceased but also by sect, i.e. Sunni and Shia.

In spite of the right to inherit under the Shari'a law, many women do not inherit in practice. Women do not inherit property and widows customarily lose their right to inheritance if they remarry outside of the family of the deceased husband even though the law prescribes otherwise. In addition, because land holding size is a determinant of social status, and power, the desire is to keep land in the family and a woman is not considered part of the family after she marries. On the other hand, a woman may be granted inheritance but may forgo her share in favor of her brothers to prevent putting her kinship relationships at stake, since she may rely on those kin relations in a time of need. Further, a broken relationship with brothers can have an impact on her children's marriages and can lead to being ostracized from the entire kin group. Moreover, women's dowry is regarded as compensation for her inheritance in most of Pakistan.

Key NGOs Working on Women's Land Rights

Shirkat Gah

Shirkat Gah Women's Resource Centre, (SG) has a Women Law and Status program that focuses on women's legal rights specifically those related to personal laws (covered under Islamic law). It works with local women's community based organizations to, on the one hand, understand the complexity of personal law issues as they affect women in different local/ regional contexts and on the other to build capacity of local organizations through information sharing on rights (especially filling of the marriage contract), training in legal and negotiation skills, and provision of legal aid in select cases. The information and learning from the field feeds into SG's policy advocacy. Property and land rights have been the subject of discussion in the field with reference to inheritance.

SG's legal awareness and legal literacy programs have had some results. In a large number of its work areas parents now seriously fill out the marriage certificate (nikah nama) ensuring that all clauses are filled and women protected in marriage.

Aurat Foundation

AF is a leading women's rights and advocacy organization with a particular focus on women's political participation. The organization in 1999-2000 developed a number of suggestions for women politicians as measures for women's empowerment to include in their election manifestos. This was in response to government's move at the time to distribute land to the peasants. AF raised the issue that women be included in the scheme and receive half the share in the distributed land or at least be given joint ownership. It proposed that marginalized women, widows and single women should get property rights when they become heads of households. AF's position was premised on the belief that ownership of land would lead to securing economic rights and the security of property would reduce women's vulnerability.

AF also initiated a signature campaign on the issue, publicized it through the media and sent the suggestions to the government and political parties before the 2002 elections asking for:

- the inclusion of women in government's land distribution schemes;
- strict enforcement of inheritance laws and registration of property in the name of women;
- legislation to ensure that women's share in all properties and assets acquired by spouses after marriage is legally recognized and secured for her;
- land reforms and imposition of progressively scaled agricultural income tax;
- redistribution of available arable land to landless peasants ensuring half the recipients were women or had joint title deeds with men.

Roots for Equity Azra

Roots for Equity (RFE) is an organization working on land rights in the villages of Sindh. RFE conducts research and awareness raising on rural issues for women and also on land rights. Roots is planning to initiate an experimental project where it wants to lease two acre plots of land in two villages and turn them over to women to manage on their own. It wants to study the dynamics at the local level if poor women have total control over the land.

Thardeep Rural Development Programme

Thardeep has conducted a study on land rights in Tharparkar, the desert area of Sindh. The organization felt gaps in information on their work on land ownership, the status of common property grazing lands (livestock is the mainstay of the local population that has traditionally been pastoral), and other related matters and was therefore prompted to undertake the research. The study covers both men and women and is based on old records from the British times. Women of the area, like their counterparts in most of Sindh collect fodder and fetch water but do not have rights over the land they work on, nor ownership of livestock though they take care of it. Thardeep wants to use the findings of its research for its social mobilization work and will share it widely once it is published.

Women's Rights to Land and Property in Sri Lanka

Sri Lanka, formerly Ceylon, became a democratic socialist republic in 1948. The government is organized into separate executive branch, unicameral legislature, and judiciary. Sri Lanka has a highly complex legal system that has elements of English common law, Roman-Dutch civil code, two codified customary laws, and codified Shari'a law, governed by a constitution. Under Sri Lanka's constitution, land issues are matters for shared legislation and control by the central government and provincial councils.

In 2004, Sri Lanka suffered its worst natural disaster, when a major tsunami swept ashore, killing about tens of thousands of people, leaving more than 6,300 missing and 443,000 displaced, and destroying $1.5 billion in property. Government spending and reconstruction drove growth to more than seven percent in 2006, but reduced agriculture output slowed growth to about six percent in 2007.

Sri Lanka is politically unstable. Ongoing civil war, between the armed forces of the predominantly Buddhist Sinhalese government and Hindu or ChristianTamil Tiger rebels over the Tamils' right to self-rule in the north and east has intensified over thc last 20 years, killing about 64,000 people, displacing one million, and hampering the island's growth and economic development. The World Bank and Asian Development Bank considered Sri Lanka one of the "world's most politically unstable countries" in 2004 and Foreign Policy ranked Sri Lanka 20th in its annual Failed States Index for 2008.

Sri Lanka is a mostly rural and poor country. Approximately six percent of the Sri Lankan population is unemployed and twenty-two percent of the population is below the poverty line. Further, 5.6 percent of Sri Lankans still survives on less than one dollar per day and 41.7 percent exists on two dollars a day or less.

Currently, Sri Lanka's most active economic sectors are food processing, textiles and apparel, food and beverages, port construction, telecommunications, and insurance and banking. In 2006, plantation crops made up about15 percent of exports, while textiles and garments accounted for more than 60 percent. About 800,000 Sri Lankans work abroad, 90 percent of them in the Middle East; remittances sent home from these citizens living abroad account for more than $1 billion a year.

Significantly, over eighty percent of Sri Lanka's people live in rural areas. The rural poor account for 95% of Sri Lanka's poor and in 2002 the rural poverty rate was at 25 percent, compared with the urban poverty rate of 8%. Further, about 38 percent of the rural population is below the poverty line.

Disadvantaged Groups

The 1978 constitution grants primacy to Buddhism while assuring freedom of religion, Historical divisions continue to have an impact on Sri Lankan society and politics. From independence, the Tamil minority has been uneasy with Being the country's unitary form of. government and apprehensive that the Sinhalese majority would abuse Tamil rights. Being a minority in a particular area can impact access to important resources; for instance, Muslims in some areas that suffered during the Tsunami did not benefit from some reconstruction efforts as much as others, however, they did benefit from donations from Muslim support groups.

Local Land Related Challenges

Landlessness is high in Sri Lanka. Around 27%of Sri Lankans are landless and this number is project to rise; the current per capita availability of land is 0.29 hectares, and with projected population growth it is anticipated that the per capita availability of land will be further reduced to 0.22 hectares.

Natural disaster and conflict have had an impact on Sri Lanka's natural resources. Guerrilla warfare and the clearing of forests for military purposes extensively damaged the forests and environment in the North and East. Decline in forestry activities reduced the rural population's employment opportunities. Acute shortage of firewood, the primary energy source for cooking, especially affected the Jaffna peninsula that has no forests. Depletion of forest cover affects ground water levels and creates environmental problems. Unlawful operations such as illicit timber harvesting contribute to environmental degradation.

Women's Property Ownership, Activities and Employment

Since the 1940s the Sri Lankan government has invested in basic health and education; thus, indicators of Sri Lankan women's life expectancy, literacy, and maternal mortality have been impressive at a national level. The 2008 estimate of Sri Lankan women's life expectancy at birth is 77 years, compared to 72.95 year for Sri Lankan men. In 2004, adult literacy rates in

Sri Lanka were estimated at 89.1% for women, and 92.3% for men and men, while for children 15 years of age and younger it is 96.1 percent for girls and 95.1 percent for boys. Similarly, Sri Lanka's net primary school enrollment rate was 98 percent for women and 99 percent for men, with 93 percent of women progressing through grade 5 and 91 percent of them completing their primary education.

Customs and traditions vary across different regions and religions and affect Sri Lankan women in different ways. Sri Lankan women face gender barriers in the labor market and in the political arena. All national and local assemblies have been consistently male-dominated. The proportion of women members in parliament or the national state assembly has never exceeded five percent since 1931. Most women are employed in the informal sector; in 2006, Sri Lankan women's labor force participation rate 35 percent, as compared to men whose rate of participation 68.1 percent.

In one study that covered three locations in Sri Lanka, about 30% of women owned property. Of these women, 54% owned only a house but not the land that the house was on. Also, the majority of female landowners had received their property through inheritance. Nineteen percent of rural households in the North and East are female-headed households.

Land Policy and Reform

The Land Development Ordinance (LDO) of 1935 regulates state agricultural lands given by state-issued permits to Sri Lankan citizens. The LDO is gender neutral, but its implementation has favored males. A widow or a woman who previously owned land qualifies; however, on remarriage a widow loses the right to cultivate if she has not been nominated, and she cannot nominate a successor.

Legal and Customary Land Rights for Women

Present-day Sri Lankan law is a highly complex admixture of custom-based legal systems made up of Roman-Dutch civil law and English common law, customary laws – Kandyan and Tesawalami – and Shari'a laws.

Roman-Dutch Law now generally applies in Sri Lanka when statutes and indigenous laws do not regulate the issue in question. Relevant laws from this tradition are the General Law of Matrimonial Rights and Inheritance Ordinance and the Married Women's Property Ordinance.

Kandyan Law applies to ethnic Sinhalese whose can trace their lineage back to the Kandyan provinces during the period of the Kandyan monarchy in central Sri Lanka which ended in the 1850s. Kandyan Sinhalese are covered by Kandyan law unless they choose to opt out, and complete the necessary administrative steps.

Theswalamai Law is based on ancient customs of Jaffna Tamils in Sri Lanka. It applies to lands situated in the Northern Province and is not applicable to all Tamils, just those Tamils who are inhabitants of the Jaffna Peninsula in Northern Sri Lanka. The relevant Thesawalamai law is the Matrimonial Rights and Inheritance Ordinance of 1911.

The personal laws of Islam apply to all Muslims in Sri Lanka. When a Muslim marries another Muslim, the bride and the groom do not have the option of getting married under the General Law, unlike in the case of Kandyan Sinhalese. Marriage, divorce and other related issues involving Muslims are governed by the Marriage and Divorce (Muslim) Act, and any subsequent amendments. It also regulates the Quazi courts applying that law. Issues related to interstate succession and donations, involving Muslims, are dealt with under the Muslim Interstate Succession Ordinance, and any subsequent amendments.

Marriage

Kandyan personal laws distinguish between diga and binna marriages. A binna marriage is matrilocal, meaning that the bridegroom shifts to the bride's house upon marriage. A diga marriage is patrilocal, meaning the bride moves to the bridegroom's house upon marriage. These designations have an impact on the woman's right to inherit ancestral property. Polygamy is permitted for Muslims and Muslims are excluded from the penal code which criminalizes bigamy. However, the Muslim Marriage Divorce Act requires notification in the event of a Muslim male wishing to enter into a polygamous marriage.

In Sinhalese culture, which is dominant, the bride is given a dowry separate from any other gifts. This is her own property, controlled and managed by the bride.

In many Sri Lankan cultures, cross-cousin marriage is preferred. It is most acceptable person for man to marry is the daughter of his father's sister and in many villages, people spend their entire childhood with a clear knowledge of their future marriage plans and in close proximity to their future spouses.

Divorce, Separation and Abandonment

For Muslims, the Muslim Marriage Divorce Act provides detailed rules regarding the registration of divorce by the husband and the wife. A husband who "intends to pronounce the talaq on his wife" shall give notice to the Quazi of the area where she is resident, and the Quazi's duty is to attempt to effect a reconciliation, with the help of the relatives of both parties, as well as elders and influential Muslims of the area.

While legal divorce is easy to obtain, and divorces of customary marriages occur through mutual consent of the partners in consultation with their extended families, most marriages do not end in divorce because of the social pressure and support exerted by kin of both the husband and the wife."

The grounds for divorce under Kandyan personal laws continue to be discriminatory towards women; they are required to prove adultery coupled with gross cruelty or incest, while men need prove only adultery. Under the General law, divorce is based on the concept of "fault" the legal grounds for divorce, however, are the same for both parties.

Inheritance and Division of Property Inheritance for Muslims is guided by the uncodified Muslim law governing the sect to which the deceased belongs. Generally this means that a female in a class of heirs will typically receive one half of the share of a male in the same class of heirs.

Kandyan inheritance laws distinguish between diga and binna marriages. In a binna marriage if the bride's father dies, she receives an equal share of the father's ancestral (paraveni) property together with her brothers, unmarried sisters and other sisters in binna marriages. In a diga marriage, if the bride's father dies, she does not receive any share of his ancestral property. A diga married daughter is precluded from claiming parental property unless she has acquired binna rights or returns to the mulgedera (family home). However, daughters who marry in diga after the death of her father must transfer for fair market value any ancestral property she inherited to her siblings who also inherited before the conclusion of one year.

Under the Theasawalmai, a widow keeps separate property; widow receives half of property acquired during marriage and half shared equally amongst children (sons and daughters); widow has no right to ancestral property and children (sons and daughters) inherit equally.

For all others, the Matrimonial Rights and Inheritance Ordinance applies, in which a widow inherits one half share of the deceased's property and one half shared among descendants (sons and daughters)

Region, ethnic group, and religion can play a part in what whether a women inherits family land in practice. For instance, in both Tamil and Muslim communities of the North East Province, inheritance follows the matrilineal line.

Key NGOs Working on Women's Land Rights

Sri Lanka Women's NGO Forum

The main objective of this organization is to act as a lobbying and advocacy body at regional, national, and international levels. It focuses in particular on raising awareness on women's issues and rights in Sri Lanka.

Centre for Women's Research (CENWOR)

The main objective of CENWOR is to support women in realizing their full potential and to achieving equality in all spheres of life. Information is one of the key functions of CENWOR. CENWOR thus took a leading role in the development of a research database, which has subsequently been used for lobbying and advocacy. The centre offers training and publishes original research. It also produces posters, leaflets, manuals and bibliographies.

Muslim Women's Research and Action Forum

The objectives of the MWRAF are specifically focused on awareness raising, empowering, and promoting the cause of Muslim women in Sri Lanka. They also seek advocate on behalf of Muslim women's groups and create an active network with groups working with similar objectives at local, national, and international levels.

Their activities are focused on action research, mobilization, legal counseling and legal aid. Action research focuses on the formal and customary legal and social and issues facing Muslim women and leads to proposals for reform. Mobilization efforts focus on legal literacy of urban and rural Muslim women. Their legal counseling and legal aid services focus on clients identified in their mobilization efforts.

Approaches to Designing Interventions

Women's inheritance rights are beset with both legal and cultural obstacles. These obstacles are highly contextual, and can vary widely among countries, regions, religions, tribes, clans, ethnic groups, castes, and class. What is feasible in one community may not be in another. Yet, field studies on inheritance practices are rare. Even rarer are documented perspectives of women on what interventions would help secure their rights to property. Designing interventions from a distance without adequate information from the field may run the risk of being inappropriate for the context or, in some cases, may make things worse for women. The following interventions are thus intentionally generalized in nature and are geared more towards raising awareness, raising flags that will require study for their relevance in a given setting, and identifying possible means to address the cultural change that will be required to ensure equity in property rights for women and men.

Speak to Women about Property Rights for Women

Before any action is taken to amend discriminatory laws or design a land-related intervention, it is imperative that it be driven by what is feasible, possible and desired by the women that the intervention seeks to assist. Since customary rules often govern women's lives, attempting to change custom can be very threatening to women and men alike. Any planned intervention must include significant efforts to solicit information from women about the rights that they want for themselves, their daughters, their children, and their future with regard to safety, protection, survival.

Work with Men to Champion the Property Rights of Women

Gaining inheritance rights for women requires social and cultural change. In patriarchal cultures, men are the powerbrokers; gender equity in property rights cannot be achieved unless some critical mass of men are convinced that it is worthy of their support. Thus, projects intended to promote gender equity must explicitly target men as well as women. Engaging men, especially opinion leaders and those who wield local influence, is a critical and oft-overlooked strategy in assisting that change. Understand the specific role of customary, religious and formal laws for women noting that the relevant roles may be different across regions, tribes, clans and class. Research and generate baseline information on women's land rights under customary, religious, and formal laws.

Legal Awareness, Legal Literacy, and Legal Aid

Many NGOs have identified in their assessments that there is a general lack of awareness amongst women and men about women's property rights and how they can be effectuated. One NGO in Pakistan, Shirkat Gah, has had some successes by doing something as simple as assisting parents in completing the marriage certificate correctly. In Pakistan, under

Shari'a law the marriage certificate is the one place where the property arrangements between spouses are recorded. In their research, Shirkat Gah found that these certificates were not completed correctly by parents and that later, if there was an issue in the marriage or a death, the woman's property rights as agreed to at the beginning of the marriage were not recorded anywhere, and there was thus no evidence of the agreement that had been made. They found that by helping parents fill in the form, the forms became legitimate protection for the woman's rights in the relationship.

Initiate debate with policy makers, NGOs, networks, and advocates towards creating social legitimacy for women's land rights and control over resources. Advocacy and lobbying may be one of the most common types of interventions amongst the NGOs identified. The Aga Khan foundation in Bangladesh works directly with locally elected female officials, to improve their knowledge of the factors which prevent women from realizing their property rights, with the view that they will become political advocates on those issues. Another NGO in Bangladesh takes a slightly different approach with its advocacy campaigns. The Center for Development Services (CDS) conducts interactive and informative media campaigns on women's property rights, taking a human rights based approach. The CDS focus, however, is on the boys and girls who will be the women and men of the next generation. Similarly, in Pakistan, the Aurat Foundation works specifically on publicizing the issues around property rights for women in the mainstream media during election times. The basic premise being that women and men both can use their voting power to affect the policy position of candidates running for election. They have advocated for including women in land rights distribution schemes, enforcement of inheritance laws, and changes in laws that will permit equal ownership of property that has been purchased by both spouses.

Legal Change

While it is true that legal change alone is insufficient to ensure women's inheritance rights in face of customary laws, a strong legal foundation can be an important and necessary first step. However, some legal reforms may be more readily acceptable to women and men than others, and part of the process of legal change must involve listening to the women to understand what legal rights are most important to them, as recommended above. In India, the Women's Resource Access Programme (WRAP) does this via a network of grass roots civil society organizations. It seeks to train and strengthen the capacity of civil-society organizations to listen, document and share rural poor women's views and perceptions on the importance of resource access to increase their ability to influence local, national and international decision-making processes. Likewise, the Nepalese Forum for Women, Law and Development (FWLD) is an NGO whose mission is to eliminate all forms of gender discrimination in Nepal. Among other things, they conduct research on socio-legal issues facing women, lobby for legal reform, and then seek to use laws as instruments of social change.

Land Leasing, Purchase, or Allocation Programs for Women

Recognizing that some land reforms of the past were not addressing the issues of women's rights, some state governments of India have begun allocating land to landless families in the name of the wife in the family. In West Bengal, a new government allocation program identifies landless and homestead-less families in the target area and purchases land from large landowners who are willing to sell at the market price. The family receives a transfer deed, or patta which is in the name of the wife. West Bengal also has a longstanding program to expropriate private land owned above a statutorily set ceiling and allocating that land to landless families. Providing the pattas in the sole name of the wife is a recent revision to the program which has provided land to approximately 1.5 million families. The underlying expectation is that a woman will gain more power within the household and thus be less prone to abandonment or domestic abuse if she is the owner of the land that the family relies on for its survival.

In South Asia, as in many regions of the world, women do not usually inherit land. The reasons for this are many and varied and can be different for different groups of people. On the one hand, formal law may be discriminatory. On the other hand, formal law that is equitable is often largely irrelevant in the face of customary law that does not recognize equitable property rights for women. Such customary rules related to marriage and other social relations often significantly constrain a woman's right to inherit.In addition, other social pressures, related to poverty, women's lack of mobility and lack of financial security may influence whether a woman will claim any legal right to inherit she may possess.Understanding the complexities of formal and customary personal laws is the key to any intervention that seeks to address women's inheritance rights to land property. Also, because inheritance involves cultural practices, changes in inheritance behavior require cultural change. Changing norms and behavior is no simple task, but there are many NGOs operating in South Asia who seek to do just that.

Towards Real Rights

The UN-HABITAT led Global Campaign for Secure Tenure emphasizes that "securing tenure for the household does not necessarily secure tenure for women and children. In undertaking the Global Campaign for Secure Tenure, the extension of secure tenure must benefit women and men equally…."So far, women's land and property rights have remained mainly illusory rather than substantive and the majority of women have therefore not been able to enjoy these rights.

The Habitat Agenda, Millennium Development Goals, various Resolutions of the UN Commission on Human Rights and of the UN-Habitat Governing Council, provide the mandate to UN-HABITAT to be on the forefront of efforts to improve women's land, housing and property rights, including their equal secure tenure. On the basis of ongoing research, UN-HABITAT, together with various governments, and partner organizations at international, regional, national and local level, is working on identifying and developing strategies and tools towards women's enjoyment of land and property rights. Some of the activities currently undertaken are:

(a) *Advocacy* for further participatory law and policy reform with a holistic approach (linking laws and policies related to rural and urban land, housing, water, credit, marital property, inheritance, and gender). Ongoing research is identifying particular needs for law and policy reform in specific countries and the Global Campaigns for Secure Tenure and Urban Good Governance can use those research findings as advocacy entry points, while linking up with various lobbying and advocacy alliances already working towards law and policy reform;

(b) *Technical advice* on how to include women's rights, concerns and needs in regulations and guidelines for the implementation of laws and policies;

(c) *Technical advice* on gender inclusive adjudication;

(d) *Technical advice and advocacy* on innovative, affordable and flexible land tenure systems;

(e) *Training* of judges, police officers, Members of Parliament, local councilors, land officials etc. on gender awareness and women's land and property rights (this activity is carried out by UN-HABITAT partners and others);

(f) *Training of paralegal networks* who disseminate information on women's land, housing and property rights in their communities, intervene in disputes and have been seen to successfully prevent evictions of widows etc. and who are challenging local customs when discriminating against women (this activity is carried out by UN-HABITAT partners and others);

(g) *Awareness raising*: wide dissemination of international and regional human rights instruments recognizing women's equal land, housing and property rights;

(h) *Linking up and supporting* the already existing initiatives of women slum dwellers who through innovative approaches have managed to collectively gain access to land and housing, e.g. through saving schemes and cooperatives;

(i) *Identifying joint tenure types* that improve women's security of tenure and mechanisms to increase independent registration of land and housing in women's names;

(j) *Gender perspective in slum upgrading*: ensuring that in slum upgrading and regularization programs, women's rights and specific needs and interests are actively taken into account;

(k) *Women's inclusion in decision-making*: ensuring that women are well represented in all decision-making processes surrounding slum upgrading and regularization.

Women's equal rights to land, housing and property are human rights, recognized in various international human rights instruments. The recent Women's Rights Protocol to the African Charter on Human and Peoples' Rights is a very welcome regional addition to such instruments. Various positive developments have taken place in terms of law and policy reform in many countries, while other countries have not yet taken such steps. In general, a more holistic and inclusive approach is still needed in the reform of laws and policies that links laws related to inheritance and the division of marital property to laws and policies on land, housing, credit and gender. Urban and peri-urban land issues should also be brought within the national land policy and linked to rural land issues. Gender should be a true cross cutting perspective, also included in budgeting. Implementation of such laws and policies remains a huge challenge and require concerted efforts from all levels in order for women's rights to land and property to become reality.

References

Agarwal, Bina. 1994. "Gender and Command over Property: A Critical Gap in Economic Analysis and Policy in South Asia." *World Development* 22(10): 1455-1478.

Allendorf, Keera. 2007. Do Women's Land Rights Promote Empowerment and Child Health in Nepal? *World Development* 35(11): 1975-1988.

armen Diana and Cheryl R. Doss. 2008. "Gender and the Distribution of Wealth in Developing Countries" in James B. Davies, ed. *Personal Wealth from a Global Perspective*, pp. 353-372. New York: Oxford University Press.

Besley, T., and M. Ghatak. 2009. "Property Rights and Economic Development," in *Handbook of Development Economics,* ed. By D. Rodrik, and M. Rosenzweig. North Holland.

Panda, Pradeep and Bina Agarwal. 2005. *Marital violence, human development and women's property status in India*. World Development 33(5): 823-850.

Steinzor, Nadia. 2003. "Women's Property and Inheritance Rights: Improving Lives in a Changing Time." Development Alternatives, Inc.

4

Women's Rights to Health

The importance of good health and education to a woman's well-being - and that of her family and society - cannot be overstated. Without reproductive health and freedom, women cannot fully exercise their fundamental human rights, such as those relating to education and employment. Yet around the world, the right to health, and especially reproductive and sexual health, is far from a reality for many women. According to the World Bank, a full one-third of the illness among women ages 15-44 in developing countries is related to pregnancy, childbirth, abortion, reproductive tract infections, and human immunodeficiency virus and acquired immune deficiency syndrome (HIV/AIDS).

Women's disproportionate poverty, low social status, and reproductive role expose them to high health risks, resulting in needless and largely preventable suffering and deaths. Many of the women and girls who die each year during pregnancy and childbirth could have been saved by relatively low-cost improvements in reproductive healthcare; yet high levels of maternal mortality persist. The benefits of eliminating the harmful and painful practice of female genital mutilation are easily demonstrated, yet it persists for cultural and traditional reasons. And a large proportion of abortions, some resulting in death and injury, would be avoided if women and men had access to safe, affordable and effective means of contraception.

Women's health status is affected by complex biological, social and cultural factors which are interrelated and can only be addressed in a comprehensive manner. Reproductive health is determined not only by the quality and availability of health care, but also by socio-economic development levels, lifestyles and women's position in society. In fact, the International Federation of Gynecology and Obstetrics asserts that improvements in women's health require state action to correct injustices to women. In its 1994 World Report on Women's Health, the Federation states that women's health is often compromised not by lack of medical knowledge, but by infringements on women's human rights.

The health status of both women and men is affected by their biological characteristics but also by the influence of gender divisions on their social, cultural and economic circumstances. For women the effects of gender are predominantly negative. The impact on men is more difficult to assess since male status involves a more complex mixture of risks and benefits.

Social and economic inequalities mean that in many countries women have difficulty in acquiring the basic necessities for a healthy life. Of course the degree of their deprivation will vary depending on the community in which they live but the "feminization" of poverty remains a constant theme. "Cultural devaluation" is also important though it is difficult to measure or even to define. Because they belong to a group that is seen by society to be less worthwhile, many women find it difficult to develop positive mental health. This process begins in childhood with girls in many cultures being less valued than boys and continues into later life where "caring work" is given lower status and less rewards. These gender inequalities are further reinforced by women's lack of power and the obstacles they face in trying to effect social change.

The prevailing tendency is to view as pathological what are normal processes in women's physical and mental health. For example, pregnancy and child birth are normal physiological processes under most circumstances. Unlike diseases affecting males, they are not diseases or surgical events. In many societies pregnancy and child birth have been medicalized excessively rather than treated as healthy processes. Gender inequalities preventing access to quality health services doubly disadvantage women already at risk because of their life-giving role.

The nature of female labour itself may affect women's health. Household work and child care can be exhausting and debilitating especially if they are done with inadequate resources and combined, as they are for many women, with pregnancy and subsistence agriculture. It can also damage mental health when they are given little recognition and carried out in isolation. The time consumed by caring for others leads to neglect by women of their own health. For women, domestic life and labour also carry the threat of violence since the home is the arena in which they are most likely to be abused. The emphasis on their domestic roles also means that women suffer more severe consequences than men when a family member is a substance user or if they use substances themselves. Even in the context of paid work, "female" jobs often pose particular hazards that receive little attention.

Gender-based violence is a risk factor for many women. Not only is it a violation of their human rights but it has wide ranging consequences for their physical and mental health and the health system. Women are victims of assault as a result of inequalities in society, and are most at risk of abuse from their partners and close relatives.

The sexual subordination of girls and women has increased their vulnerability to STDs, HIV and AIDS, exacerbating the burden of disease among them and greatly reducing life expectancy and quality of life. In addition girls and women with HIV and AIDS are exposed to stigma and mistreatment in most circumstances.

Women are under represented as policy makers, decision-makers and educators in many segments of the health sector. Inequality in access to training and education is one reason. This translates into reduced access to resources and a lack of attention to women's needs and priorities.

Thus far it is women and their advocates who have paid most attention to the impact of gender divisions on health. However new questions are now being raised about the possible health hazards of being a man and these may also need to be addressed in the development of gender-sensitive policies.

On the face of it, "maleness" can only be health promoting since it is likely to give a man greater power, wealth and status than a woman in the equivalent social situation. However certain disadvantages have also been identified. In the context of renumerated work for instance, the idea of the "male breadwinner" has meant that in many societies men have felt compelled to take on the most dangerous jobs. As a result male rates of industrial accidents and diseases have historically been higher than female rates and deaths from occupational causes more common among men than among women.

Men in the majority of societies are also more likely than women to adopt a variety of unhealthy habits - using licit and illicit psychoactive substances - as well as dangerous sports. These activities are linked in most cultures to ideas about masculinity so that young men in particular may feel pressure to indulge in risk taking behaviour in order to show that they are "real men". Similar concepts have been used to explain the high rates of male on male violence found in many parts of the world. In the area of mental health too, some men are now arguing that gender stereotyping narrows the range of emotions they are allowed to express, making it difficult for them to admit weakness, for example, or other feelings regarded as "feminine". Gender inequalities affect men's behaviour and may affect relationships between women and men. They have impeded men's appreciation of their responsibility for the health hazards of violence in relationships between women and men.

Right to Health

The Fourth World Conference on Women defined "Women and Health" as one critical area of concern in the Platform for Action and established five strategic objectives. In doing so, it emphasized the importance of a holistic and life-cycle approach to women's health. The objectives are:

— increase women's access throughout the life cycle to appropriate, affordable and quality health care, information and related services;

— strengthen preventive programmes that promote women's health;

— undertake gender-sensitive initiatives that address sexually transmitted diseases, HIV/AIDS, and sexual and reproductive health issues;

— promote research and disseminate information on women's health;

— increase resources, and monitor follow-up for women's health.

The Platform also addressed, a number of specific health causes, such as mental health, cancer, occupational health, disability issues, tropical diseases and suggested to "increase financial and other support from all sources for preventive, appropriate biomedical, behavioral, epidemiological and health service research on women's health issues and for research on the social, economic and political causes of women's health problems, and their consequences, including the impact of gender and age inequalities, especially with respect to chronic and non-communicable diseases, particularly cardiovascular diseases and conditions, cancers, reproductive tract infections and injuries, HIV/AIDS and other sexually transmitted diseases, domestic violence, occupational health, disabilities, environmentally related health problems, tropical diseases and health aspects of ageing".

As the strategy leading to implementing the tasks set under all critical areas of concern, including health and achieving equality between women and men, the Platform recommended gender mainstreaming. The definition of gender mainstreaming has been further elaborated in the Agreed Conclusions on mainstreaming the gender perspective into all programmes and policies of the United Nations, which state that "mainstreaming a gender perspective is the process of assessing the implications for women and men of any planned action, including legislation, policies and programmes, in all area and at all levels.

Women's health rights are also addressed in the Convention on the Elimination of All Forms of Discrimination against Women through its various provisions including those specifically on health care. The Convention as an international legal instrument should be used by all actors to make Governments accountable for the implementation of its provisions and the eradication of discrimination against women in all its forms including in the area of health. The Declaration and the Programme of Action of the 1993 World Conference on Human Rights stated that women's rights are human rights.

Occupational and Environmental Health

Men as well as women are exposed to a variety of health hazards in the workplace. However, women are more likely to suffer from occupational stress and musculo-skeletal disorders due to their work as unskilled or semi-skilled workers in agriculture and the informal sector. Occupational stress is likely to result from their multiple overlapping roles (as housewives, mothers and workers), repetitive monotonous jobs, sexual harassment at the workplace and shift-work. Musculo-skeletal disorders in women are caused by combined manual work, household work and poorly designed tools and work stations. Exposure to chemicals in the workplace such as solvents in small-scale industries and pesticides in agriculture have been known to result in adverse reproductive outcomes both in males and females.

There is some evidence that a number of persistent environmental chemicals are associated with long-term health hazards in women and men. Exposure of the foetus in utero to compounds such as DDT and polychlorinated biphenyls (PCBs) may cause endocrine disruption manifesting as disease at a later stage.

More research needs to be carried out on the environmental and other risks posed to women's health by their occupational activities in both rural and urban settings with synergistic effects of heavy household work, malnutrition, multiple pregnancies, adverse climatic conditions as they affect millions of poor women in developing countries. There is also need for ergonomic redesigning of tools, equipment and work stations to reduce most occupational morbidity in women.

Sexual and Reproductive Health

Socio-economic differences between women and men are even more important than biological differences in determining the sexual and reproductive health status in women. Lack of autonomy, failure to enforce laws in women's favour, discrimination in laws such as the criminalization of abortion, inadequate allocation of health resources and failure by governments to implement remedial measures sanctioned by international agreements, all contribute to their relatively poor health status in many societies.

The enormous impact of gender inequality is demonstrated by the estimated 586,000 maternal deaths each year, many as the result of unsafe abortion and the millions who become infected with HIV and AIDS by their partners. For poor women who often lack support from their partners and social services, pregnancy is an additional burden. Adolescent and adult women face obstacles to fertility regulation including restricted access to information and services.In most countries women are primarily valued as mothers and the interruption of pregnancy is socially censured. Gender discrimination is a determining factor in legal, political and religious barriers to women's access to safe abortion. Unsafe abortion continues to be a major public health problem, causing widespread damage to women's physical and mental health. Women with low incomes, rural woman, young women and and adolescent girls are particularly vulnerable to these risks.

In order to change traditional male attitudes towards women, boys should be socialized to treat girls as equals at an early age. Sex education for boys as well as girls should be provided so as to reduce the incidence of unwanted pregnancy, unsafe abortion, STDs, HIV and AIDS. Quality sexual and reproductive health information and services, including emergency contraception, should be made accessible and acceptable.

Women should be fully involved up to the highest level of health service planning so as to ensure that their sexual and reproductive health needs are met throughout the life cycle from infancy to old age. The same applies to decisions taken on funding research on women's health.

Right to Life

Every minute, a woman dies somewhere in the developing world as a result of pregnancy and childbirth. These young women, in the prime of their lives die from causes which can be prevented or treated. But, it is a question of how much the life of a woman is considered to be worth. When societies invest less in girls and underestimate the economic contribution of women and when few women are in decision-making positions, it should be no surprise, in resource-poor settings, that a low priority is given to saving the lives of mothers.

Maternal mortality should not be ranked for priority against other disease problems. Maternity is not a disease. It is the means by which the human species is propagated. Societies have an obligation to protect women's right to life when they go through the risky process of giving us life. Safe motherhood is a human rights issue to which countries should be held accountable.

Disease Control Programmes

Communicable diseases such as tuberculosis, malaria, and to a growing extent, HIV and AIDS, are diseases of poverty. Poor women are especially vulnerable because of their low nutritional status, restricted access to education and gainful employment, and heavy workloads. The stigma attached to many communicable diseases, particularly those involving disfigurement, leads to hiding of the disease and a decrease in life opportunities, including marriage.

Once infected, women are more likely to self treat and to postpone seeking professional care because of gender-based constraints including domestic responsibilities, caring for others and the cost of travel and treatment. Having sought treatment they receive low priority due to their low social status. Health services thus miss an important opportunity to provide women, the main health providers within the household, with the information required to perform the role of providing effective medial care at the right time and more effectively.

Gender bias begins at a young age: girl children are less likely to be brought to health services for immunization and early diagnosis and treatment of communicable diseases. Hence epidemiological information based on health statistics do not reflect the true distribution of disease. Men also should be involved in health decision-making with respect to their children. Research has shown that fathers= participation in the decision to immunize their children increased the timely completion of the immunization schedule.

Little research has been conducted on how communicable diseases affect women and men differently, and what is known is not taken into account in planning services. There is need for gender sensitivity education of health professionals at all levels, and ensuring the necessary resources for programming. Women, health advocates and non-governmental organizations (NGOs) should also be involved from the earliest stage in planning, research and delivery of services.

Mental Health

Depression, anxiety and stress are more prevalent in women whereas disorders arising from substance abuse are more common in men. World Bank data on DALYs (Disability Adjusted Life Years) shows that 30 per cent of mental disability in women is from depression as compared with 13 per cent in men. Conversely 31 per cent of mental disability in men is caused by dependence upon alcohol or other drugs as compared with only seven per cent in women. Studies show that depression is more common among poor working-class women (who usually experience more severe adverse life events and have to cope with chronic sources of stress). It may be that men externalize their mental suffering through substance abuse, and under-report their mental distress, whereas women express depression, anxiety and psychological trauma.

Research indicates that women who use substances suffer from more serious psychological, social and economic consequences than do men. In addition, factors that contribute to their use of substances differ from those experienced by men (e.g., sexual abuse, substance use by male partner or family member).

Poverty, domestic isolation, powerlessness (resulting from illiteracy, low education, economic dependence, and patriarchal oppression) are all associated with the higher prevalence of psychiatric morbidity in women, compounded by sexual and physical violence. Family and social abuse of women have a devastating effect on their physical and mental health. Good quality mental health services need to be integrated with other services, in particular with legal, educational and other social services and law enforcement services in order to deal with mental illness resulting from, or aggravated by, violence and other forms of abuse to women.

Inappropriate medication of emotional distress and psychological illness should be avoided as it can result in silencing women and men rather than dealing with the root causes of their problems. It should not be assumed that female relatives are able to provide the full range of mental health care within the home setting to those with serious mental illness. Mental health services should be integrated into, and viewed as part of, basic health care.

Reproductive Rights of Women

Reproductive rights are a series of legal rights and freedoms relating to reproduction and reproductive health. The World Health Organisation defines reproductive rights as follows:

> Reproductive rights rest on the recognition of the basic right of all couples and individuals to decide freely and responsibly the number, spacing and timing of their children and to have the information and means to do so, and the right to attain the highest standard of sexual and reproductive health. They also include the right of all to make decisions concerning reproduction free of discrimination, coercion and violence.

Reproductive rights began to develop a subset of human rights at the United Nation's 1968 International Conference on Human Rights. The resulting non binding Proclamation of Teheran was the first international document to recognize one of these rights when it stated that parents have a basic human right to determine freely and responsibly the number and the spacing of their children.

States, though, have been slow in incorporating these rights in internationally legally binding instruments. Thus, while some of these rights have already been recognized in hard law, that is, in legally binding international human rights instruments, others have been mentioned only in non binding recommendations and, therefore, have at best the status of soft law in international law, while a further group is yet to be accepted by the international community and therefore remains at the level of advocacy.

According to Knudsen, issues related to reproductive rights are some of the most vigorously contested rights' issues worldwide, regardless of the population's socioeconomic level, religion or culture.

Reproductive rights may include some or all of the following: the right to legal or safe abortion, the right to birth control, the right to access quality reproductive healthcare, and the right to education and access in order to make reproductive choices free from coercion, discrimination, and violence.

Reproductive rights may also include the right to receive education about contraception and sexually transmitted infections, and freedom from coerced sterilization, abortion, and contraception, and protection from gender-based practices such as female genital cutting (FGC) and male genital mutilation (MGM).

In 1945, the UN Charter included the obligation "to promote... universal respect for, and observance of, human rights and fundamental freedoms for all without discrimination as to race, sex, language, or religion". However, the Charter did not define these rights. Three years later, the UN adopted the Universal Declaration of Human Rights (UDHR), the first international legal document to delineate human rights; the UDHR does not mention reproductive rights. Reproductive rights began to appear as a subset of human rights in the 1968 Proclamation of Teheran, which states: "Parents have a basic right to decide freely and responsibly on the number and spacing of their children and a right to adequate education and information in this respect".This right was affirmed by the UN General Assembly in the 1974 Declaration on Social Progress and Development which states "The family as a basic unit of society and the natural environment for the growth and well-being of all its members, particularly children and youth, should be assisted and protected so that it may fully assume its responsibilities within the community. Parents have the exclusive right to determine freely and responsibly the number and spacing of their children." The 1975 UN International Women's Year Conference echoed the Proclamation of Teheran.

The twenty year "Cairo Programme of Action" was adopted in 1994 at the International Conference on Population and Development (ICPD) in Cairo. The non binding Programme of Action asserted that governments have a responsibility to meet individuals' reproductive needs, rather than demographic targets. It recommended that Family planning services be provided in the context of other reproductive health services, including services for healthy and safe childbirth, care for sexually transmitted infections, and post-abortion care. The ICPD also addressed issues such as violence against women, sex trafficking, and adolescent health.

The Cairo Program is the first international policy document to define reproductive health, stating:

> Reproductive health is a state of complete physical, mental and social well-being and not merely the absence of disease or infirmity, in all matters relating to the reproductive system and its functions and processes. Reproductive health therefore implies that people are able to have a satisfying and safe sex life and that they have the capability to reproduce and the freedom to decide if, when and how often to do so. Implicit in this last condition are the right of men and women to be informed [about] and to have access to safe, effective, affordable and acceptable methods of family planning of their choice, as well as other methods for regulation of fertility which are not against the law, and the right of access to appropriate health-care services that will enable women to go safely through pregnancy and childbirth and provide couples with the best chance of having a healthy infant [para. 72].

Unlike previous population conferences, a wide range of interests from grassroots to government level were represented in Cairo. 179 nations attended the ICPD and overall eleven thousand representatives from governments, NGOs, international agencies and citizen activists participated. The ICPD did not address the far-reaching implications of the HIV/AIDS epidemic. In 1999, recommendations at the ICPD+5 were expanded to include commitment to AIDS education, research, and prevention of mother-to-child transmission, as well as to the development of vaccines and microbicides.The Cairo Programme of Action was adopted by 184 UN member states. Nevertheless, many Latin American and Islamic States made formal reservations to the programme, in particular, to its concept of reproductive rights and sexual freedom, to its treatment of abortion, and to its potential incompatibility with Islamic Law.

The 1995 Fourth World Conference on Women in Beijing, in its non binding Declaration and Platform for Action, supported the Cairo Programme's definition of reproductive health, but established a broader context of reproductive rights:

> The human rights of women include their right to have control over and decide freely and responsibly on matters related to their sexuality, including sexual and reproductive health, free of coercion, discrimination and violence.

> Equal relationships between women and men in matters of sexual relations and reproduction, including full respect for the integrity of the person, require mutual respect, consent and shared responsibility for sexual behavior and its consequences [para. 96].

The Beijing Platform demarcated twelve interrelated critical areas of the human rights of women that require advocacy. The Platform framed women's reproductive rights as "indivisible, universal and inalienable human rights."

Reproductive Rights as Human Rights

Since most existing legally binding international human rights instruments do not explicitly mention sexual and reproductive rights, a broad coalition of NGOs, civil servants, and experts working in international organizations has been promoting successfully a reinterpretation of those instruments to link the realization of the already internationally recognized human rights with the realization of reproductive rights.

An example of this linkage is provided by the 1994 Cairo Programme of Action:

> "reproductive rights embrace certain human rights that are already recognized in national laws, international human rights documents and other relevant United Nations consensus documents. These rights rest on the recognition of the basic right of all couples and individuals to decide freely and responsibly the number, spacing and timing of their children and to have the information and means to do so, and the right to attain the highest standard of sexual and reproductive health. It also includes the right of all to make decisions concerning reproduction free of discrimination, coercion and violence as expressed in human rights documents. In the exercise of this right, they should take into account the needs of their living and future children and their responsibilities towards the community."

Similarly, Amnesty International has argued that the realisation of reproductive rights is linked with the realisation of a series of recognised human rights, including the right to health, the right to freedom from discrimination, the right to privacy, and the right not to be subjected to torture or ill-treatment.

However, not all states have accepted the inclusion of reproductive rights in the body of internationally recognized human rights. At the Cairo Conference, several states made formal reservations either to the concept of reproductive rights or to its specific content. Ecuador, for instance, stated that:

> "With regard to the Programme of Action of the Cairo International Conference on Population and Development and in accordance with the provisions of the Constitution and laws of Ecuador and the norms of international law, the delegation of Ecuador reaffirms, inter alia, the following principles embodied in its Constitution: the inviolability of life, the protection of children from the moment of conception, freedom of conscience and religion, the protection of the family as the fundamental unit of society, responsible paternity, the right of parents to bring up their children and the formulation of population and development plans by the Government in accordance with the principles of respect for sovereignty. Accordingly, the delegation of Ecuador enters a reservation with respect to all terms such as "regulation of fertility", "interruption of pregnancy", "reproductive health", "reproductive rights" and "unwanted children", which in one way or another, within the context of the Programme of Action, could involve abortion."

Similar reservations were made by Argentina, Dominican Republic, El Salvador, Honduras, Malta, Nicaragua, Paraguay, Peru and the Holy See. Islamic Countries, such as Brunei Darussalam, Djibouti, Iran, Jordan, Kuwait, Libya, Syria, United Arab Emirates, and Yemen made broad reservations against any element of the programme that could be interpreted as contrary to the Sharia. Guatemala even questioned whether the conference could legally proclaim new human rights.

The United Nations Population Fund (UNFPA) and the World Health Organization (WHO) advocate for reproductive rights with a primary emphasis on women's rights. In this respect the UN and WHO focus on a range of issues, including access to family planning services, sex education, menopause, and the reduction of obstetric fistula, to the relationship between reproductive health and economic status.

The reproductive rights of women are advanced in the context of the right to freedom from discrimination and the social and economic status of women. The group Development Alternatives with Women for a New Era (DAWN) explained the link in the following statement:

Control over reproduction is a basic need and a basic right for all women. Linked as it is to women's health and social status, as well as the powerful social structures of religion, state control and administrative inertia, and private profit, it is from the perspective of poor women that this right can best be understood and affirmed. Women know that childbearing is a social, not a purely personal, phenomenon; nor do we deny that world population trends are likely to exert considerable pressure on resources and institutions by the end of this century. But our bodies have become a pawn in the struggles among states, religions, male heads of households, and private corporations. Programs that do not take the interests of women into account are unlikely to succeed...

Attempts have been made to analyse the socioeconomic conditions that affect the realisation of a woman's reproductive rights. The term reproductive justice has been used to describe these broader social and economic issues. Proponents of reproductive justice argue that while the right to legalized abortion and contraception applies to everyone, these choices are only meaningful to those with resources, and that there is a growing gap between access and affordability.

Reproductive Health Care

Over the past decade the percentage of surveyed women who say they do not want to have more children has grown substantially in every region except sub-Saharan Africa. Even in Africa, although most women want large families, there is great interest in spacing births. In nearly all sub-Saharan countries surveyed by the Demographic and Health Surveys (DHS), between one-third and one-half of married women said that they wanted to space their next births by at least two years. Such statistics imply large potential demand for family planning services.

Even though contraceptive use has risen substantially in recent years, in most surveyed countries between 20% and 30% of married women of reproductive age report that they are not using contraception but do not want any more children or else want to delay their next birth at least two years. Rates of abortion, even where abortion is illegal and unsafe, also testify to women's strong desire to control their own fertility. Demographers describe women who are not using contraception but want to space or limit births as having an unmet need for family planning.

Using this definition, Population Reports has estimated, based on DHS data, that 120 million married women of reproductive age in developing countries have an unmet need for contraception. Ruth Dixon-Mueller and Adrienne Germain suggest widening the definition of unmet need to include unmarried women, women who need better or more suitable contraceptive methods, women who need abortion services, and women who need more comprehensive reproductive health services than are currently available. These numbers cannot be easily estimated, but they would surely add substantially to the 120 million figure.

Men also have unmet needs for family planning. In DHS in Burundi, Egypt, Ghana, Kenya, and Pakistan, over half of men approve of family planning, but very few are using a contraceptive method. In smaller, qualitative studies as well, men have asked for more information about reproductive health services including both contraception and treatment for sexually transmitted diseases. Effectively serving all who want to avoid pregnancy but are not using contraception could help reconcile the dual goals of (1) serving individual clients and (2) slowing global population growth.

Family planning programs replace demographic objectives with the objective of meeting unmet need. In 9 of 12 countries studied, levels of contraceptive use would be higher if all unmet need were met than if current demographic objectives were reached. To translate this unmet need to control fertility into utilization of reproductive health services, policy makers must let clients know that these services are a safe and effective way to achieve their personal goals. Reproductive health programs can identify the obstacles that prevent women from using services and can design services and communication that will help overcome some of those obstacles.

Obstacles may range from lack of supplies and services to dissatisfaction with current services to fears of contraceptive side effects, to social limits on women's mobility or decision-making. Beyond the need to control their own fertility, women also need other reproductive health services, and family planning programs may be able to meet these needs, as well.

Family Planning Clients

Serving clients' needs requires learning and heeding what clients want. Since most family planning clients are women, women should be involved at all levels in population and reproductive health programs and policy-making. Women can offer valuable insights as policy-makers, program managers, and health professionals. Most importantly, programs should consult with clients about their reproductive health care priorities. Policy-makers can use various means to learn what clients and the public want. A recent review has identified a range of approaches. Many of these approaches are routinely used in the audience research that is part of designing and monitoring family planning communication programs:

— Observation of client-provider interactions,

— Feedback from "mystery" or "simulated" clients-people who use services and then report on their experience,

— Patient flow studies to determine how long patients spend in such activities as waiting and talking to providers,

— Focus-group discussions with clients and potential clients about their experience and their preferences,

— Exit interviews or other postservice interviews with clients,

— Interviews with service personnel about what they think would constitute a good client visit and what they see as difficulties,

— Involving women directly in program design as program administrators or on advisory groups,

— Working with women's health advocacy groups to benefit from their analyses of women's health needs,

— Open discussion meetings in the community, sometimes specifically for women or for men, and

— Learning from other programs with services that clients like.

Some women's grass-roots organizations have identified their own reproductive needs and responded to them. For example, the Working Women's Forum in India and the Mothers' Clubs in South Korea offer family planning services that complement the economic help and other services that they provide to members. The seven clinics run by the Bangladesh Women's Health Coalition each have a local advisory committee to ensure that the clinics meets local needs.

Some women's organizations have focused on informing other women. In 1991 a collective of Egyptian women wrote a nontechnical book on women's reproductive health. In Peru women in focus groups helped Peru Mujer, a nongovernmental organization, design educational materials for nonliterate women like themselves. Women in Fiji made videos for women's groups on topics that they wanted discussed, such as sexually transmitted diseases and women's attitudes toward menstruation and family planning. Other family planning organizations can learn from such groups and perhaps collaborate with them.

Involving women more deeply in program design should not mean excluding men. Men and women share responsibility for reproductive health. Policies and programs will work best if they are planned by, and for, both women and men. Ideally, the insight and experiences of both women and men will create better programs that improve the lives of all clients. Improving the lives of women and men should be a primary goal of population policy. Reproductive health care programs contribute by enabling men and women to live healthier lives and to plan when they will have children. Women, and men who enjoy better health and more control over their reproductive lives can have more opportunity to fulfill their hopes for their children, themselves, their families, and their communities. Women confront many obstacles to better lives. Women need change in many areas simultaneously. Thus the agenda for policies to give women more opportunities must be broad. In addition to assuring women's ability to control their own fertility, important elements include efforts to:

Improve health: In the nations with the best health care, the life expectancy of women is 10% longer than that of men. In developing countries, however, women's life expectancy is closer to or shorter than men's. This occurs because women receive less than their fair share of health care and food, often beginning in childhood. As adults, many women do not get the food and health care needed for healthy childbearing.

Encourage education: Over the last 20 years more and more girls have been going to school, but boys still get more education than girls. An estimated two-thirds of the 300 million children without access to education are girls. Two-thirds of the 960 million nonliterate adults are women.

Ensure job opportunities and fair pay: Most women work long and hard, and they earn less for it than men do. Even in developed countries, for example, women earn 75% or less of what men earn. Much of women's work is unpaid. Women's unpaid household labor accounts for about one-third of the world's economic production. When unpaid agricultural work and housework are considered along with wage labor, women work more hours than men.

Guarantee legal protection: Legal codes often sanction inequality between husband and wife. They may allow marriage of very young women, marriage without the woman's consent, unequal ownership and control over family assets including land and other property, unequal inheritance rights, and unequal access to divorce and to support after divorce. In many cases the law does not recognize women as adults with the same capacities and right to make decisions as their husbands. Laws that do protect women's rights often are not enforced.

Permit access to reproductive health care: The International Planned Parenthood Federation (IPPF) has reported that 46 of 94 surveyed countries require spousal consent for contraception, abortion, or voluntary sterilization-services used primarily or exclusively by women. Worldwide, 54 countries require a woman to obtain her husband's approval before voluntary sterilization, but only 20 of these countries also require a man to have his wife's approval. Young women and unmarried women often have little or no access to reproductive health services. Yet surveys in eight sub-Saharan countries, for example, find that 20% to 47% of adolescent women become pregnant before marriage.

Prevent violence against women: Many women live every day in fear of violence, often from their husbands. In surveys in Chile, Colombia, Kenya, India, Mexico, Pakistan, Papua New Guinea, San Salvador, South Korea, and Thailand, 40% to 99% of women reported physical abuse by their husbands. Most of these women have no choice but to live with this abuse and fear. Leaving the marriage is often not a realistic option when women, denied education, jobs, and inheritance rights, are economically dependent on their husbands.

Unwanted sexual intercourse is a major form of violence against women. In a US national sample survey, 13% of women reported that they had been raped at some time in their lives, not counting marital rape. This amounts to one woman raped every minute. Half of these women were under age 18 when raped, and 75% knew the man who raped them.

Fear of desertion or violence prevents women from acting in their own best interests. For example, in Egypt many women do not seek care for gynecological problems such as vaginal discharge or fistula because they fear that their husbands will divorce them for spending time and money on their own health. Threats of violence prevent some women even from participating in development projects.

Increase respect for women: Since most societies value females less than males, many women grow up believing that they are inferior to males. Such perceptions are difficult to change. For example, China has promoted equal roles and rights for women for 40 years. Still, 30% of Chinese women surveyed in 1990 thought that men are born to be more important than women, and 33% agreed that women should hold back so that they are not more successful than their husbands.

Improvement Programs

Programs to help women often focus on their economic or legal position. Women themselves have started many of these programs. For example, women in India formed the Self-Employed Women's Association (SEWA) in 1972 and the Working Women's Forum (WWF) in 1977 to change local ordinances that interfered with their ability to work as market traders. Both groups broadened their agendas as members began to request help with health, education, and other needs. Development planners have developed two broad approaches to assessing women's needs and designing programs to address them:

— The status of women approach compares the positions of women and men in a society or cross-nationally. After identifying the areas in which women are disadvantaged, planners design programs to address the problems.

— The empowerment of women approach aims to help women gain more control of their lives. This approach often begins with women identifying and prioritizing their own needs. Program organizers then help women to design programs that meet those needs.

Both approaches have advantages. Focusing on objective measures of women's status documents the problem for top-level policy-makers and helps motivate their support for policy changes. The United Nations has based its efforts to eliminate discrimination against women on status measures such as years of education and hourly wages. The empowerment approach may bring faster results for individual women, although usually on a smaller scale. Involving women in solving their own problems builds their skills and self-confidence and finds solutions that are locally appropriate.

Using both approaches could speed improvements for women, and in practice the two approaches are not always distinct. Program organizers can use the status-of-women approach to influence policy nationally and to evaluate its impact and at the same time can use community-based empowerment programs to begin change locally. Some of the most successful community programs at first address a need that women clearly recognize, such as the need for income, and then build skills that women can use in many areas of life.

Women's advocates are asking that development plans pay more attention to the effects of planned changes on women's lives. Some development plans have required, for example, male labor migration or female volunteer labor, which place additional burdens on women. "Gender planning," as the approach is called, considers the impact of a proposed program on women, men, and their relationship. Its goals are to ensure that development programs do not inadvertently harm the lives of men or women and to see that women's situation is improved.

Daughter Neglect

In some countries parents tend to prefer sons and to treat them better than daughters. Boys sometimes get more to eat and more medical care, while girls are slighted in education and jobs and in some cases are neglected, abused, and even killed. While the majority of studies on son preference come from countries in South Asia and North Africa, where son preference is believed to be strongest, son preference appears to exist to some degree in other regions of the world as well. The preference for sons is both a symptom and a cause of limited opportunities for women.

A common index of preference for sons comes from survey responses: the ratio of the number of parents who say that they prefer their next child to be male to the number who prefer their next child to be female. A ratio also can be derived from survey responses about desire for additional children among women with different numbers of living daughters and sons.

Among countries surveyed, those with strong preference for sons-indices of 1.6 or above-are Bangladesh, Jordan, Nepal, Pakistan, South Korea, and Syria. Moderate preference for sons has been documented in many other countries, including the Dominican Republic, Egypt, Mexico, Senegal, Sudan, Turkey, Nigeria, Tunisia, and Yemen. Some countries, such as Colombia, Ghana, and Indonesia, show no preference, and two-Jamaica and Venezuela-show a slight preference for daughters. In most countries parents desire at least one daughter as well as sons.

There are many reason for son preference:

— *Economic security*: In many developing countries sons are their parents' only source of security in old age. Particularly where women have little economic independence or cannot inherit property, sons are insurance for a mother against the loss of her husband's support due to death or desertion. Where women have few opportunities to earn income, investing household resources in female children, who will marry and leave the family, is likely to have little pay-off, and so poor families tend to invest what little they have in sons. In cultures with dowry systems, such as India's, daughters are more expensive to marry off than sons.

— *Cultural factors*: In many countries kinship systems, tradition, and religion value males over females. In parts of Bangladesh, China, Egypt, India, and Tanzania, for example, traditional patrilineal kinship systems require women to marry out of their families of origin and then not to provide financial or even emotional support to their own parents. In both Hindu and Confucian traditions, practiced throughout Asia, only sons can pray for and release the souls of dead parents, and only males can perform birth, death, and marriage rituals.

Effects to Female Children

Although females are thought to be genetically more resistant to respiratory and other infectious diseases than males and more likely to survive infancy, in some developing countries this advantage rapidly disappears as female babies grow up. Females are more likely than males to die in early childhood (ages 1 to 4), particularly in South Asia, the Near East, and North Africa. Poorer nutrition and health care are important reasons.

— *Nutrition*: In some places boys get more and better food than girls. Breastfeeding and weaning practices also seem to favor boys in some countries. In the Indian state of Punjab, for example, boys from both wealthy and poor households are better nourished than girls. An analysis of DHS data from 18 countries, however, found few significant differences in the nutritional status of boys and girls.

— *Medical care*: Girls are sick as often as boys, but boys sometimes receive more treatment and more medicine. For example, boys were seen 66% more often than girls at a diarrhea treatment center in Bangladesh even though the center provided free ambulance transport and treatment. Parents bought drugs and sought medical care three times more often for boys than for girls. Girls often receive less preventive health care, as well. Studies in Latin America and India show that girls often are immunized later than boys or not at all.

— *Female infanticide*: Some unwanted female children are killed or abandoned soon after birth. It is not clear how common or widespread the practice is, but some demographers have long suspected its existence. They base their conclusions largely on reported sex ratios at birth. Others argue that underreporting explains the discrepancy. In China, where sex ratios show that 5% of all infant girls born are unaccounted for, some observers suspect that female infanticide accounts for at least some of these missing girls, although informal adoptions, sending girls to faraway relatives, or raising the girls covertly probably explain most of the cases.

— *Abortion of female fetuses*: Selective abortion of female fetuses reportedly is widespread in such Asian countries as China, India, and South Korea. Increasing use of prenatal ultrasound and amniocentesis procedures, which make selective abortion possible by revealing the sex of a fetus, may be contributing to a growing gap in the number of males and females born in some countries.

Higher Fertility and Contraceptive Use

In general, where most couples have large families, son preference has little impact on fertility levels because most couples will have at least one son by biological chance. As contraceptive use becomes more widespread and average family size decreases, however, in some countries the desire to have at least one son begins to affect fertility decisions: Trying for a son, many couples have more children than they would otherwise.

A recent study in Matlab, Bangladesh, indicates that son preference can have a strong effect on contraceptive use and fertility. In Matlab, where intensive family planning services are available, contraceptive prevalence now tops 50%, and couples average four children, researchers calculated that eliminating preference for sons would increase contraceptive use by 10% and continuation rates by 15%. These increases would avert nearly one birth for every two couples.

Attempts to improve the position of girls in society often focus on economics. Increasing economic opportunities for women and raising the value of women's labor increases the likelihood that parents will see daughters as economic assets and not as liabilities. Also, increasing girls' education may increase their income-earning potential and, thus, their economic value to their parents. Other recommendations include better access to food and medical care so that parents will not have to choose between male and female children in allocating household resources.

Also, better access to pension plans and other forms of old-age security that do not depend on children would relieve some of the pressure to have sons. While specific measures can help, some researchers insist that only far-reaching improvements in the cultural, social, legal, and economic position of women will improve the well-being of female children.

Changes in Women's Lives

The Demographic and Health Surveys (DHS) are varies widely among surveyed countries, from over 60% in 4 of 30 countries to 5% or lower in 3 countries. The surveys reveal that in countries where contraceptive use is widespread, women:

— Are older when they have their first child,

— Complete their childbearing earlier,

— Spend fewer years pregnant, and

— Spend fewer years with young children in the household.

Age at First and Last Births

Where total contraceptive use is above 40% (the average for use of modern methods in developing countries), women ages 25 to 29 at the time of the surveys first gave birth on average about three years later than in countries where contraceptive use is below the average. First births come soon after marriage in most countries.

Still, on average women in the countries with higher contraceptive prevalance first give birth more than two years after marriage, while women in countries with lower than average prevalence give birth about a year and a half after marriage. Last births come sooner in countries where contraceptive use is above average levels. Where contraceptive use exceeds 40%, most women had their last births in their early thirties, while in countries with lower levels of contraceptive use, women last gave birth in their late thirties.

Age at last birth for women ages 40 to 49 at the time of the survey, the age group most likely to have completed childbearing. This analysis may underestimate the impact of contraceptive use on average age at last birth, because women in this age group are the least likely to have been affected by recent rises in the use of contraception in many countries. The median age at last birth ranges from 31 years in a few Caribbean countries where contraceptive use is widespread to 38 or 39 years in several African countries where there is little use of contraception. Of course, other factors besides contraceptive use help to determine the age at last birth, including age-related sterility, divorce, widowhood, and reduced coital frequency at older ages.

The number of years that women can expect to live after the birth of their last child varies tremendously. This difference reflects both a woman's age at the birth of her last child and her life expectancy. Life expectancy tends to be longer in the more developed countries, where also age at last birth is lower. In all surveyed countries where contraceptive prevalence is above 40% except Peru, a woman still has more than half of her life ahead of her when she last gives birth. In contrast, in most countries where contraceptive prevalence is below 40%, women average fewer years of life after their last birth than before it.

Duration of the Childbearing Years

Where the level of contraceptive use is above average, women devote less of their lives to childbearing and childraising. Also, within countries the length of the childbearing period has decreased as contraceptive use has spread.

Differences across countries: The interval between average ages at first and last births among women ages 40 to 49 ranges from just 11 years in Trinidad and Tobago and in Thailand, where contraception is widely used, to nearly twice as long in Zambia and Senegal, where contraception is little used. In Trinidad and Tobago women ages 40 to 49 averaged four children. The first child was born when the mother was 20 years old, and the last, when she was 31. In contrast, in Zambia women ages 40 to 49 had given birth to an average of seven children.

The first was born when the mother was 18, and the last, when she was 38. Because contraceptive use is increasing in nearly every country, the childbearing years probably will be shorter for women who are now in their 20s or 30s. By comparison, US women have fewer children over a shorter period of time. In the US, where about three-quarters of married women use contraception, those born between 1940 and 1949-and thus about the same age as women ages 40 to 49 in DHS surveys-married at a median age of 20.5 years. They first gave birth a little over a year after marriage and had their last child at age 30. They gave birth to an average of 2.8 children over the course of approximately eight years, and their life expectancy at the time of their last birth was 47.5 more years. Both the number of children that women have and the spacing of their births influence the number of years that mothers spend with young children. In countries where use of contraception is widespread, women spend an average of 14 years with at least one of their children under the age of six. Where contraceptive prevalence is low, women have young children for an average of 20 years.

Changes over time: Women's childbearing patterns have changed as contraceptive prevalence has risen. In 16 countries at least two comparable surveys have been conducted since the 1970s. Where contraceptive use has increased most, the childbearing period has decreased most. Also, in all 16 countries the time that women had a child under age six in the household decreased, but in some countries the decline was small. The changes are most obvious in the five countries where three surveys have been taken. For example, in Morocco, where the level of contraceptive use more than doubled between 1979-80 and 1992, women's average childbearing period decreased by almost two years.

The number of years spent with a child under age six fell by almost three years. In the Java-Bali region of Indonesia, contraceptive prevalence rose from 26% to 53% between 1976 and 1991. Over the same period the childbearing period decreased by 3.5 years, and the amount of time spent with at least one young child at home declined by five years. Age at last birth declined substantially in Colombia, the Dominican Republic, and Peru, and so did the length of the childbearing period. Because the DHS are internationally comparable surveys, they offer a unique comparison of women's lives across a large number of countries with varying levels of contraceptive use. But they cannot tell the whole story.

Cross-sectional surveys such as the DHS cannot explain much of how contraceptive use affects individual women. This is because surveys usually have not recorded the sequence of events such as the timing of contraceptive use, births, and employment. Also, surveys can reveal full childbearing patterns only for women whose reproductive years have ended. As noted, these women's experience is least likely to reflect recent changes in contraceptive use.

Not enough is known about the way contraceptive use affects women's lives. Researchers know that women's education, economic position, household characteristics, and social status influence use of contraception and thus fertility. In contrast, little is known about the opposite perspective-how changes in contraceptive use and thus in fertility affect other aspects of women's lives, particularly the ability to take on new roles.

Assessing current understanding of this issue, Sawon Hong and Judith Seltzer observed, "

— good data and rigorous analysis are scarce;

— the relationship is complex and varies by social, cultural, and economic setting; and

— no simple conceptual model has yet been set forth".

To improve understanding of how contraceptive use affects women's lives, the United States Agency for International Development has funded a 5-year, US$8.6 million research project, begun in late 1993 by Family Health International. Its purposes are

— to support social and behavioral research on the immediate and long-term consequences for women of both family planning programs and contraceptive methods and

— to help improve family planning and related reproductive health policies and programs through increased knowledge of the needs and perspectives of women. The project will support qualitative and quantitative research in six to eight countries. In-country advisory committees will help establish the research agenda. Based on its findings, the project will recommend improvements in program design and implementation from the perspective of women's interests and needs.

Reproductive Decisions

Family planning programs can better serve their clients, both male and female, if they can answer these questions. They also can better find ways to help women express their needs and to help men understand and respect women's concerns.

Complex Decisions

The reproductive decision-making process reflects tradition, religious belief, community norms, family structure, household economics and the value of children, and access to new ideas and innovations, all expressed in peoples' attitudes and opinions. Research on the reproductive decision-making process is limited and scattered, but a study in areas of North and South India illustrates the complexity of the process. Women in southern India are valued agricultural workers, marry later than women in the North, have more contact with and support from their parents and families, and are closer emotionally to their husbands.

Their daughters are less likely to die in infancy. Women in southern India are better treated because they marry within their own extended families-groups of people who depend upon each other for continuing support. In contrast, women in northern India marry out of their extended families into families that have no on-going relationship with the women's parents and other relatives and that permit married women little contact with their own families. Meanwhile, men's families form close, mutually supportive groups.

Most men are not close to their wives. In the northern system women have little value to their own parents and are valued by their husbands' families chiefly when they produce sons. Women in the southern kinship system are better able to make reproductive choices such as using contraception because they are more valued, less isolated, and more autonomous. They also are under less pressure to produce sons.

While the web of influences on decision-making is complex, people nonetheless have perceptions of who actually makes decisions in the household or who has the most say. Here and there surveys and focus-group research have asked people who makes household decisions including decisions about reproduction.

Within marriage, in many cultures men typically have more say than women in the decision to use contraception and in the number of children that the couple will have. In Ghana, for example, both Demographic and Health Survey (DHS) data and focus-group research reveal that the husband is usually the effective decision-maker about fertility. Furthermore, husbands' family planning attitudes and fertility goals usually are not influenced by those of their wives. When partners disagree on whether to use family planning, the man's preference usually dominates.

Within marriage some women make the decision to use family planning. In the few studies comparing various household decisions, women seem to have more say about using contraception than about most other important decisions. In Turkey, for example, 62% of the semi-urban wives surveyed made their own decisions about contraceptive use. In general, better educated women have more decision-making power within marriage, including more influence over decisions about reproduction and family planning.

Some women decide to use contraception without telling their husbands. In DHS in African countries, a small minority of women report doing so because they think that their husbands would disapprove. In rural Nigeria, as elsewhere around the world, some women secretly use contraceptives, use patent medicines as abortifacients, or make secret trips for abortions even though they risk eviction from their homes if found out.

Many unmarried women make reproductive decisions by themselves, of course. These decisions add up; in many countries women spend much of their lives outside marriage. For example, in Botswana women older than age 20 spend an average of 46% of their remaining reproductive years unmarried. In Colombia women spend an average of 40% of their entire reproductive lives unmarried.

Partners and Joint Decision-Making

Married couples together sometimes make household decisions of various kinds, including the decision to use contraception. Whether a couple discusses family planning can affect the decision to use contraception. In many places such communication is the exception rather than the rule, however. In Kenya, for example, lack of communication between spouses proved to be a more common obstacle to contraceptive use than male opposition. In a study of monogamous couples in Ghana, 35% of the wives and 39% of the husbands reported discussing family planning during the previous year. Focus-group discussions in Tanzania found that different people had different reasons for not discussing contraception. Older people did not discuss using contraceptives because they believed that God determined the number of their children or because they used abstinence or herbal medicines to space pregnancies. Women did not discuss the topic because they thought that their husbands did not approve of contraception. Married men said that discussion was unnecessary because the women decided on their own the number and timing of pregnancies. Young people did not talk about contraceptives for fear of being considered promiscuous.

Program managers need to be aware of the variety of ways that individuals and couples make decisions about contraception-a variety that reflects not only the social position of women relative to men but also the different types of sexual relationships, from longterm monogamous marriages to one-time contacts between strangers. Communication campaigns and counseling are most likely to be effective when they recognize existing patterns of communication and decision-making. In some cases that means reaching out to couples.

Gender Perspective in Health Care

The Commonwealth has been pioneering the introduction of Gender Management Systems (GMSs), both at the level of the national government and within the health sector in member states. Adapted to the specific conditions and requirements of each country, GMSs are a potentially very effective tool for mainstreaming gender within policies and programme.

In a series of multi-national, multi-sectoral workshops, frameworks have been developed for national action plans for the introduction of GMSs in the health sector, subsequently to be completed and implemented by each national group. Among the important issues that have emerged during the process, two are seen as particularly critical.

Firstly, there is a great need for sensitization and training of actors at all levels of the health sector, government and public administration in gender concepts, which are generally poorly understood.

Secondly, the factor that emerges as the single most important determinant of progress is the degree of political commitment at the highest levels.

The process is unlikely to proceed beyond a few token steps unless the Health Minister and senior cabinet colleagues become closely involved. External actors such as international organizations and local players such as NGOs can play vital catalytic roles in helping to secure this political commitment.

Applying a fully comprehensive gender perspective would require that all health statistics be disaggregated by sex and that a comprehensive women's health profile be constructed. The International Council of Nurses (ICN), for example, has developed guidelines for countries to develop such a profile covering demographics, socio-economics, health status, lifestyle, environment, health care services, health service use, sexuality, and policy development. Mainstreaming of the gender perspective includes consideration of basic health care as a human right. Even in countries, where education is provided free of charge as a human right, health care is often free only for certain groups.

In the interests of mainstreaming the gender perspective, ICN has issued guidelines to its affiliates which include eliminating negative cultural practices such as female genital mutilation; supporting programmes to reduce violence against women; promoting women's access to comprehensive health services and education (including that of girls and elderly women) and researching women's non-reproductive health needs (e.g., protection against pesticides, solvents, occupational strain, chronic stress).

International organizations and agencies should provide technical assistance for national and regional programmes to deal with gender concerns in health care systems only if they can be shown to integrate fully a gender perspective. It should be noted that for nursing, as a female dominated profession, the industrial models of management have created a lot of dissatisfaction and staff turnover.These trends can only be alleviated by main-streaming a gender perspective into the management of human and financial resources in nursing and within the health delivery system.

Health Canada (Canada's Federal Department of Health) has established five Centres of Excellence for Women's Health across the country with a mandate to conduct policy-oriented research on women's health. The goal is to improve women's health by generating knowledge, information and policy advice that can be applied to make the health system more responsive to women's health needs. Research is generated in each centre through a partnership of academics, researchers, health care providers and community-based women's and women's health organizations. The Centres examine current health system issues such as the impact of health reform on women and women's health; patterns of health service provision to women ; women's experience with the health system; and the health needs of particular groups of women.

Health Reform and Financing

The adverse effects of poverty on the health of women are well established and reflected in the health services available to them under different systems of financing health care. Individually financed services based on private payment for services, and those based on third party insurance whereby health coverage is paid for by individuals and employers, leave large groups of the population, especially women (as they fall into the lower economic groups and have less resources) without coverage. Female-headed households and elderly women are characteristically impoverished and dependent on the family and the state for health care services.State financed health services, in which the state pays for all health care, and social insurance systems, whereby an essential health care package is provided for the whole population with additional services provided under other schemes, can also raise gender issues by increasing the gap between rich and poor in terms of health status and access to quality care. An equitable division of coverage by the public and private sectors is required to avoid all non-profit services being automatically assumed by the public sector.

Currently decentralization of management is being proposed to bring health services nearer to communities and to strengthen their accountability over resources. This should be accompanied by the provision of adequate resource allocations to local levels in order to provide basic health services. Otherwise, health care providers, the majority of whom are women, carry a burden of increased workload, as do women who are required to provide home care because of limited services available.

Standards of care should be set through gender-sensitive programmes and based on best practices. This will need greatly improved information systems and more gender-sensitive methodologies than the currently used DALY measurement and include qualitative as well as quantitative data.

Partnership for Health

A number of actors and stake holders have an important role to play in mainstreaming gender into the health sector. While the Ministry of Health is usually in charge of the health sector within the Government, other Ministries can also have an impact on health care. Parliamentarians can play a crucial role in the establishment of gender-sensitive health policies and in introducing legislation. Relevant parliamentary commissions on human rights or budget for instance can also be involved as appropriate, in monitoring the application of policies dealing with abuses to women's right to health or preparing budgetary allocations for the health sector. Political will at the highest level is a prerequisite. For instance, the Heads of States of Government of the Southern African Development Community (SADC) in their Declaration on Gender and Developmentcommitted themselves to recognizing, protecting and promoting the reproductive and sexual rights of women and girl children.

District and local authorities are important in the delivery of health care services, in particular when services are decentralized. Local authorities often have a better understanding of the realities in various cities or regions and can have better access to the communities involved. The WHO "healthy cities" initiative demonstrates the leading role that can be played by local governments in improving access to and quality of care. The example of the Women's Total Health Care Programme (PAISM) in Sao Paulo (Brazil) shows that it is necessary to establish women's health advising and coordinating offices, to do epidemiological diagnosis and health planning with a gender perspective at the district level. Of particular importance is intersectoral networking and networking with women's organizations. It is also crucial that women move into decision-making positions at the district level.

NGOs can play an effective role in promoting a gender approach to health care by acting as advocates for the protection of women's rights as human rights, e.g., by exposing violence against women, by calling attention to the needs of the girl child and by promoting and developing a comprehensive, holistic and rights-based approach to health services for women. They should convince the key stake holders, whether they work in government, in administration, or as providers of the necessary funding, of the need to bring about the necessary changes, by ensuring that the electorate understands and supports the changes which need to be made.

NGOs also have extensive experience of advocacy which involves the identification of key decision-makers; preparation of position papers; lobbying; contacting the media by means of press releases and press conferences and arranging press visits and encounters. Most key government departments concerned with health care tend to be male-dominated and may be expected to include some who are resistant to the introduction of a gender approach to health care. It is particularly important to involve health professional associations in advocacy, because their members are likely to be among the first to be affected by the changes. Their officers are also likely to be in touch with members of parliament and may have influential contacts in government. A co-ordinated approach by NGOs is needed to the departments concerned, involving NGOs with different constituencies such as the health professions, women, development issues etc.

Many NGOs have already developed training programmes in gender sensitivity which can easily be adapted to take account of the special needs of the health sector and of departments of government that are involved in providing health services such as finance and planning and even transport such as ambulance services. Health professional associations will also need to sensitize their own members at all levels of health service activities as they play a crucial role in providing services. They should take account of the working relationships between male and female health professionals and with other health workers as women are often less well trained and less well paid. Governments should therefore invite suitably experienced NGOs to act as partners in the development of training programmes on the gender approach to health care.

CEDAW and Women's Health Rights

The Convention on the Elimination of All Forms of Discrimination against Women (CEDAW) was adopted in 1979 by the United Nations General Assembly and entered into force in 1981. While all the human rights treaties protect and promote the rights of all peoples, the CEDAW specifically addresses the rights of women and girls. As of 2 November 2006, 185 countries – over ninety percent of the members of the United Nations – are party to the Convention.

Equality of rights for women is a basic principle of the United Nations. The Universal Declaration of Human Rights proclaims the entitlement of everyone to equality before the law and to the enjoyment of human rights and fundamental freedom, without distinction of any kind, including sex. The International Covenant on Economic, Social and Cultural Rights and the International Covenant on Civil and Political Rights, both of which entered into force in 1966, translate the principles of the Declaration into legally binding form and clearly specify that the stated rights are applicable to all persons, without distinction of any kind, including distinction based on an individual's sex.

The Commission on the Status of Women was established in 1946 with the mandate to elaborate the general guarantees of non-discrimination from a gender perspective. The Commission was originally established as a subsidiary body of the Commission on Human Rights but was granted the status of a full commission as a result of pressure exerted by women's activists. In 1972, the Commission asked the Secretary-General to call upon United Nations Member States to consider the possibility of preparing a legally binding treaty that would give normative force to the provisions of the Declaration. In 1974, it was agreed that a single, binding treaty on the elimination of discrimination against women should be drafted. The text of the CEDAW was prepared by working groups of the Commission during 1976 and was the subject of extensive deliberations by a working group of the Third Committee of the General Assembly between 1977 and 1979. The CEDAW was adopted by the General Assembly in 1979. On 2 September 1981, 30 days after the twentieth Member State had ratified it, the Convention entered into force.

The Committee on Elimination of All Forms of Discrimination against Women (CEDAW Committee) was established under Article 17 of the CEDAW, with the mandate to monitor States' compliance with their obligations under the Convention.

CEDAW defines discrimination against women in Article 1 as "... any distinction, exclusion or restriction made on the basis of sex which has the effect or purpose of impairing or nullifying the recognition, enjoyment or exercise by women, irrespective of their marital status, on a basis of equality of men and women, of human rights and fundamental freedoms in the political, economic, social, cultural, civil or any other field." The CEDAW gives the basis for realising equality between women and men by ensuring equal access to and equal opportunities for women in political and public life, education, employment and health.

The CEDAW contains a number of articles that are directly related to WHO's objective of assisting governments in protecting and improving women's health. These articles enshrine the right to non-discrimination and equal rights to education, to seek, receive and impart information, to marry and found a family and equality in private and family life.

Duty of States

The duty of States to ensure, on a basis of equality of men and women, access to health care services, information and education, implies an obligation to respect, protect and fulfil human rights related to women's health. States have the responsibility to ensure that legislation, executive action and policy comply with these three obligations.

The obligation to respect rights requires States Parties to refrain from obstructing action taken by women in pursuit of their health goals. States Parties should not restrict women's access to health services on the grounds that women do not have the authorisation of husbands, partners, parents or health authorities, because they are unmarried or because they are women.

The obligation to protect women's rights relating to health requires States Parties, their agents and officials to take action to prevent and to impose sanctions for violations of rights by private persons and organisations. For instance, as gender-based violence is a critical health issue for women, States Parties should ensure:

— The enactment and effective enforcement of laws and the formulation of policies to address violence against women, including sexual abuse of girls, and the provision of appropriate health services;

— The enactment and effective enforcement of laws that prohibit female genital mutilation and forced marriage of girls and other harmful traditional practices;

— Gender-sensitive training to enable health-care workers to detect and manage the health consequences of gender-based violence; and

— Fair and protective procedures for hearing complaints and imposing appropriate sanctions on health-care professionals guilty of sexual abuse of patients.

The duty to fulfil rights places an obligation on States Parties to take appropriate legislative, judicial, administrative, budgetary, economic and other measures to the maximum extent of their available resources to ensure that women realise their rights to health care. High maternal mortality and morbidity rates worldwide, for example, are an important indication for States Parties of possible breaches of their duty to ensure women's access to reproductive health care services.

Importance of a Multisectoral Approach

In many States Parties to the CEDAW, national bodies for the advancement of women are entrusted with the responsibility of implementing the Convention. Such bodies facilitate and support gender mainstreaming and play a role in ensuring that governments fully consider the gender implications of laws, programes and policies in all areas of their responsibility. Although national bodies for the advancement of women vary considerably, they tend to be located within governments, with the involvement of ministries for women, children or social welfare, and are the official bodies responsible for promoting women's issues, gender mainstreaming and gender equality across government sectors.

Although the respect and protection of human rights in the context of health are increasingly understood to be multisectoral, implementation of CEDAW often falls under the responsibility of ministries of women's affairs or their equivalent, while women's health issues are dealt with by the ministry of health. Addressing women's health and rights, however, requires the involvement of a variety of government ministries and national partners.

Relevance of States Parties' Reservations

In ratifying the Convention, a State can enter reservations to the Convention, indicating that, while it consents to be legally bound by most of the provisions, it does not agree to be bound by certain others. A number of States Parties have entered reservations to particular articles on the grounds that their national laws, traditions, religion or culture are incongruent with those principles. The CEDAW Committee identified two articles that are core provisions of the Convention and should not, therefore, be subject to reservations:

— Article 2, dealing with the various legislative and other measures to be introduced to combat discrimination against women; and

— Article 16, covering the elimination of discrimination against women in all matters relating to marriage and family relations, including the right of women to decide freely and responsibly on the number and spacing of their children.

Nevertheless, despite the fundamental nature of these provisions, some States Parties have entered reservations to them. The Committee is concerned about the number and extent of such reservations. The Committee also called upon States to question the validity and legal effect of reservations to the Convention in the context of reservations with regard to other human rights treaties and to reconsider their reservations with a view to strengthening the implementation of all human rights treaties.

Role of CEDAW Committee

The CEDAW Committee was established in 1982. It consists of 23 members with expertise in international women's human rights, who serve in their personal capacity and not as representatives of their governments. Originally, the Committee met twice a year, usually in January or February and June or July, to review States' efforts to bring their laws, policies and practices into compliance with the CEDAW.

The threefold mandate of the Committee is:

1. To review national reports submitted by each State Party within one year of ratification or accession and thereafter every four years;
2. To make recommendations on any issue affecting women to which it believes the States Parties should devote more attention, or the Committee's view of the obligations assumed under the Convention requires further elaboration; and
3. To receive and consider complaints from individuals or groups within its jurisdiction, as recognised by those States that have ratified the Optional Protocol to the Convention.

Monitoring

Each State that has ratified the CEDAW is required to submit a report to the Committee at least every four years, detailing its efforts to implement the Convention and progress in achieving women's rights. At a formal meeting following submission of the country report, Committee members have an opportunity to discuss the content of the report with country representatives. These exchanges are a major strength of the reporting process and provide opportunities for a number of groups to improve government compliance with the Convention. Committee members then issue concluding comments to the reporting government, which are compiled in an annual report and sent to the United Nations General Assembly.

Normative Function: General Recommendations

Article 21 of the Convention empowers the Committee to make General Recommendations about specific provisions of the Convention and on the relation between the articles and issues that the Committee has described as "cross-cutting". As of January 2004, the CEDAW Committee had adopted 25 General Recommendations. That most relevant to health is General Recommendation 24 on women and health. Other General Recommendations that address issues of women's health include:

— No. 14, on female circumcision, 1990;

— No. 15, on women and AIDS, 1990;

— No. 18, on disabled women, 1991;
— No. 19, on violence against women, 1992;
— No. 21, on equality in marriage and family relations, 1994; and
— No. 25, 1995, on Article 4(1), temporary special measures, 2004.

The Committee's interpretation of non-discrimination in the context of women's health is based on the programe of action elaborated at the 1994 International Conference on Population and Development and the platform of action adopted at the 1995 Fourth World Conference on Women.

General Recommendation 24 on Women and Health

General recommendations give the Committee's views of the obligations assumed under the Convention. General Recommendation 24 on women and health states the Committee's definitive interpretation of the Convention and:.

— Requires governments to eliminate discrimination against women in their access to health care services, throughout the life cycle, particularly in the areas of family planning, pregnancy, confinement and during the postnatal period;

— Provides specific direction to governments on their obligations to end discrimination against women under Article 12. The health status of vulnerable groups of women—rural, minority, older and disabled—is also of interest to the CEDAW.

— In relation to maternal health issues, directs governments to include information on measures they have taken to ensure appropriate services for pregnancy, confinement and the postnatal period, and on the rates at which these measures have reduced maternal mortality and morbidity in the country in general and in vulnerable groups, regions and communities in particular;

— Recommends a number of actions for governments to consider in eliminating discrimination against women, for example: implementing a comprehensive national strategy to promote women's health throughout their lifespan;

WHO's role in formulation of General Recommendations

In 1997, the Committee adopted a three-stage process for formulating General Recommendations:

— Open discussions among the Committee, nongovernmental organisations, United Nations agencies and others on topics for General Recommendations;

— Initial drafting of General Recommendations for discussion at the session; and

— Adoption of a revised draft by the Committee.

United Nations agencies, including WHO, are thus invited to contribute and to make statements during the first step.

The CEDAW Optional Protocol

The Optional Protocol to the CEDAW provides two additional mechanisms for holding governments that have ratified it accountable for their obligations under the CEDAW:

— A communications procedure, which gives individuals and groups the right to lodge complaints with the CEDAW Committee, and

— An inquiry procedure, which allows the CEDAW Committee to conduct inquiries into serious or systematic abuses of women's rights.

WHO and the Optional Protocol

The Committee invites United Nations bodies and specialised agencies to include descriptions of efforts made to supporting ratification of the Optional Protocol in their country-specific reports.

Relevance to WHO's Work

As a member of the United Nations family, WHO is committed to making human rights a central concern, and its Constitution reaffirms this commitment. Monitoring the implementation of the CEDAW—one of the key means by which the United Nations promotes and protects the rights of women—can potentially contribute to advancing the right to health and other health-related rights of women and girls around the world.

The Committee has emphasised the importance it attaches to assistance from and cooperation with specialised agencies in implementing its mandate under the Convention and the Beijing Platform of Action.

As the main purpose of monitoring the CEDAW is to encourage governments to comply fully with their treaty obligations for women's rights, including the elimination of discrimination in health care, WHO can use the monitoring process to strengthen the technical support it gives to countries.

Participation of the United Nations in monitoring the implementation of the CEDAW might be coordinated by a United Nations agency, such as the United Nations Development Fund for Women (UNIFEM), the United Nations Development Programe (UNDP), the Office of the High Commission of Human Rights (OHCHR), or by the United Nations resident coordinator. If there is no coordination, WHO might liaise directly with the ministry of health and other relevant ministries.

Working with United Nations Country Teams

United Nations country teams are in a unique position to use the treaty body system in field activities, in a common effort to strengthen national systems for the protection of human rights.

— The human rights treaties form a reference system and minimum standard for the action of country teams, as they clarify the meaning of universal human rights standards. They serve as;

a) A tool for benchmarking current knowledge and implementing relevant human rights obligations;

b) A tool for assessing gaps between human rights obligations and the experience of the population in general and children, women and minorities in particular, as well as the capacity of institutions and mechanisms to address the situation;

c) A tool for emphasising the legal responsibilities of governments for protecting and promoting human rights during dialogue with governments;

d) An opportunity to establish national mechanisms for monitoring the implementation of various human rights treaties;

e) An opportunity for public scrutiny of government policies and the participation of various sectors of society in the formulation, evaluation and review of policies; and

f) an entry point and platform for national dialogue on human rights among relevant stakeholders, including government agencies, the media, national human rights institutions, nongovernmental organisations, parliaments, women and young people and civil society as a whole.

— The concluding observations and recommendations of treaty bodies identify specific human rights concerns, which can be used to help set priorities at national level. These can provide a framework for joint action by governments, United Nations agencies, nongovernmental organisations and other partners and serve as a reference for programming consistent with the provisions of the relevant treaties.

— International human rights standards and the output of treaty bodies, including their General Comments, form a reference system for national courts and a framework for human rights accountability at international and national levels.

— Treaty bodies provide information for national human rights institutions, whose responsibilities often include encouraging ratification or accession to international human rights instruments and ensuring their implementation, as well as contributing to reporting.

WHO can provide support to governments throughout monitoring.

Step 1. Preparation of States Parties reports and their submission

Once States Parties have ratified the CEDAW, they are under an obligation to submit periodic reports to the Committee on the legislative, judicial, administrative or other measures that they have adopted to implement the Convention. The initial report must be submitted within one year.

The Committee has adopted guidelines to help States to prepare these reports. According to these guidelines, the initial report should be a detailed, comprehensive description of the position of women in the country at the time of submission, to be used as a benchmark against which progress can be measured. Subsequent periodic reports are to focus on the concerns and recommendations resulting from the Committee's consideration of the previous report, giving details of significant developments over the past four years, noting key trends and identifying obstacles to full implementation of the Convention. The Committee specifically requests that governments provide information on health and health-related issues that are compatible with WHO's indicators.

In many countries, a ministry of women's affairs or its equivalent coordinates interaction with the CEDAW Committee, including preparation and submission of reports. In some countries, the ministry of foreign affairs may be the institution that coordinates interaction with United Nations treaty monitoring bodies, with support from other ministries. WHO can provide valuable support to a government and assist the ministry of health during preparation of a report, in particular by:

— Informing the ministry of health about the reporting schedule of the CEDAW Committee and about how the ministry can contribute to the report;

— Contributing to discussions to ensure that health-related issues are adequately reflected throughout the report;

— Ensuring that the data provided are relevant to the articles of the Convention, especially to Article 12 and General Recommendation 24 on women and health, and help the government to identify relevant data and their interpretation; and

— Assisting in ensuring that the report submitted to the Committee is accurate, objective and responsive to the questions presented in relation to health and health-related issues.

Step 2. Pre-sessional review

In order to consider States' reports adequately, the Committee holds pre-sessional working group meetings prior to each regular session. The list of issues and questions resulting from the pre-sessional review indicates issues to which the Committee wishes to pay particular attention during the formal review session and includes requests for further information that arose during discussions. Specialised agencies, United Nations bodies and intergovernmental and nongovernmental organisations are invited to submit information, orally or in writing, to the pre-sessional review of State Party reports in areas within the scope of their activities. During the meeting, Committee members can pose questions to the representatives of the United Nations and nongovernmental organisations. United Nations agencies can ask that the representatives of nongovernmental organisations and other observers be excluded when they are presenting their reports if they are confidential.

Step 3. The session

The Committee meets twice or, in exceptional circumstances, three times a year for three weeks. During the sessions, the Committee discusses the States

Parties' reports with government delegations. The objective is to hold constructive dialogues with government representatives about implementation of the Convention and to raise any concerns that the Committee might have on the basis of a State Party report.

The meetings between government delegations and the Committee typically last 1–2 days. The delegation usually includes high-level officials with the authority to speak on behalf of the government, as well as persons more directly involved in implementation of the treaty. State representatives are given the opportunity to introduce their reports orally, and Committee members then raise questions relating to specific articles of the Convention.

As at the pre-sessional meeting, specialised agencies, United Nations bodies and intergovernmental and nongovernmental organisations are invited to submit information, orally or in writing, regarding the States Parties' reports. During the meeting, which usually takes place at the beginning of the session, Committee members can pose questions to these representatives. The plenary session, unlike the pre-sessional meeting, is held in public, unless the Committee decides otherwise, and the media and the public can attend.

The outcome of this meeting is a series of concluding comments, prepared in the light of the State Party report, discussions held with the government delegation and other national stakeholders, including nongovernmental organisations and United Nations agencies.

The concluding comments start with an introduction, followed by an acknowledgement of the positive steps that the State Party has made towards implementing the Convention. Then, the principal areas of concern are outlined, with recommendations. The comments then contain a request for wide dissemination of the concluding comments, so that government officials, politicians, parliamentarians and women's nongovernmental organisations, are made aware of the steps taken to ensure equality for women and the future steps required.

The CEDAW Committee has repeatedly stressed during its meetings that the quality of its review of country reports depends on the availability of accurate, understandable information, including sex-disaggregated data. As health-related issues tend to receive little attention in States Parties' reports, they are sometimes discussed less comprehensively than other issues during the pre-sessional review and session.

WHO could increase the visibility of health issues in a number of ways. Staff at WHO Headquarters could organise informal meetings with Committee members on various women's health issues, perhaps held in collaboration with other United Nations agencies and nongovernmental organisations. Such briefings could give Committee members who are not health professionals up-to-date data on specific public health matters and give them a better insight into the health data presented.

The Division for the Advancement of Women at the United Nations serves as the secretariat for the Committee and notifies the Director-General of WHO of the opening date, duration, place and agenda of each session of the Committee and of the pre-sessional working groups. Upon receiving this notification, WHO Headquarters should send all appropriate information, including the States Parties' reports, to the relevant regional and country offices.

WHO staff could prepare technical reports to be submitted to the Committee for consideration during the pre-sessional review and the session. These reports should provide technical information and a description of the health of women in a country. Selection of countries and preparation of WHO reports requires collaboration between Headquarters and regional and country offices; however, as the Committee considers reports from States in various regions during the same session, preparation and submission of the reports should be coordinated by Headquarters.

Step 4. Implementation of concluding comments at country level

The Committee adopts its concluding comments before closure of the session. The comments are the result of constructive dialogue during the session. They reflect the main discussion points, highlight problems in implementation of the Convention and recommend action.

The concluding comments are sent to the appropriate representatives of the State Party and are freely available on the website of the United Nations Division for the Advancement of Women and the Office of the United Nations High Commissioner for Human Rights.

Follow-up to the concluding comments is essential to ensure that all the relevant national actors participate in implementing the recommendations. Their issuance therefore presents an opportunity to enlist support and resources from all appropriate government sectors, as well as other partners such as donor governments and nongovernmental organisations. The follow-up can include:

— General dissemination of the concluding observations;
— Establishment of a multi-stakeholder mechanism; and
— Assessment and revision of national laws, policies and programes.

In order to involve various national stakeholders, the responsible body can convene a meeting with the relevant ministries and other actors, disseminate the comments and design an implementation plan. The media can use the concluding comments to draw attention to specific women's rights issues in the country.

WHO's Role in Following up the concluding Comments

Provided that the concluding comments give clear guidance to governments on the measures to be taken to ensure health and health-related rights, WHO can support government and other national actors in following up the concluding comments and translating them into laws, policies and programes. This is also an opportunity to build multisectoral collaboration for addressing women's health issues from a human rights perspective.

At country level, Headquarters, Regional and Country offices can collaborate in:

— Facilitating multisectoral communication among national stakeholders, including ministries of health, women's affairs, education and finance, nongovernmental organisations, professional associations and academics for implementing the concluding comments related to women's health;
— Facilitating implementation of the concluding comments by revising or drawing up laws and policies on women's health issues and integrating the provisions of the Convention into programes. Current WHO-assisted programes and dissemination of WHO guidelines can help to improve women's health and implement the concluding comments.
— Training health managers on human rights and how they relate to women's health, as well as how the Convention can be used in line with other, related international and regional treaties, as a framework for policy and programes;
— Assisting States in monitoring, evaluating and documenting efforts made and obstacles encountered in fulfilling the recommendations; and

— Collaborating with other United Nations agencies to ensure follow-up and implementation of the concluding comments.

At the regional level, WHO Headquarters and regional and country offices can collaborate with other United Nations agencies to organise regional workshops involving persons from countries that have recently reported or are about to report to the CEDAW Committee, to discuss how monitoring can promote and protect women's right to health and health-related rights.

Overcoming Gender Bias in Healthcare

Most health-related research continues to be carried out within the biomedical tradition. Though social factors are beginning to be taken more seriously, by far the largest proportion of resources is still spent on projects falling within the formal domain of biomedicine. This applies not just to clinical and epidemiological research but also to the routine collection of morbidity and mortality statistics which continue to be framed within standard medical categories. There is a lack of qualitative research. As a result the information collected and the findings generated are often inadequate for the implementation of gender-sensitive policies.

It is therefore important to develop more adequate health information systems to inform policy and programme decision-making. This should include locally collected data (both qualitative and quantitative) that is more sensitive than existing DALYs (Disability Adjusted Life Years) to both socio-economic conditions and gender issues. The data can then be used to set priorities through a process that includes a systematic gender analysis.

Most medical research continues to be based on the unstated assumption that women and men are physiologically similar in all respects apart from their reproductive systems. Other biological differences are ignored as are the social differences which have such a major impact on health. The consequence of this approach is the generation of biased knowledge. In the context of routine data collection, statistics are not always disaggregated by sex and age, making it difficult to plan for the specific needs of women and men. Similarly many clinical studies leave women out altogether or fail to treat sex and gender as important variables in the analysis.

As a result both preventive and curative strategies are often applied to women when they have only been tested on men. Particular concern has been expressed about this in relation to coronary heart disease and also HIV and AIDS. There is also growing evidence that sex and gender differences may be important in a range of infectious and parasitic diseases including tuberculosis and malaria. Sex- related biological differences may affect both susceptibility and immunity while gender differences in patterns of behaviour and access to resources may influence the degree of exposure to infection and its consequences. However, without more accurate information it is difficult to translate these observations into more effective policy making or clinical practice.

Similar concerns have been raised about gender bias in access to medical care and in the quality of care received. There is considerable evidence to show that women experience gender-related constraints on their access to health services and that this affects the poorest women in particular. The obstacles they face include lack of culturally appropriate care, inadequate resources, lack of transport, stigma and sometimes the refusal of their husband or other family members to give permission to access. Limited public expenditure on health care will affect men as well as women but in conditions of scarcity it is often the females in the family whose needs are given the least priority.

If they do gain access to health care, there is also evidence that the quality of care women receive is inferior to that of men. Too many women report that their experiences are distressing and demeaning. The gender bias and superiority stance of medical and health professionals of both sexes too often intimidate women, giving them no voice in decisions about their own bodies and their own health.

When women are excluded from the decision-making process, gender bias in staff deployment, promotion, postings and the career development of health personnel obstruct health seeking behaviour of women.

Mainstreaming Gender in Health Research

Gender inequalities in the wider society are also reflected in the way medical research is carried out. If this is to be changed, women's health should have a more prominent place in the research process. A formal set of policies will be needed to ensure that their interests are represented.

One of the most basic problems facing many policy makers is lack of specific information on the situation of women. The failure to separate women from men in national and regional statistics can make it difficult to plan effectively to meet the particular needs of either group. It is essential therefore that data is collected about both sex and gender differences in health status and that the results are clearly presented for easy use. The conceptual framework for this data collection process should be appropriate to the setting in which it is being used and should also recognize the diversity of women's experiences over the lifespan.

Older women and young girls for example, may have particular health problems, making it essential that factors such as their nutritional status, or their access to health care are routinely monitored. This will require the development of appropriate indicators for measuring different aspects of their health and quality of life. Other groups of women whose vulnerability may require special attention include rural women, industrial workers, sex workers, refugee or migrant women, women bringing up children alone and women coping with chronic disease or long-term disabilities. For example, research has shown that women suffering from stigmatizing or disfiguring diseases such as tuberculosis and leprosy were more isolated than men from all activities and treated as outcasts, even within the family setting.

In many developing countries, the lack of data on women's health reflects in part the very limited nature of the vital registration system, which affects both sexes. However, this is often compounded by a failure on the part of the relevant authorities to recognize the importance of gender issues and a lack of understanding of the complex social pressures that may render women's health problems invisible. Health statistics are based on clinical records in which male data is more prominent and hence females are under-represented. In the case of maternal mortality also, a wide range of religious, cultural and social factors can contribute to serious underreporting. Process indicators have now been identified and these need to be used routinely by those responsible for monitoring community health.

Similar problems are evident in relation to the identification and measurement of rape, domestic violence and sexual abuse. This represents a huge public health problem which has not yet been adequately documented. To fill this knowledge gap, individual countries need to move forward with the development of ethical and culturally appropriate methods for the collection of relevant data in their own particular settings. This can be facilitated by co-operation with international organizations such as WHO which have already developed a range of resources for work in this area.

Gaps in the availability of information on women's lives are now beginning to be filled, providing new sources of accessible data. For instance, the recent elaboration by the United Nations Development Programme (UNDP) of a number of new gender-related indicators, offers important tools with which individual countries can assess the levels of gender equality in their own society. Indicators for reproductive health have been established by WHO and UNFPA. Also, a number of specialized programmes in WHO are now focusing on sex and gender differences in the impact of specific diseases such as malaria, leprosy, onchocerciasis and tuberculosis. However, there is still a need for national governments and international organizations to work together to develop more specific health-related measures combining both biomedical and socio-economic data to monitor the epidemiological profile of women's and men's health, particularly with respect to emerging epidemics such as tuberculosis, HIV, tobacco, and neglected areas such as occupational, mental health and substance use.

Few women are currently involved in what has been the male-dominated arena of medical research either as researchers or as subjects. However strategies for change are beginning to emerge. Concerns about bias in medical research have led to attempts in a number of countries to include women in study samples wherever appropriate. However, it is essential that this is only done with the relevant ethical safeguards, such as informed consent protocols. Long-term studies have also been initiated to investigate the particular problems of women as they move through the life cycle and more of these are needed in different socio-economic and cultural settings. Attempts to involve women in the determination of research priorities have included formal dialogues between researchers and women's health advocates, particularly in reproductive health services.

Reforming biomedical research can only be a partial strategy for extending understanding of sex and gender inequalities in health and illness. Social science research is also needed if the full range of influences on human health is to be understood. In particular, governments should encourage multidisciplinary research involving social, environmental and biomedical researchers as co-investigators, and use their findings to develop more comprehensive health promotion policies.

The most useful studies are often those that have used both quantitative and qualitative methods in which statistical data are enriched by in-depth information from people's own experiences. Good examples of this kind of work can now be found in the areas of sexual and reproductive health, tropical diseases, mental health, occupational and environmental health, where new techniques have been developed to explore the intimate concerns of women and men which would otherwise remain hidden. For example, research on onchocerciasis and lymphatic filariasis has shown that women are concerned about the impact of the disease on their physical appearance while men are troubled by sexual performance and virility.

It is essential that strategies to improve the health of women and men are grounded in a rigorous analysis of the whole range of reproductive and productive activities undertaken across the lifespan. In the case of women this is especially problematic because of many of their activities are invisible. Femaleness cannot be equated with motherhood and the scope of health research needs to shift accordingly. Hence planners need to acquire much more information on the risks women face both in the home and in the workplace.

Until recently, few researchers had examined the occupational and environmental risks associated with domestic work. This is now beginning to change as new techniques are being developed to explore the interior of the family. This has revealed a number of hazards that are especially dangerous for the poorest women. Analysis of the relationship between patterns of energy consumption and the volume of household work for instance suggests that some women's responsibilities impose long-term damage on their health. A range of environmental risks have also been identified including lung damage caused by pollution from cooking stoves as well as a range of unregulated but toxic substances in the household.

Women's work outside the home also needs much more attention from both researchers and policy makers. Though health records show that male workers die more often than females from work-related causes, women's work-related disease and disability is rapidly increasing in many parts of the world. Evidence is now emerging that traditionally "female" jobs such as nursing and clerical work can pose both physical and psychological risks. The millions of women now taking on traditionally "male" jobs may also be facing serious risks especially if they are forced to combine heavy physical labour with domestic work and with reproduction.

Occupational health researchers need to develop greater gender sensitivity in their methods of investigation as well as a clearer understanding of the differences between women and men. Their findings need to reflect both the different jobs done by women and men and also the biological and social differences that mediate the impact of waged work on health and well-being. Only then will regulatory bodies have accurate information on which to base health and safety at work policies that can benefit women and men equally.

The strategies should be adopted to make health and health services research more gender-sensitive and, therefore, more appropriate as a base for national and international policy making. However, a great deal of information on gender issues is already available and it is essential that health planners and policy makers use the most up-to-date and gender-sensitive resources as the basis for developing their services.

The mainstreaming of gender concerns is vital at every stage of the policy process from policy formulation, planning, delivery and implementation to monitoring and evaluation. Lack of awareness or "gender blindness" on the part of policy makers and planners frequently leads to gender bias and to the prioritization of male interests in decision-making. If this is to be avoided those involved need to have not only a clear understanding of the relevant issues but also the political will to reduce the inequalities between women and men.

In mainstreaming gender into the health sector, establishing effective partnerships with women and men's groups is critically important. While the Ministry of Health usually has the mandate to deliver health services, interventions from other ministries especially Finance, Education, Women's Affairs and Social Welfare, Environment and Youth should be encouraged. Alliances between the ministries, target population, local authorities, the private sector, international organizations and donors should be formed. The private sector, in particular employers of men and women with potential occupational health concerns should be key partners in the provision of health.

Both sexes should not be treated in exactly the same way. Despite their commonalities, women and men will also have their own particular needs. Hence adherence to the principle of equality is required to ensure that these different needs are met. Nor does it mean that all women or all men should receive the same treatment. Their varying circumstances will mean that here too a range of strategies will be needed if equality is to be achieved between women and between men.

In order to achieve these goals, there should be a serious commitment at the highest levels of government. Experience shows that little is likely to change unless there is the necessary political will, the responsibility for the achievement of greater gender equality, both in health and elsewhere, is clearly allocated and the goal itself is given a high priority. Ministries of Health, Finance, Education and Environment should allocate special resources to mainstreaming gender in health service delivery through, for example, the creation and support of gender focal points, and by establishing the necessary budget line items.

Political will can be generated in different ways. One strategy should be to use examples demonstrating the cost-effectiveness of gender intervention in order to strengthen arguments based on equality and human rights considerations. The media can also be used, particularly through the publicizing of individual cases. In addition, strategic networks can be deployed to campaign for change.

Individuals and groups in civil society should press for public sector reforms and good governance mechanisms. These will lead to a more transparent system and to the greater availability of data that can be used to make the necessary arguments to politicians about gender priorities for action. International organizations also play a role encouraging governments to implement their commitments to gender equality.

If the goal of developing gender-sensitive policies is to be achieved, it needs to be built explicitly into the original objective of the programme in a way that can be used later for evaluation purposes. This will require a preliminary analysis of the context in which the policy will be operating and a clear understanding of the gender issues involved. It will involve a comparison of the numbers of males and females in the target population and an assessment of the gender patterns in current service use.

In order to do this the following questions inter alia should be answered:

— Do gender differences in daily life expose women and men to different kinds of health risks?

— How are existing gender differences in the use of services to be explained?

— Can any differences be observed in the quality of care women and men currently receive?

— In what ways are health services themselves gendered ? Do gender relations within health services affect the experiences of users?

— Who currently controls access to health-related resources and do the allocation criteria take into account the different needs of women and men?

— Are health sector reforms likely to have a differential impact on women and men and what will the impact be on gender equality and access to care?

To make the planning process gender-sensitive the following steps should be taken:

— Women themselves and health advocates including NGOs need to be more involved in the design, implementation and evaluation of all services as well as in the definition of strategies related to women's health;

— An appropriate form of consultation should be devised either with representative organizations, community groups, or directly with those requiring services;

— Tools, methods and training material should be developed to assist in conducting gender analysis in policies and programmes and in implementing gender impact assessment.

Health sector reforms have failed until now to take into account gender issues that are critical if a negative impact, particularly on women, is to be avoided. The impact of user charges often negatively affect poor women who tend to be more vulnerable than men for reasons of economic dependency or limited access to paid work.

Institutional changes in the national health systems to address inefficiencies and to raise levels of service coverage, without consideration of the specific health risks and needs of women and men, have often resulted in maintaining or reinforcing gender roles and relations that have an adverse impact on health.

A health sector reform has a direct impact on staff composition, and unless it is done in a gender-sensitive way, may run the risk of reinforcing occupational segregation between women's and men's jobs. Gender disadvantages are reflected in occupational segregation between female and male health staff with women being posted to more marginal areas and rarely in senior positions.

In order to achieve a balance of the sexes throughout the process of health sector reform, attempts should not be restricted to improvements in managerial and administrative skills. There are a number of often unrecognized issues which adversely affect the contribution of women health providers. Examples include civil service regulations, "old-boy" networks, rigid hierarchy and seniority patterns, and failure to provide incentives for gender-sensitive performance.

Decentralization is perceived as an alternative policy to the centralized one and as a way of transferring resources, functions and authority to the periphery. However, due to the existing interregional inequalities within developing countries, less wealthy districts will be unable to raise funds to protect the most vulnerable population groups such as orphans, widows, unsupported elderly, landless and female-headed households.

Developing Framework for Gender Planning

In order to mainstream gender issues in health service, it will be necessary to create a national or regional policy framework within which both the planning process itself and delivery of services can be located. Though there is no single model for such a framework, a range of options already exists in countries with varying political and legal structures.

The issue of setting targets for service delivery needs to be examined carefully on a case by case basis, particularly where there are built-in incentives for the service providers. There are many examples where human rights have been violated, gender inequalities perpetuated and priorities distorted by the application of incentive driven programmes, especially in the field of sexual and reproductive health and mass screening.

Capacity Building

The effective operation of the service will require a strategy for educating health workers to understand the full significance of gender issues in health. Capacity-building programmes should be designed for both female and male workers. They should focus not just on "women's issues" but on the wider topic of gender itself, human rights and gender identities of female and male health providers. They may include broadly based "gender awareness" courses and participatory approaches at every level.

It is important that these programmes be culturally appropriate to the settings in which they are to be used but a number of models already exist which can be used as the foundation for their development. Courses of this kind, taught by competent gender experts and advocates need to be provided for qualified health workers at all levels and also need to be formally built into the curriculum for all those undertaking health care education and training. Medical and nursing curricula in particular need to be very carefully shaped so that gender issues are properly embedded in the future planning and delivery of services.

The attitudes of many doctors and nurses often constitute particular obstacles to women seeking informed decisions concerning their own health. Therefore, one of the most important goals of the capacity building should be to inculcate in all health workers a respect for the dignity and human rights of all service users, including the formal right to full information about their condition and available treatments. This should be expressed in an explicit charters of rights.

Accountability, Monitoring and Evaluation

Gender dimensions which cross all aspects of health systems should be subject to accountability as an essential part of good management practice. Access to education and information alone will rarely be enough to ensure appropriate and ethical treatment. Therefore a range of mechanisms is needed to ensure that women have access to advocacy services. The existence of formal and easily accessible opportunities for complaint and redress through an independent system is needed as well.

It is essential that all policies include gender issues in their strategies for monitoring and evaluation. This will enable service providers to measure the differential impact of the policy on women and men in their roles as both users and workers. The results will then provide the basis to plan any changes needed to promote greater gender equality and equity in health. The lessons learned can be more widely disseminated to help those at an earlier stage of innovation. These monitoring and evaluation strategies need to be culturally sensitive and designed to reflect and change existing patterns of gender relations.

Intersectoral Collaboration

While intersectoral coordination is important, it does not, in itself, solve women's health problems because of the gender inequality in decision-making within and between sectors and financial allocation. Good governance to ensure women's participation in health decision-making is essential. The first principle is that health is a human right and that includes women's human rights. The second is a gendered democracy or parity democracy that ensures women's equal political participation. Accountability and transparency are also vital.

The framework for intersectoral coordination should be based on the agreements made in the Beijing Platform for Action in which twelve critical areas of concern were identified. This document, combined with the Convention on the Elimination of All Forms of Discrimination Against Women and other international human rights instruments, provides strategies and recommendations to improve the political, economic, social and cultural well-being of women. However, these need to be more systematically integrated and linked across sectors to women's health.

Health care is only one of the influences on health itself. If, therefore, gender inequalities in health are to be tackled successfully the strategy also needs to include a range of other public policies in areas as diverse as education, law and order, agriculture, industry, transport, social security and the legal system. In each of these areas gender equality needs to be a specific goal and targeted interventions need to be introduced to tackle traditional patterns of gender disadvantage. Only then will the root causes of gender inequalities in health be challenged.

In the development of macro-economic policies for example, attention needs to be paid to the informal sector, to unpaid labour and to the "care economy" so that the implications of any decisions for women's work receive appropriate attention. Similarly, legislation is required to create a "level playing field" through the control of gender discrimination in access to social and economic resources. Looking at more specific areas of public policy, targeted interventions that can reduce gender inequalities in health include the development of an integrated policy to meet women's practical energy needs, female literacy programmes, special subsidies to meet the transport needs of rural women, strategies to increase women's management of agrochemicals, water resources and more provision of credit for women especially in the agricultural sector.

It is essential that all policy makers recognize that gender inequalities cross all determinants of health, such as class, ethnicity and socio-economic status. Policies to improve the health of women and men should also take factors such as these into account. Intersectoral coordination should, furthermore, be implemented across sectors and at all levels, from the local to the global level, by a variety of actors. Recognizing that countries vary according to their infrastructure, capability and history of intersectoral planning, the main focus should be to ensure gender mainstreaming in all policies and programmes.

The following examples illustrate the challenges and some best practices of intersectoral coordination that include a gender perspective:

(i) *Gender-based violence, trafficking of women and child prostitution*: The Pan American Health Organization (PAHO) coordinates a prevention programme on gender violence in seven Central American and three Andean countries that involves criminal justice, law enforcement, health, employment and a broad group of actors including women's NGOs;

(ii) *Environmental health*: Sweden has adopted Agenda 21 of the Earth Summit and applied it on a national and municipal level with ombudsmen to ensure integration of gender equality into environment programmes. Examples in Asia are found in water and sanitation programmes in which women's participation combined with good intersectoral coordination were key in achieving success;

(iii) *Occupational health and women worker's access to health services:* In the 1970s, women's unions in Hong Kong improved occupational health in the free trade zones by educating women on the labour laws. This included more than maternity leave and covered safety and environmental conditions. In Botswana, Cuba and the Netherlands, national policies striving for universal access to health helped to ensure unpaid household working women and those in the informal sector access to health services;

(iv) *Promotion and prevention*: In Zimbabwe, the HIV and AIDS programme uses a wide intersectoral approach involving women's NGOs, the media, schools and various governmental agencies. Some anti-smoking programmes in the USA, including those which reach out to young women have been successful in reducing smoking through intersectoral cooperation;

(v) *Community health:* In the Women's Total Health Care Programme (PAISM) in Sao Paulo, women and their organizations played a key role in setting up community based health systems with a strong gender component. In collaboration with the Municipal Government's Women's Health Office and its local health centres, women participated in designing and applying epidemiological surveys, based on their needs, establishing priorities and monitoring their application. Outcomes of this programme include free access to family planning including emergency contraception, abortion and counselling services for women in special situations and establishment of Maternal Mortality Prevention and Survey Committees;

(vi) *Sexual and reproductive health:* The initiative to eradicate FGM in the Sabini community in Uganda demonstrates effective horizontal collaboration at the local level. These efforts involve health workers, NGOs, community-based organizations and traditional leaders who provide information, education and communication on the dangers of FGM;

(vii) *Tropical diseases*: The positive role of the private sector, combined with community involvement of women, is illustrated in the partnership of the African Programme for Onchocerciasis Control (APOC) in which a pharmaceutical company provides free medication (Ivermectin) for prevention to many countries in Africa and the Americas.

References

Amnesty International (1991). *Women in the Frontline: Human Rights Violations Against Women.* Amnesty International, NY.

Bunch, Charlotte (1995). "The Global Campaign for Women's Human Rights: Where Next After Vienna?" *St. John's Law Review*, 69(1-2):171-178.

Cook, Rebecca (1995). "International Human Rights and Women's Reproductive Health." *Studies in Family Planning*, 24,73.

Charo, R. Alta (1995). "Women's Health and Human Rights: The Promotion and Protection of Women's Health Through International Human Rights Law." *Journal of Law, Medicine & Ethics* v23, n2 (Summer, 1995):195-198.

Macklin, Ruth (1993). "Women's health: an ethical perspective." (Proceedings of the Third International Conference on Health Law and Ethics) *Journal of Law, Medicine & Ethics* v21, n1 (Spring, 1993):23-29.

Stark, Barbara (1991). "Nurturing Rights: An Essay on Women, Peace, and International Human Rights." *Michigan Journal of International Law*, 13:144.

5

Violence against Women

Violence affects the lives of millions of women worldwide, in all socio-economic and educational classes. It cuts across cultural and religious barriers, impeding the right of women to participate fully in society.

Violence against women takes a dismaying variety of forms, from domestic abuse and rape to child marriages and female circumcision. All are violations of the most fundamental human rights.

In a statement to the Fourth World Conference on Women in Beijing in September 1995, the United Nations Secretary-General, Boutros Boutros-Ghali, said that violence against women is a universal problem that must be universally condemned. But he said that the problem continues to grow.

The Secretary-General noted that domestic violence alone is on the increase. Studies in 10 countries, he said, have found that between 17 per cent and 38 per cent of women have suffered physical assaults by a partner.

In the Platform for Action, the core document of the Beijing Conference, Governments declared that "violence against women constitutes a violation of basic human rights and is an obstacle to the achievement of the objectives of equality, development and peace".

Some females fall prey to violence before they are born, when expectant parents abort their unborn daughters, hoping for sons instead. In other societies, girls are subjected to such traditional practices as circumcision, which leave them maimed and traumatized. In others, they are compelled to marry at an early age, before they are physically, mentally or emotionally mature.

Women are victims of incest, rape and domestic violence that often lead to trauma, physical handicap or death.

And rape is still being used as a weapon of war, a strategy used to subjugate and terrify entire communities. Soldiers deliberately impregnate women of different ethnic groups and abandon them when it is too late to get an abortion.

The Platform for Action adopted at the Fourth World Conference on Women declared that rape in armed conflict is a war crime — and could, under certain circumstances, be considered genocide.

Secretary-General Boutros-Ghali told the Beijing Conference that more women today were suffering directly from the effects of war and conflict than ever before in history.

"There is a deplorable trend towards the organized humiliation of women, including the crime of mass rape", the Secretary-General said. "We will press for international legal action against those who perpetrate organized violence against women in time of conflict."

A preliminary report in 1994 by the Special Rapporteur, Ms. Radhika Coomaraswamy, focused on three areas of concern where women are particularly vulnerable: in the family (including domestic violence, traditional practices, infanticide); in the community (including rape, sexual assault, commercialized violence such as trafficking in women, labour exploitation, female migrant workers etc.); and by the State (including violence against women in detention as well as violence against women in situations of armed conflict and against refugee women).

In the Platform for Action adopted at the Beijing Conference, violence against women and the human rights of women are 2 of the 12 critical areas of concern identified as the main obstacles to the advancement of women.

Governments agreed to adopt and implement national legislation to end violence against women and to work actively to ratify all international agreements that relate to violence against women. They agreed that there should be shelters, legal aid and other services for girls and women at risk, and counselling and rehabilitation for perpetrators.

Governments also pledged to adopt appropriate measures in the field of education to modify the social and cultural patterns of conduct of men and women. And the Platform called on media professionals to develop self-regulatory guidelines to address violent, degrading and pornographic materials while encouraging non-stereotyped, balanced and diverse images of women.

Defining Gender-based Abuse

The Declaration on the Elimination of Violence against Women is the first international human rights instrument to exclusively and explicitly address the issue of violence against women. It affirms that the phenomenon violates, impairs or nullifies women's human rights and their exercise of fundamental freedoms.

The Declaration provides a definition of gender-based abuse, calling it "any act of gender-based violence that results in, or is likely to result in, physical, sexual or psychological harm or suffering to women, including threats of such acts, coercion or arbitrary deprivation of liberty, whether occurring in public or in private life".

The definition is amplified in article 2 of the Declaration, which identifies three areas in which violence commonly takes place:

— Physical, sexual and psychological violence that occurs in the family, including battering; sexual abuse of female children in the household; dowry-related violence; marital rape; female genital mutilation and other traditional practices harmful to women; non-spousal violence; and violence related to exploitation;

— Physical, sexual and psychological violence that occurs within the general community, including rape; sexual abuse; sexual harassment and intimidation at work, in educational institutions and elsewhere; trafficking in women; and forced prostitution;

— Physical, sexual and psychological violence perpetrated or condoned by the State, wherever it occurs.

The importance of the question of violence against women was emphasized over the last decade through the holding of several expert group meetings sponsored by the United Nations to draw attention to the extent and severity of the problem.

In September 1992, the United Nations Commission on the Status of Women established a special Working Group and gave it a mandate to draw up a draft declaration on violence against women.

The following year, the United Nations Commission for Human Rights, in resolution 1993/46 of 3 March, condemned all forms of violence and violations of human rights directed specifically against women.

The World Conference on Human Rights, held in Vienna in June 1993, laid extensive groundwork for eliminating violence against women. In the Vienna Declaration and Programme of Action, Governments declared that the United Nations system and Member States should work towards the elimination of violence against women in public and private life; of all forms of sexual harassment, exploitation and trafficking in women; of gender bias in the administration of justice; and of any conflicts arising between the rights of women and the harmful effects of certain traditional or customary practices, cultural prejudices and religious extremism.

The document also declared that "violations of the human rights of women in situations of armed conflicts are violations of the fundamental principles of international human rights and humanitarian law", and that all violations of this kind — including murder, systematic rape, sexual slavery and forced pregnancy — "require a particularly effective response".

Discrimination in Family

While the type of discrimination varied from region to region, women throughout the world found that their relationship to a male relative or husband determined their rights. The third world countries continued to use statutory and customary law to discriminate against women with regard to property ownership and inheritance. The explosive increase in numbers of young widows with children as a result of the Human Immunodeficiency Virus/Acquired Immunodeficiency Syndrome (HIV/AIDS) pandemic and wars in these regions starkly exposed the critical link between denial of women's rights and extreme poverty.

Personal status laws of women in the third world countries, continued to curtail women's rights entering into marriage, during marriage, and at the dissolution of marriage. In Islamic states, the minimum age for marriage was eighteen for boys and seventeen for girls. If a woman over the age of seventeen married without the consent of a male guardian, the guardian could demand the annulment of the marriage if the husband was not of the same social standing as the wife, and as long as the wife was not pregnant. A wife's "disobedience" could lead to forfeiture of her husband's responsibility to provide support. A man could legally have up to four wives simultaneously, while a woman could have only one husband. Women did not have the same rights as men to end marriage: while the personal status law provided for the unilateral and unconditional right of a husband to effect divorce by repudiation, a woman seeking divorce was required to go to court and prove that her husband had neglected his marital duties.

A serious consequence of limitations on women's equality in their private lives, such as whom to marry, was loss of citizenship for themselves and/or their children. Nationality laws in such disparate countries as Egypt, Sri Lanka, and Bangladesh denied women the right to transfer citizenship to their children. These laws, designed in part to curtail immigration and thus maintain the purity, loyalty, and cohesion of the nation, demonstrated the way in which discrimination on the bases of national origin and gender intersected to further entrench women's subordinate status in the family and in society.

Despite years of protest and lawsuits by women's human rights groups, in May 2001 the State Consultative Council of Egypt dismissed the recent parliamentary plea to amend the 1975 Nationality Law. Under this law, which contradicted the constitution, an Egyptian man could automatically transfer his nationality to his children while an Egyptian woman could do so only under limited circumstances: when the child was born in Egypt to a stateless father or to a father of unknown nationality, or when the child's relationship to his or her father could not be legally established. The Egyptian Center for Women's Rights estimated that thousands of women married to foreigners and as many as one million children continued to suffer discrimination under this law.

Domestic Violence

Violence against women in the family occurs in developed and developing countries alike. It has long been considered a private matter by bystanders — including neighbours, the community and government. But such private matters have a tendency to become public tragedies.

In the United States, a woman is beaten every 18 minutes. Indeed, domestic violence is the leading cause of injury among women of reproductive age in the United States. Between 22 and 35 per cent of women who visit emergency rooms are there for that reason.

The highly publicized trial of O. J. Simpson, the retired United States football player acquitted of the murder of his former wife and a male friend of hers, helped focus international media attention on the issue of domestic violence and spousal abuse.

In Peru, 70 per cent of all crimes reported to the police involve women beaten by their husbands.

In Pakistan, Prime Minister Benazir Bhutto strongly defended a 35-year-old mother of two who was severely burned by her husband in a domestic dispute.

"There is no excuse for such a behaviour", the Prime Minister declared after visiting the hospitalized victim. "My presence here is to send a message to all those who violate Islamic teachings and defy laws of the land with their inhuman treatment of women. This will not be tolerated."

According to the Human Rights Commission of Pakistan, in the 400 cases of domestic violence reported in 1993 in the province of Punjab, nearly half ended with the death of the wife.

Many Governments now recognize the importance of protecting victims of domestic abuse and taking action to punish perpetrators. The establishment of structures allowing officials to deal with cases of domestic violence and its consequences is a significant step towards the elimination of violence against women in the family.

The UN Special Rapporteur's report highlights the importance of adopting legislation that provides for prosecution of the offender. It also stresses the importance of specialized training for law enforcement authorities as well as medical and legal professionals, and of the establishment of community support services for victims, including access to information and shelters.

In many countries, women fall victim to traditional practices that violate their human rights. The persistence of the problem has much to do with the fact that most of these physically and psychologically harmful customs are deeply rooted in the tradition and culture of society.

Female Genital Mutilation

According to the World Health Organization, 85 million to 115 million girls and women in the population have undergone some form of female genital mutilation and suffer from its adverse health effects.

Every year an estimated 2 million young girls undergo this procedure. Most live in Africa and Asia — but an increasing number can be found among immigrant and refugee families in Western Europe and North America. Indeed, the practice has been outlawed in some European countries.

In France, a Malian was convicted in a criminal court after his baby girl died of a female circumcision-related infection. The procedure had been performed on the infant at home.

In Canada, fear of being forced to undergo circumcision can be grounds for asylum. A Nigerian woman was granted refugee status since she felt that she might be persecuted in her home country because of her refusal to inflict genital mutilation on her baby daughter.

There is a growing consensus that the best way to eliminate these practices is through educational campaigns that emphasize their dangerous health consequences. Several Governments have been actively promoting such campaigns in their countries.

Son Preference

Son preference affects women in many countries, particularly in Asia. Its consequences can be anything from foetal or female infanticide to neglect of the girl child over her brother in terms of such essential needs as nutrition, basic health care and education.

In China and India, some women choose to terminate their pregnancies when expecting daughters but carry their pregnancies to term when expecting sons. According to reports from India, genetic testing for sex selection has become a booming business, especially in the country's northern regions. Indian gender-detection clinics drew protests from women's groups after the appearance of advertisements suggesting that it was better to spend $38 now to terminate a female foetus than $3,800 later on her dowry.

A study of amniocentesis procedures conducted in a large Bombay hospital found that 95.5 per cent of foetuses identified as female were aborted, compared with a far smaller percentage of male foetuses. The problem of son preference is present in many other countries as well. Asked how many children he had fathered, the former United States boxing champion Muhammad Ali told an interviewer: "One boy and seven mistakes."

Dowry-related Violence

In some countries, weddings are preceded by the payment of an agreed-upon dowry by the bride's family. Failure to pay the dowry can lead to violence.

In Bangladesh, a bride whose dowry was deemed too small was disfigured after her husband threw acid on her face. In India, an average of five women a day are burned in dowry-related disputes — and many more cases are never reported.

Early marriage, especially without the consent of the girl, is another form of human rights violation. Early marriage followed by multiple pregnancies can affect the health of women for life.

Dowry deaths are reported in various South Asian countries such as India, Pakistan, and Bangladesh. Dowry death is considered one of the many categories of violence against women in South Asia.

Most dowry deaths occur when the young woman, unable to bear the harassment and torture, commits suicide. Most of these suicides are by hanging, poisoning or by fire. Sometimes the woman is killed by setting her on fire; this is known as "bride burning", and sometimes disguised as suicide or accident. According to Indian police, every year it receives over 2,500 reports of bride-burning, while human rights organisations in Pakistan report over 300 deaths per year. The Indian National Crime Records Bureau (NCRB) reports that there were about 6787 dowry death cases registered in India in 2005.Incidents of dowry deaths during the year 2005 (6,787) have increased significantly by 46.0 per cent over 1995 level (4,648).

'The 1961 Dowry Prohibition Act' prohibits the request, payment or acceptance of a dowry, "as consideration for the marriage". where "dowry" is defined as a gift demanded or given as a precondition for a marriage. Gifts given without a precondition are not considered dowry, and are legal. Asking or giving of dowry can be punished by an imprisonment of up to six months, or a fine of up to Rs. 5000. It replaced several pieces of anti-dowry legislation that had been enacted by various Indian states. Indian women's rights activists campaigned for more than 40 years to contain dowry deaths without much success. The Dowry Prohibition Act 1961 and the more stringent Section 498a of IPC (enacted in 1983) did not achieve the desired result. Using the Protection of Women from Domestic Violence Act 2005 (PWDVA) implemented in 2006, a woman can put a stop to the dowry harassment by approaching a domestic violence protection officer. Due to demands by women's rights activists, the Indian government has modified property inheritance laws and permitted daughters to claim equal rights to their parental property. Some religious groups have urged the people to curb the extravagant spendings during the marriages.

Child Marriage

Child marriage usually refers to two separate social phenomena which are practiced in some societies. The first and more widespread practice is that of marrying a young child (generally defined as below the age of fifteen) to an adult. In practice, it is almost always a young girl married to a man.

The second practice is a form of arranged marriage in which the parents of two children from different families arrange a future marriage. In this practice, the individuals who become betrothed often do not meet one another until the wedding ceremony, which occurs when they are both considered to be of a marriageable age.

An increase in the advocation of human rights, whether as women's rights or as children's rights, has caused the traditions of child marriage to decrease greatly as it was considered unfair and dangerous for the children.

Child marriages may have many purposes. The aristocracy of some cultures tend to use child marriage among different factions or states as a method to secure political ties between them. For example, the son or daughter of the royal family of a weaker power would sometimes be arranged to marry into the royal family of a stronger neighbouring power, thus preventing itself from being assimilated. In the lower classes, if they were fortunate, families could use child marriages as means to gain financial ties with wealthier people, ensuring their successions.

In child betrothals, a child's parents arrange a match with the parents of a child from another family (social standing, wealth and expected education all play a part), thus unilaterally determining the child's future at a young age. It is thought by adherents that physical attraction is not a suitable foundation upon which to build a marriage and a family. A separate consideration is the age at which the wedding, as opposed to the engagement, takes place.

Families are able to cement political and/or financial ties by having their children inter-marry. The betrothal is considered a binding contract upon the families and the children. The breaking of a betrothal can have serious consequences both for the families and for the betrothed individuals themselves.

Discrimination at Workplace

In many countries, women faced severe discrimination in employment practices and violence in the workplace, including sexual harassment, with little or no protection. In Taliban-controlled Afghanistan, women were not permitted to work outside the home, unless they were healthcare professionals, or widows. The latter, estimated to number 40,000 in Kabul alone, were mostly unable to obtain paid employment and were reduced to begging to support their families and faced constant harassment and violence at the hands of the religious police. In Guatemala, where domestic workers number tens of thousands and domestic labor is one of the principal forms of employment for poor, especially indigenous women, the adoption of specific legislation to protect domestic workers remained a low priority for the government. Under threat of losing its beneficiary status under the U.S. Generalised System of Preferences (GSP) trade act, Guatemala reformed its labor code with respect to freedom of association during 2001, to bring it more in line with International Labor Organisation conventions. However, the government missed an opportunity to remedy the unequal treatment of domestic workers who, under the current labor code, suffered discrimination as a group: the code denied domestic workers the right to the eight-hour workday and the minimum wage, limited their right to national holidays and rest, and based access to healthcare on employer largesse. Guatemala also systematically denied women workers the enjoyment of full labor rights, continuing to discriminate against women on the grounds of reproductive status. Some factories required job seekers to state whether they were pregnant, and denied full benefits to employees who became pregnant post-hire.

In USA, live-in domestic workers remained explicitly excluded from protection under the National Labor Relations Act, the Occupational Safety and Health Act, and the overtime provisions of the Fair Labor Standards Act. The exclusion of domestic workers from basic U.S. labor rights and protections was based on gender stereotypes and perceptions about the role of domestic workers in the family, and had a disproportionate impact on women, thus constituting disparate impact sex discrimination. In post-apartheid South Africa, the government made efforts to overcome the legacy of apartheid in commercial farming areas: new laws provided full labor rights for farmworkers, including women. Yet, in practice, racist and sexist attitudes remained pervasive on farms: women farmworkers were the lowest paid, had the fewest benefits, were often forced to become squatters, and were targets of harassment and violence by farmers and farmworkers alike. The situation of women on South African farms was precarious: personal relationships were divided on racial and patriarchal lines, with women subjected to discrimination, violence, and abuse. Women farmworkers were more likely to be seasonal or temporary workers than men, and usually did more menial, less remunerative work, such as planting or harvesting. Employers viewed women's labor as a supplement to men's labor even in situations in which women did the same types of jobs and worked as long hours as men.

Rape

Rape can occur anywhere, even in the family, where it can take the form of marital rape or incest. It occurs in the community, where a woman can fall prey to any abuser. It also occurs in situations of armed conflict and in refugee camps.

In the United States, national statistics indicate that a women is raped every six minutes. In 1995, the case of a Brazilian jogger raped and murdered in New York City's Central Park drew international attention once again to the problem. The incident occurred only a few years after an earlier sensational jogger-assault case in which the victim — an American assaulted in the same general area of the park — barely survived after her assailants left her for dead.

Relations between residents of the Japanese island of Okinawa and American GIs were thrown into turmoil in 1995 after two marines and a sailor allegedly kidnapped and raped a 12-year-old girl.

Sexual Assault within Marriage

In many countries sexual assault by a husband on his wife is not considered to be a crime: a wife is expected to submit. It is thus very difficult in practice for a woman to prove that sexual assault has occurred unless she can demonstrate serious injury.

Sexual Harassment

Sexual harassment in the workplace is a growing concern for women.

Employers abuse their authority to seek sexual favours from their female co-workers or subordinates, sometimes promising promotions or other forms of career advancement or simply creating an untenable and hostile work environment. Women who refuse to give in to such unwanted sexual advances often run the risk of anything from demotion to dismissal.

But in recent years more women have been coming forward to report such practices — some taking their cases to court. Sexual harassment constitutes a form of sex discrimination. It not only degrades the woman, but reinforces and reflects the idea of non-professionalism on the part of women workers, who are consequently regarded as less able to perform their duties than their male colleagues.

Prostitution and Trafficking

Many women are forced into prostitution either by their parents, husbands or boyfriends — or as a result of the difficult economic and social conditions in which they find themselves. They are also lured into prostitution, sometimes by "mail-order bride" agencies that promise to find them a husband or a job in a foreign country. As a result, they very often find themselves illegally confined in brothels in slavery-like conditions where they are physically abused and their passports withheld.

Most women initially victimized by sexual traffickers have little inkling of what awaits them. They generally get a very small percentage of what the customer pays to the pimp or the brothel owner. Once they are caught up in the system there is practically no way out, and they find themselves in a very vulnerable situation.

Since prostitution is illegal in many countries, it is difficult for prostitutes to come forward and ask for protection if they become victims of rape or want to escape from brothels. Customers, on the other hand, are rarely the object of penal laws.

In Thailand, prostitutes who complain to the police are often arrested and sent back to the brothels upon payment of a fine.

The extent of trafficking in women and girl children has reached alarming proportions, especially in Asian countries.

Many women and girl children are trafficked across borders, often with the complicity of border guards. In one incident, five young prostitutes burned to death in a brothel fire because they had been chained to their beds.

At the same time, sex tours of developing countries are a well-organized industry in several European and other industrialized countries.

Traffickers moved their human victims around the globe, held them in debt bondage, seized their passports, and threatened them or their families with harm if they resisted. Ever-tightening border controls and the lack of legal opportunities to migrate often forced women to turn to traffickers, increasing their vulnerability to abuse. Sold as chattel and forced to work for little or no pay, trafficked persons feared local law enforcement authorities, perceiving, in many cases correctly, that an appeal to police would end in prosecution and deportation, rather than protection.

Trafficking victims from ethnic minority commu-nities faced an even more daunting situation, including at its worst xenophobic violence, racism, and, in the case of trafficked hilltribe women and girls in Thailand, statelessness. States continued to fail to combat trafficking. The token prosecutions of traffickers merely proved the rule. One positive development brightened the picture slightly in 2001. The opening for signature of the Protocol to Prevent, Suppress, and Punish Trafficking in Persons, Especially Women and Children, Supplementing the United Nations Convention against Transnational Organised Crime, marked a small step forward in the battle against trafficking. By late November, one hundred countries had signed the protocol, committing their governments to punish traffickers and protect the human rights of trafficking victims, but only three had ratified it.

Even countries that ratified the protocol, such as Nigeria, failed to adhere to those commitments. Women's organisations protested that Nigeria fell far short in the effective investigation and prosecution of individuals engaged in trafficking of women and children. The 2001 U.S. State Department report on trafficking in persons cited widespread corruption among law enforcement officials as a major stumbling block to combating trafficking in Nigeria. Trafficking victims alleged that some Nigerian immigration officials colluded with traffickers, assisting them in forging documents and bringing persons across borders, and accused others of actively engaging in trafficking. Nigerian citizens, mostly women and children, facing stark conditions and oppressive poverty, chose to migrate but found themselves preyed upon by traffickers who transported them to Lagos and other cities and forced them into domestic servitude or prostitution. Traffickers seized all wages to pay off the trafficking victims' debt.

Traffickers and employers held women trafficked from Ukraine, Moldova, and Romania in debt bondage in brothels throughout Bosnia and Herzegovina. Trafficked women reported to the United Nations that their employers sometimes forced them to provide free sexual services to local police officers. In a handful of cases, Bosnian police actively participated in trafficking, either as part owners or employees of the clubs, or by procuring false documents for traffickers. Trafficking victims, terrified of retaliation by traffickers, feared reporting the abuse to law enforcement authorities. Eager to fan that fear, employers routinely claimed that they counted police officers among their friends. The U.N. also stood accused of complicity in trafficking when allegations emerged that International Police Task Force (IPTF) officers—United Nations police charged with monitoring local Bosnian police—had gone to brothels as clients and, in a small number of cases, purchased women for personal use.

In March 1999, the UN stepped in to facilitate voluntary repatriation of trafficking victims through an International Organisation for Migration (IOM) program, but some trafficked women fell through the cracks of the screening process, serving thirty-day sentences in Bosnian prisons before facing deportation. By October 2001, the IOM had completed over three hundred voluntary repatriations of victims ranging in age from thirteen to thirty-six years old. Government authorities in Colombia, another signatory to the protocol, estimated that between two and ten women were trafficked from Colombia each day, the vast majority of them to Europe. In July 2001, new anti-trafficking legislation went into effect; however, the legislation only treated trafficking victims as those who had been trafficked outside of Colombia for forced prostitution, failing to protect persons trafficked into other forms of forced labor. In addition, NGOs lamented that the law established prison sentences of just four to six years for traffickers. In mid-2001, the Colombian Congress began debating an anti-trafficking bill that would enhance the definition of trafficking, the range of victims protected, and the severity of the penalties for the crime.

In Japan, women trafficked into the sex industry accounted for a significant proportion of the estimated 260,000 undocumented migrants. Yet, the government, a non-signatory to the protocol, took no concrete steps to prevent trafficking and continued to treat trafficked women as illegal immigrants, detaining them and failing to provide them human rights protections. The minority of trafficked women who managed to escape from their employers with the help of NGOs or their embassies found themselves placed in detention and then deported as illegal aliens, unable to seek redress or sue for compensation. Thailand continued to be a major country of origin for women trafficked into the Japan's so-called snack bars. Discrimination against minority groups in Thailand heightened some women's vulnerability to trafficking. Hilltribe women, denied citizenship and rights by the Thai government, suffered from extremely limited educational and employment opportunities. Since births among the hilltribe communities were often not registered, and because hilltribe people did not possess official Thai citizenship, hilltribe people were left effectively stateless.

Meanwhile, Israel is failed to provide even minimal human rights protections for persons trafficked into its territory for domestic servitude, agricultural labor, forced prostitution, and construction work despite the passage of an anti-trafficking law in 2000. Trafficking victims feared cooperating with law enforcement officials and had no incentive to do so, absent witness protection, shelter, and relief from deportation, or legal assistance. State complicity and corruption also played a role in trafficking into Israel. In March 2001, the Hotline for Migrant Workers, an Israeli NGO working with trafficking victims, reported to the United Nations Human Rights Commission that six trafficking cases involved policemen: in one case a policeman stood accused of managing a brothel; in four cases police officers tipped brothel owners off on upcoming raids; and in another case a policeman faced charges of selling a trafficked woman to another brothel owner after arresting her. Israeli authorities continued to treat trafficked women as criminals rather than victims, and failed to prosecute those responsible for trafficking.

Violence against Women Migrant Workers

Female migrant workers typically leave their countries for better living conditions and better pay — but the real benefits accrue to both the host countries and the countries of origin. For home countries, money sent home by migrant workers is an important source of hard currency, while receiving countries are able to find workers for low-paying jobs that might otherwise go unfilled. But migrant workers themselves fare badly, and sometimes tragically. Many become virtual slaves, subject to abuse and rape by their employers. In the Middle East and Persian Gulf region, there are an estimated 1.2 million women, mainly Asians, who are employed as domestic servants.

According to the independent human rights group Middle East Watch, female migrant workers in Kuwait often suffer beatings and sexual assaults at the hands of their employers.

The police are often of little help. In many cases, women who report being raped by their employers are sent back to the employer — or are even assaulted at the police station. Working conditions are often appalling, and employers prevent women from escaping by seizing their passports or identity papers.

Pornography

Another concern highlighted in the Special Rapporteur's report is pornography, which represents a form of violence against women that "glamorizes the degradation and maltreatment of women and asserts their subordinate function as mere receptacles for male lust".

Custodial Violence

Violence against women by the very people who are supposed to protect them — members of the law enforcement and criminal justice systems — is widespread. Women are physically or verbally abused; they also suffer sexual and physical torture. According to Amnesty International, thousands of women held in custody are routinely raped in police detention centres worldwide. The report of the Special Rapporteur underlines the necessity for States to prosecute those accused of abusing women while in detention and to hold them accountable for their actions.

Violence Against Women in Situations of Armed Conflict

Rape has been widely used as a weapon of war whenever armed conflicts arise between different parties. It has been used all over the world: in Chiapas, Mexico, in Rwanda, in Kuwait, in Haiti, in Colombia. Women and girl children are frequently victims of gang rape committed by soldiers from all sides of a conflict. Such acts are done mainly to trample the dignity of the victims. Rape has been used to reinforce the policy of ethnic cleansing in the war that has been tearing apart the former Yugoslavia.

The so-called "comfort women" — young girls of colonized or occupied countries who became sexual slaves to Japanese soldiers during the Second World War — have dramatized the problem in a historical context. Many of these women are now coming forward and demanding compensation for their suffering from Japanese authorities. "Such rape is the symbolic rape of the community, the destruction of the fundamental elements of a society and culture — the ultimate humiliation of the male enemy", the report by the Special Rapporteur noted. It stressed the need to hold the perpetrators of such crimes fully accountable.

Women continuously suffered conflict-related abuse or its sequelae, and waited in vain for justice. Rape and sexual assault, in particular, were employed to achieve specific military or political objectives. When women sought refuge in other countries, they continued to experience sexual and other forms of physical violence in and around refugee camps. While acts of sexual violence in the context of armed conflict were recognised internationally as a war crime and a crime against humanity, perpetrators were rarely brought to justice. Moreover, in armed conflicts, women suffered from a broad array of abuses not limited to violence by combatants.

The Organisation for Security and Cooperation in Europe (OSCE) released a scathing report in October 2000, detailing how women victims of sexual violence in Kosovo confronted discrimination, intimidation, and bias in the criminal justice system.

A follow-up report issued by the OSCE in early 2001 indicated that the Kosovo judicial system had failed to remedy those ongoing problems and continued to handle sexual assault cases "superficially... illustrating disregard for the serious nature of such cases for both the alleged victim and the defendant."

The OSCE reported that the majority of rape and sexual assault cases involved juvenile victims. In Indonesia, despite substantial evidence of the frequent occurrence of sexual violence in the conflict in Aceh between Indonesian security forces and the armed insurgent Free Aceh Movement (GAM), very few cases were reported to the authorities—and one particularly notorious case showed why.

The case involved five women from South Aceh district who reported being sexually abused by members of the Indonesian paramilitary police, Brimob, in February 2001.

Human rights NGOs brought the women to Banda Aceh, the provincial capital, where the case and their identities were widely publicised. Taken into police custody for questioning, the women publicly recanted their stories, instead saying it was members of the armed insurgency, GAM, who had abducted them and forced them to say that Brimob had assaulted them.

The lack of protection for victims of sexual violence and NGOs' inexperience in handling such a case in a highly politicised context made the women into pawns of the police. The end result was that the relevant human rights violations remained uninvestigated and unpunished.

In an ongoing conflict largely ignored by the international community, the Congolese Rally for Democracy (RCD) and its Rwandan allies, along with Hutu rebels and Mai Mai forces, continued to abduct women and commit sexual violence against them in eastern Congo.

In 2001, these groups had raped thousands of women and girls of all ethnic groups. In many cases, Mai Mai and Rwandan Hutu rebels raped women, often in front of their husbands, families, or community as a public humiliation and demonstration of power, when families fled an area under control by a certain group, and moved into what was perceived as the "enemy's" territory. Mai Mai and Rwandan Hutu rebels took women and girls hostage and kept them as "wives" for several weeks or months, releasing them after capturing other women.

Even after fleeing conflict in search of sanctuary from violence, women refugees frequently found that there was no meaningful refuge—they simply escaped violence in conflict to be confronted by different types of violence in refugee camps or en route to refugee camps. Guinean security personnel and civilians, during the relocation of some 60,000 Liberian and Sierra Leonese refugees from the border to the interior of the country, regularly harassed refugees.

Checkpoints along the roads were particularly dangerous places, where Guinean security forces often subjected refugees to arbitrary strip searches, beatings, sexual assault, and extortion—while allegedly screening refugees for the presence of rebel marks.

Violence against Refugee and Displaced Women

Women and children form the great majority of refugee populations all over the world and are especially vulnerable to violence and exploitation. In refugee camps, they are raped and abused by military and immigration personnel, bandit groups, male refugees and rival ethnic groups. They are also forced into prostitution. In her report, the Special Rapporteur proposes the following measures to be taken for the protection of women and girls in refugee camps: improvement of security, deployment of trained female officers at all points of the refugees' journey, participation of women in organizational structures of the camps and prosecution of government and military personnel responsible for abuse against refugee women.

Threats of Violence

Threats of violence is ever-present in women's public and private lives. In situations of political upheaval, state custody, domestic contexts, and other situations involving private actors and NGOs, women's physical and sexual integrity was at risk in all regions. Since it came to power in 1980, the Zimbabwe government had promised to enact land reform measures to redistribute to black Zimbabweans lands taken under white ownership during colonial rule, though without making significant progress before the end of 2000. In 2001, however, groups of ruling party supporters and reputed veterans of the war against colonial rule seized control of many white-owned farms by force in what the government described as a "spontaneous and popular uprising." Many black farmworkers, as well as white farmworkers and their families, were assaulted in the process. Some were killed. Many women on farms and in rural areas were raped or sexually assaulted with impunity.

In the U.S., the California State Legislature held hearings in January 2001 to address reports of continuing mental, physical, and sexual abuse, as well as medical neglect in the state's women's prisons. The hearings were prompted by the deaths of nine women at the Central California Women's Facility within a two-month period at the end of 2000. Legislators expressed concern over reports that some women inmates who requested medical attention prior to their deaths did not receive immediate attention. In one case, the cellmates of a deceased prisoner alleged that corrections officers had mocked the dying woman's pleas for assistance shortly before she died. There was particular concern that medical technical assistants (MTAs), prison guards with minimal medical training, were responsible for determining whether women inmates should see medical staff.

In Uzbekistan, local officials and community leaders coerced women into remaining with abusive partners, often thwarting their efforts to escape the violence by leaving their marriages. In some cases, local authorities refused to provide documents to women attempting to file for divorce. More frequently, officials and medical doctors sought to convince the women to return to violent spouses in order to "save the family," and be "better wives."

Dimensions of Gender-based Violence

Violence against women and girls is often perceived as an individual problem and as isolated incidents. However, a glance at empirical evidence presents an alarming picture. The World Bank estimates that violence against women is as serious a cause of death and incapacity among women of reproductive age as cancer and is a greater cause of ill health than traffic accidents and malaria put together. Viewed in this light, it becomes obvious that – besides being a fundamental violation of human rights violence against women represents one of the most critical public health challenges and is a major factor contributing to poverty. Therefore, reducing violence against women and girls is also a key to achieving the Millennium Development Goals.

The international recognition of violence against women as a human rights violation was the result of years of dedicated campaigning by women's rights activists and survivors of violence. In 1993, the Vienna World Conference on Human Rights finally recognised that women's rights are human rights, a position that has been reaffirmed at all subsequent world summits. Since the Vienna conference, violence against women has left the private domain and became an established issue within public debates. However, greater efforts and more resources need to be harnessed in order to adequately address the sheer scale and multidimensional nature of the problem.

In 1993 the UN General Assembly put forward a comprehensive definition of violence against women. The resulting Declaration on the Elimination of Violence against Women was duly adopted by the Assembly members and is by now widely used: For the purposes of this declaration, the term "violence against women" means any act of gender-based violence that results in, or is likely to result in, physical, sexual or psychological harm or suffering to women, including threats of such acts, coercion or arbitrary deprivation of liberty, whether occurring in public or in private life.

Violence against women shall be understood to encompass, but not be limited to, the following:

(a) Physical, sexual and psychological violence occurring in the family, including battering, sexual abuse of female children in the household, dowry-related violence, marital rape, female genital mutilation and other traditional practices harmful to women, non-spousal violence and violence related to exploitation;

(b) Physical, sexual and psychological violence occurring within the general community, including rape, sexual abuse, sexual harassment and intimidation at work, in educational institutions and elsewhere, trafficking in women and forced prostitution;

(c) Physical, sexual and psychological violence perpetrated or condoned by the State, wherever it occurs.

There are numerous reasons why violence exists and there are many different expressions of violence. In a recent seven-volume work on violence and freedom, one author establishes nearly twenty different categories and justifications to explain violent behavior. Most of these justifications are formulated in the form: "in defence of...X". Within this framework, violence is justified in defence of one's homeland, as self-defence, or in defence of class, creed, honour, authority, race and culture.

It is worth considering here how violence against women might fit into such a framework. Why are men overwhelmingly responsible for perpetrating violence against women? Therefore, the causes of violence against women are rooted in gender concepts, inequalities and hierarchies.

The term 'gender' is used to describe a set of qualities and behaviors that societies expect from men and women. These expectations stem from the idea that certain qualities, behaviors, characteristics and roles are "natural" for men, while other qualities and roles are "natural" for women. However, rather than being natural or biological, gender is created; it is socially defined and learned. Gender concepts are part of social, political and economic transformation processes. Therefore, gender roles are influenced by families, schools, the media, civil society and the state. Sophisticated policies and legal frameworks are important for this purpose because contradictory or competing gender concepts often coexist within such transformation processes. In each individual context, one should first study the specific situation in order to give the best possible support to the change agents, e.g. through development cooperation.

Many gender norms that are widely accepted around the world are based on a set of beliefs that tend to value men over women. In general, the roles and traits associated with men are seen as more valuable than those associated with women. This shows how gender hierarchies are part of the wider economic and social power relations.

Thus, gender helps to shape hierarchies and fosters inequalities. Gender is about power relations between the sexes that tend to privilege men over women and attach preference to some groups over others; e.g. heterosexuals over gay, bisexual, lesbian or transgendered individuals. Violence against women acts as a "policing mechanism" to create, manifest, defend or reinforce these unfair hierarchies.

Violence and Male Role Models

Men are not innately violent towards women and children; rather, they become violent as a result of beliefs and norms about what it means to be a man. When looking at male violence it is worth examining two aspects of men's gender norms in particular. The first is men's sense of "entitlement" to certain privileges over women, while the second concerns some of the most common masculine norms.

Men and boys are taught that they are entitled to different types of privilege over women. Examples of male advantages can include: greater power and access over women in the public sphere, control over their economic activities, income and mobility; and an entitlement to sex, obedience and other services from them within the home.

To differing degrees boys and men in different societies learn that it is acceptable to use violence against women to assert these "entitlements". For example, the 2002 WHO World Report on Violence and Health states that "the events that trigger violence in abusive relationships are remarkably consistent. They include disobeying or arguing with the man; questioning him about money or girlfriends; not having food ready on time; not caring adequately for the children or home; refusing to have sex; and suspecting a woman of infidelity." In fact, many men explain their own violent behavior as a result of the women's faults and deny any responsibility. If their wives demand family support and criticise their husbands' spending on girlfriends many men react with violence.

Aside from a sense of privilege, gender norms play an important part in socialising men to use violence. Most people, regardless of where they live, can list specific characteristics and roles that are attributable to women and men.

The world's rich cultural diversity has created many different expressions of gender norms. However, there are also many common elements that are shared across cultures. These "dominant" gender norms are essentially idealised visions of how women and men should behave. As a consequence, people and particularly women often have little choice in how they choose to interpret these norms.

Many of the norms commonly associated with women have a tendency to relegate them to "caring roles" and to seek to ensure that women remain passive and weaker in relation to men. Whether they have children or not, women are expected to take care of households, children and the sick, as well as fulfilling other supportive and care-giving roles in the workplace and at home. In many instances, women are also socialised to be sexually attractive and compliant to men. In contrast, dominant masculine norms prise strength, courage and the ability to control situations and emotions. Frequently men are also socialised to feel entitled to privileges over women such as higher status and better pay; as well as the ability to command respect and pleasure from women.

How do these dominant gender norms affect men's perceptions of violence? Being raised to be "brave" and "in control" is key to understanding men's use of violence. When threatened, such attributes can also translate into a readiness to fight and to use violence to assert control.

These dominant gender norms help to explain why the victims and perpetrators of all forms of violence are usually men and especially young men. In general, men fight more than women, be it in wars, in the home, at school or in the street. Militaries around the world are almost always composed of men. It is also primarily men who are drafted into civil conflicts or who perpetrate acts of terrorism. Men are also more likely to be violent towards themselves. For example, statistics show that men commit suicide more often than women.

These dominant notions of masculinity present numerous challenges to men in the public and private parts of their lives. If men do not "succeed" in being masculine in the public domain – i.e. by achieving status, economic gain and/or security – they may resort to intimate partner violence within the private sphere. Such failure is compounded when wives react to a husband's failure by challenging his misconduct. Both the failure itself and the wife's challenges, which undermine his masculinity, make the husband feel humiliated"

This same set of restrictive gender norms leaves many women with a limited choice of roles in the public sphere or within family and private relations. This is especially the case in post-conflict societies, where concepts of violent masculinity predominate. It is always important to take the political and social developments as well as the current power structures into account and sustain dominant gender norms – and, therefore, the imbalances between women and men – are the same issues that foster contexts where violence against women is allowed to take place. These factors can be mapped across the environment in which violence against women occurs.

Factors Contributing to Violence Against Women

Violence against women is not simply perpetrated by individual men operating within in a vacuum: violence has structural, as well as personal, roots. On a personal level, violence against women stems from the pressures, fears and stifled emotions that lie beneath many of the dominant forms of manhood. Personal experience adds to these factors: individuals experience and learn about violence through the family, the media, the community and/or other institutions.

However, gender norms are structural: they are defined and maintained across all levels of society. The factors that shape

For Individual Men

Many aspects of an individual's attitudes and behavior, as well as past experiences, can influence his risk of using violence. These include:

- Witnessing violence against women as a child
- Experiencing sexual abuse or child abuse
- Lack of positive role models
- Sense of entitlement and control over women
- Social isolation and depression
- Alcohol and drug use
- Attitudes and beliefs supportive of sexual violence
- High potential for aggression and violence
- Perception of violence as an accepted way to safeguard individual interests

— Violent behavior is an integral part of the positive self-image
— Fear to loose control over situations
— Lack of self-confidence /little self-esteem
— Attitudes of entitlement and male privilege
— Conflicts about power and control within intimate relationships
— Patterns of poor interpersonal communication
— Male dominance in a relationship or family setting
— Economic stress, unemployment
— Emotionally unsupportive family environment
— Family honour considered more important than the health and safety of individuals
— Lack of peaceful strategies for conflict solving.

In Communities

Community environments such as villages, schools, workplaces, and neighbourhoods, all help to shape an individual's behavior and beliefs. Factors that increase the risk of violence within these arenas include:

— Living in communities that tolerate violence against women
— Attitudes and gender norms prevalent in the community that support violence against women
— Gender socialisation that promotes unequal power between men and women
— Lack of support from police and the judicial system
— Weak community sanctions against violence against women
— Poverty and economic inequality
— Little or no community engagement in violence prevention
— Sanctions against use of violence are almost non-existent
— Lack of measures for the prevention of violence by governmental institutions, religion and the media.

In Society at Large

Broader societal forces, such as economic interests, social norms, cultural beliefs, laws and policies, institutional practices, and political ideologies, heavily influence personal relationships and community interactions. Risk factors that contribute to violence against women at this level include:

— Historical and societal patterns that glorify violence, and particular violence against women
— Traditional gender norms that support male superiority and sexual entitlement
— Weak institutional responses to violence against women
— Religious or cultural belief systems that support expressions of violence against women
— Economic and social policies that create or sustain gaps and tensions between groups of people
— Stereotyped portrayal of women and men in the media
— Sexist reports on gender based violence and a high level of violent and dehumanising pornography
— Weak laws and policies related to violence against women
— Weak laws and policies related to sexism and homo phobia
— No enforcement of international legislation
— High levels of crime and other violence and all forms of sexual exploitation
— Militarism and warfare during conflict as well as in post-conflict situations
— Lack of peaceful strategies to solve conflicts.

It is clear that violence against women is rooted in prevailing hierarchical gender norms. However, it is equally apparent that these norms are unavoidable. Gender is shaped by personal behaviors and interpersonal relationships, as well as institutional and societal structures; no matter where you come from, gender is a fundamental part of your life.

Dispelling Myths

It is necessary to dispel certain myths about violence against women. Many people do not see that violence happens in their own communities or that it happens to "people like them". Some still consider violence against women a private matter, the business of spouses, partners or other family members.

It is hard to imagine people we know abusing their partners or assaulting someone sexually. However, statistics on violence emphasise that such forms of violence are remarkably prevalent in all communities. There are men in almost all cultures, classes, castes, religions and locations, who are responsible for acts of violence against women. Social, economic or educational success does not exempt someone from violent behavior; most cases of sexual abuse and rape are committed by men who are personal acquaintances of the victim and tend to be from the same social group and background. However, this interpretation misses out many of the deeper connections between gender and violence. Misconceptions about the origins and nature of violence are widespread. A study by the European Commission invited various EU citizens to choose from twelve most likely causes of violence. The results showed that 75% of EU citizens participating in the study believed that violence was caused by poverty and social exclusion, while only 59% gave priority to "the way power is shared between the sexes".

Individual acts of violence can be triggered by different circumstances such as the pressures of unemployment or living in poverty, or issues like alcohol or drug abuse. However, these "triggers" are not the underlying causes of violence against women. Yet it is important to remember that people as well as organisations, institutions and the media are ultimately responsible for constructing and maintaining these gender roles. As such, the current system of norms should not be viewed as an immutable system of ideas.

Opportunities for Change

Achieving gender equality will not necessarily end all violence. However, moves towards establishing a more equal balance of power between the sexes are an important step towards reducing violence. Both men and women have a great deal to gain from a more peaceful, non-violent world. Indeed, men are victims to many forms of violence primarily through other men. At different times in their lives, men are children, fathers, caregivers and nurturers. By drawing on more diverse notions of masculinity, men and boys can take an active role in changing the norms and behaviors that support the use of violence. Furthermore, in many societies, women are increasingly taking on leadership and decision-making roles within all spheres of society. In order to inspire real change in the amount of violence in the world, it is important for the ongoing advancement of women to continue developing and gaining strength. An expansion of gender roles for both women and men cannot only help prevent violence, it can promote a greater degree of opportunity and choice for all individuals.

International Human Rights Framework

At present there are a large number of international agreements and national laws that prohibit gender-based discrimination and violence against women and girls. This achievement was brought about by long and persistent lobbying by women's and human rights organisations. At the beginning of the UN Decade for Women violence against women had not yet developed as an issue. Even the 1979 *Convention on the Elimination of All Forms of Discrimination Against Women* did not initially include any specific provisions relating to violence. It was almost fifteen years later, in 1992, that the CEDAW Committee finally adopted General Recommendation No. 19 on "violence against women". The recommendation defines violence as a form of discrimination against women and, therefore, as a violation of CEDAW. It emphasises that because governments are responsible for eliminating all forms of discrimination against women by any person, organisation or enterprise; they are also committed to making every effort to combat violence against women, to punish these acts and to provide compensation.

The human rights of women and of the girl-child are an inalienable, integral and indivisible part of universal human rights. The full and equal participation of women in political, civil, economic, social and cultural life, at the national, regional and international levels, and the eradication of all forms of discrimination on grounds of sex are priority objectives of the international community. This position has been reaffirmed at the Cairo Conference on Population and Development, the World Conference on Women in Beijing as well as each of the subsequent World-Summits. Thus, the rights of women and girls form an inalienable and fundamental part of the universal human rights framework. The declaration clearly rejects cultural relativist critiques of human rights, which question the overall relevance of the international rights framework as a means of addressing the subordination of women. By rejecting relativism, the declaration makes it clear that the international community will no longer accept arguments based on "culture" or religion as a means of excusing violations of women's rights. In the wake of the Vienna World Conference on Human Rights, the General Assembly of the United Nations adopted the *Declaration on the Elimination of Violence against Women.*

Although the Declaration is not legally binding but a political commitment for signatory states, it provides an interpretation of existing human rights guarantees taking into account the specific situation of women to our understanding of human rights, as laid down in various, legally binding UN Covenants. These include:

— The right to life, and the right to liberty and security of persons

— The right to just and favorable conditions of work

The Declaration supplements important aspects of CEDAW and is a milestone in it's own right. Crucially, the Declaration essentially contributed in making violence against women an issue of public concern.

In 1994, the United Nations appointed a *Special Rapporteur on Violence against Women*, who is attached to the Office of the High Commissioner for Human Rights. The Rapporteur is responsible for drawing up analyses and reports on gender-based forms of violence and recommending ways of eliminating these practices.

A 21-article *Optional Protocol to CEDAW* also came into force at the end of 2000. The Protocol entitles the CEDAW-Committee to consider petitions from individual women or groups of women who have exhausted all national legal channels. Once a complaint has been filed, the Committee has the authority to adopt provisional measures to protect the victim from further harm. The Protocol also allows the Committee to conduct its own inquiries into grave or systematic violations of the Convention. Importantly, the adoption of the Optional Protocol puts CEDAW on an equal footing with the International Covenant on Civil and Political Rights; the Convention on the Elimination of All Forms of Racial Discrimination; and the Convention against Torture and other Forms of Cruel, Inhuman or Degrading Treatment or Punishment; which all have similar complaints procedures.

The Rome Statute entered into force in 2001, establishing the *International Criminal Court*. The Statute is a landmark piece of legislation, which provides international legal recognition that rape is not just a crime against personal dignity, but that it is also a war crime or a crime against humanity. In addition, forced pregnancy, enforced sterilisation, sexual slavery, enforced prostitution and any other form of sexual violence of comparable gravity were also included as crimes against humanity.

The *UN Protocol to Prevent, Suppress and Punish Trafficking in Persons, Especially Women and Children* entered into force at the end of 2003, providing a key supplement to the Convention on Transnational Organised Crime. Trafficking is viewed as a contemporary form of slavery that involves a variety of acts, actors, means and exploitative purposes. Consequently, the Protocol contains provisions that are intended to ensure that trafficked persons are not treated as criminals but as victims of crime.

In 2004, the United Nations appointed a *Special Rapporteur on trafficking in persons*, with a particular responsibility for addressing trafficking issues concerning women and children. Sigma Huda will hold the post for three years and submit annual reports to the Commission on Human Rights with recommendations on measures required to uphold and protect the rights of trafficked people.

The recognition of women's rights as universal human rights makes signatory states responsible for ensuring that women can exercise their human rights without hindrance. Importantly, such provisions raise women's status from "supplicants" and "victims", to that of equal members of society, entitled to specific legal rights.

Regional Agreements

During the 1990s the women's movement was especially active in pushing for regional versions of the key international conventions, agreements and institutions relating to women's rights. These activities mirror the general trend towards securing greater ownership of the national policy agenda.

In 1994, the Inter-American Convention on the Prevention, Punishment and Eradication of Violence against Women was adopted by member states. The Convention declares that every woman has the right to be free from violence in both public and private spheres. In particular, the standard of due diligence, i.e. the efforts made by a state to implement a right in practice, has been explicitly incorporated into the Convention. In 1998, the U.N. International Criminal Tribunal for Rwanda was the first international tribunal to judge collective rape as a form of genocide.

More recently, the Council of Europe adopted the Council of Europe Convention on Action against Trafficking in Human Beings in May 2005. This Convention is based on a strong human rights perspective and is now open for signature to 46 member states.

The Protocol to the African Charter on Human and Peoples Rights on the Rights of Women in Africa was adopted in 2003. It covers a broad range of women's rights including the protection of women from all forms of violence as well as the right to dignity and the right to life and the integrity and security of the person. Importantly, the Protocol explicitly forbids FGM. The Protocol entered into force on November 25, 2005.

In May 2005, Bangladesh, Bhutan, India, Pakistan, Maldives, Nepal and Sri Lanka adopted the Islamabad Declaration: Review and Future Action celebrating Beijing Plus Ten, 2005 at a South Asia Regional Ministerial Conference in Pakistan.

National Law Reforms

By ratifying international human rights treaties, the State parties commit themselves to international law and are obliged to respect, protect and actively fulfil these human rights. In order to comply, numerous countries have adopted laws designed to punish the perpetrators and protect women from physical, psychological and sexual violence. To date, forty-five nations have adopted legislation against violence within the family. A further twenty-one are drafting new laws and many countries have amended criminal assault laws to include domestic violence.

In *Cambodia*, the Ministry of Women's Affairs has received technical support from the German government to draft a bill to prevent domestic violence and to provide protection to victims. The National Assembly just approved the law in September 2005. In essence, the law closes a key gap in the legal framework. It adds to existing penal measures by establishing civil measures, such as temporary restraining orders, so as to provide more comprehensive protection to victims of violence. The law also enables intervention at the local level, by giving local public authorities the power to intervene in domestic violence cases.

The Ministry for Women's Affairs has developed a National Action Plan to implement the law, together with various stakeholders from relevant government ministries and civil society; and a number of national and international experts. This plan outlines measures to ensure the widespread dissemination of the law, the training of legal officials and improvements in the services for victims of violence.

Laws against domestic violence and marital rape are especially difficult to implement because these criminal acts literally take place behind closed doors. The victims are often reluctant to report incidents to anyone because of shame, fear of reprisal, or because of a lack of viable alternatives to the current situation.

In order to enhance the political and de facto commitment to effectively implementing the law, it is necessary to have government commitment and motivated stakeholders within government institutions. In addition, it is essential to have a strong civil society, which is able to exert pressure on political decision makers. In this context, the work of women's organisations and human rights organisations is of considerable importance.

In *Honduras*, GTZ has supported the implementation of the government's law against domestic violence. This legislation has been in place since 1998 and aims to protect women against physical, psychological and sexual harm and property damage resulting from intimate partner abuse. Violence is categorised here as physical violence, psychological harm, sexual violence and violence against property. The act outlines safety measures designed to stop the violence and prevent further harm.

Nevertheless, psychological, physical and sexual violence remains widespread in Honduran society. Enforcement of the new legislation is hindered by sexism, patriarchal relationships between the sexes, ignorance of formal legislation and male chauvinism within the predominantly male judiciary. Moreover, wide sections of the population regard domestic violence as a private matter and even as a so-called "peccadillo".

In response, the NGO Centro de Derechos de Mujeres has made a detailed inventory of the new law's application, so as to detect gaps between the legislation and its application. By drawing attention to these inconsistencies, the study seeks to promote the development of a legal process that is fair and capable of enforcing the victims' claims against the perpetrator.

The analysis was based on the experiences of 120 women clients at the centre, all of whom have been victims of violence. The women were prepared for their court proceedings and were given legal representation and psychological counselling.

The findings were discussed in seminars and expert discussions with judges, psychologists, doctors and social workers. These groups were sensitised to the new violence protection legislation and worked to identify the necessary steps to remedy existing implementation problems. These resources included information such as how to file a claim and how to receive child support.

Furthermore a handbook was developed for judges, which drew on CDM's experience of the cases it handled. The handbook contains detailed references about applying the law on domestic violence and aims to make it easier for the judge to reconstruct and handle the case, starting with the first indictment and continuing right up to the hearing of witnesses.

CDM forms part of the special "Inter-Institutional Commission for Monitoring Enforcement of the Law against Domestic Violence". Based on CDM's experiences, the Commission formulated a proposal for a reform of the law, which was recently presented to the congress for approval. The proposal maintains the basic principles of the law but clarifies procedure, improves certain aspects of it's application, and contemplates a more severe treatment for men who fail to comply with the measures imposed by judges.

In many countries, social norms and beliefs are often at odds with the state law, and this contributes to difficulties enforcing new legal standards. For example, female genital mutilation is still performed on two million girls and young women every year, even though legislation criminalising it exists in many countries. International conventions and action plans condemn FGM as a human rights violation and a violation of the rights of the child. The focus should be on changing attitudes of men and women of different ages, religious leaders, local leaders, nurses, doctors etc.

In countries where the reality of women is shaped by customary law, synergies should be fostered between formal legal reforms and customary rules that are consistent with human rights provisions.

According to the 1995 constitution, women in *Ethiopia* enjoy equal rights with men. However in practice, women gain few benefits from this proclamation. This is especially true in rural areas, where 85% of the population live and where most people still relate to traditional norms and customs. Harmful practices like female genital mutilation (FGM), abduction, and domestic violence are common and most men and women are unaware of the statutory laws prohibiting these forms of violence. Legal problems and most conflicts are taken to traditional courts or to elders' councils that consist primarily of men.

In this context, the local NGO HUNDEE and the bilateral German–Ethiopian Gender and Law Project Oromiya (GALPO) have been applying a cultural-sensitive approach that contributed to social change through local-level dialogue. The choice of working from within the culture arose out of an appreciation of the inadequacies of the modern legal system in protecting women from various forms of violence and abuses and an acknowledgement of the fact that culture and tradition embrace mechanisms for protecting women and girls from gender-based violence.

The approach developed by HUNDEE encompasses a number of stages. In the first step, in consultation with representatives of various government authorities at district level about 100 female and 100 male potential multipliers are identified, including local opinion leaders, traditional authorities, village elders, judges in sharia courts, and representatives of the local police, judiciary and the women's office. The women's workshops often develop into forums in which individual experiences of violence are aired in public for the first time and are recognised there as a social and structural problem.

In the moderated discussion processes the participants explore and critically illuminate the sources from which gender-based discrimination and violence derive; which elements of these practices can indeed be considered to be 'authentic' features of Oromo culture, and which of these constitute more recent manifestations instead. The village elders contribute to reawakening awareness of almost forgotten institutions, which in earlier times assured Oromo women of certain rights within the family they marry into. On the other hand they make it clear that certain practices that are today referred to as 'traditional' are relatively modern developments, as is the case with the abduction of brides or enormously inflated bride price payments. Given this historical perspective it becomes apparent that norms and practices change, and that there is no unambiguously predefined, unalterable framework of values. This insight was a key eye-opener for the people involved. The objective here is to reach a consensus on what practices and norms are considered to be worth preserving in their own culture and which should be revised.

Within the framework of these mixed workshops, jointly supported proposals are put forward for reforming local legal practices, after lengthy, lively and controversial debate. This outcome, i.e. the formal adjustment of local legal norms, was not envisaged at the start of the process, but rather emerged in the course of events as a result of the dialogue workshops. The proposals for reform that emerge in the framework of these processes are applicable to an area covering about 30 villages and take different forms in each case.

They often encompass the following issues:

— The banning of forced marriages for girls and women
— Specifying a minimum age of 16 for girls to be married
— Prohibition of bride abduction
— Prohibition of female genital mutilation
— Setting the bride price to a moderate amount.

The specific reform proposals are subsequently presented at public community conferences, where they are debated until an agreement is reached on the various legal adjustments. The final step is the performance of the "*seera tumaa*" ceremony, in other words the public completion of the new law-making process:

This public ceremony is often attended by several thousand people. In addition to the local population, the district administration, community administration and representatives of the police, judiciary and the women's offices are also present. They actively support and welcome the alignment of local and national law.

The approach developed by HUNDEE was picked up and further pursued in a bilateral project commissioned by the BMZ and implemented by the GTZ (GALPO). The GALPO team integrated representatives of the state judiciary and police and of the women's offices into its work even more closely than HUNDEE had done, and trained them to become multipliers and trainers themselves, who then each continue with the HUNDEE approach at the lower administrative level.

The work carried out by HUNDEE and GALPO has certainly not led to a complete transformation of the relationship between men and women over a wide area nor to an end of most forms of discrimination against woman and girls. It is also true that there has been resistance and setbacks. But in a total of about 30 districts for the first time a broad public debate was held about the rights of women and girls, and there are many documented individual cases, which provide evidence of the beginnings of a change of attitudes. This became possible as a result of changed attitudes by traditional authority figures and the affected parents, but also by the police and public prosecutor's office, and through active collaboration between the various parties concerned. There are quite a number of individual examples of parents who have not had their daughters circumcised and many committed male and female multipliers who perform educational work on the damaging effects of the circumcision of girls. Even if these are still only individual cases, they do have a high symbolic value and create waves.

Many women and men have developed an awareness that violence against women and girls in its various forms is neither consistent with the original elements of the Oromo culture nor with the national constitution. Many of the women involved in the discussion processes have joined together in groups, have gained self-confidence and defend themselves in the event of experiencing violence. Some of them, meanwhile – a complete novelty in the entire region – have become members of political bodies at the local level and of the elders' councils in their villages, where among other things they are involved in conflict mediation processes.

References

Chang, Das (1987). "Violence against Women in the family: a national and international perspective." *International Journal of Comparative & Applied Criminal Justice*, 11:153-7.

Elder, Betty G. (1986). "The Rights of Women: Their Status in International Law." *Crime and Social Justice*; 1986, 25, 1-39.

Freeman, Marsha A.(1994). "Women, law, and land at the local level: claiming women's human rights in domestic legal systems." *Human Rights Quarterly* v16, n3 (August, 1994):559-575.

Lederman, Joanne; Chow, Esther Ngan ling (1996). *Gender-Based Violence and International Human Rights: Women Claim Their Humanity*. American Sociological Association Paper, Washington, DC.

Nelson, Toni (1996). "Violence against women." *World Watch* v9, n4 (July-August, 1996):33.

6

Human Rights of Migrant Women

The impacts of migration on development are becoming more and more present in policy debates at both regional and international levels. Issues pertaining to migrants' rights are linked to the protection of lives and the dignity of migrants, where protecting their rights would contribute to their empowerment.

Female migrant workers engaged in domestic services are one of the most vulnerable groups of migrant workers. In host countries, many female migrants are employed in relatively low-skilled jobs within the manufacturing, domestic service or entertainment sectors, often without legal status and little access to health services. They are often subject to exploitation and/or physical and sexual violence by their employers or clients. Migrant domestic workers have become increasingly important in the labour force of receiving countries and regions. Domestic work is one area where women receive little protection and low wages, despite its contributions to economic and social development. These women and girls often lack knowledge of their rights, further heightening their vulnerability due to the lack of national legal mechanisms recognizing or protecting their rights.

Domestic workersfind themselves vulnerable to abuse in a system that leaves them with almost no effective legal protection. Labour laws often exclude domestic workers due to not being considered as employees. Furthermore domestic workers are also excluded from both labour and social protection under other national laws. Consequently, they are often excluded from health insurance and other important social and labour protections.

Reasons of Migration

Migrant women move to marry, rejoin migrant husbands and family or to work. They are domestic workers, cleaners, caretakers of the sick, the elderly and of children. They are farmers, waitresses, sweatshop workers, highly skilled professionals, teachers, nurses, entertainers, sex workers, hostesses, refugees and asylumseekers. They are young and old, married, single, divorced and widowed. Many migrate with children. Others are forced to leave them behind. Some are educated and searching for opportunities more consistent with their qualifications. Others are from lowincome or poor rural backgrounds and are seeking a better life for themselves and their children.

Marriage

Marriage has played a significant role in female migration and still does. In today's globalized world, however, marriage migration has taken on an added dimension—the growing phenomenon of international unions, including mailorder brides and arranged and forced marriages.

Arranged marriages are quite common in some cultures, especially among émigrés from the Indian subcontinent, where both men and women migrate for this purpose. For many, arranged marriages can lead to a lifelong supportive partnership. But where a woman or girl's own wishes and human rights are disregarded, such unions can be more accurately described as "forced".

Governments of receiving countries are now struggling to come to grips with the issue. In 2004, the United Kingdom established a Forced Marriage Unit in a bid to halt the practice and provide support to victims. In Australia, recent legislation includes sentences of 25 years for anyone sending a minor abroad for marriage against her will. In Denmark, authorities have established a nationwide network of crisis centres for women and girls who have been forced into marriage. The French Government has also expressed concern and plans to curb the automatic recognition of foreign unions.

In Asia, there is also a high demand for foreign brides. Migration to Taiwan, Province of China, for the purpose of marriage is skyrocketing. Foreign brides, mostly from China and SouthEast Asia, now number about 300,000—half of the total foreign population. Since the 1990s, nearly 100,000 Vietnamese women have married Taiwanese men. There is also a surge in the numbers of women migrating to the Republic of Korea to marry local men. Nevertheless, even where marriage is "consensual", women from poorer countries still face unequal terms and conditions because these unions usually involve men from wealthier countries.

When it comes to the global trade in mailorder and internet brides, women, on the whole, are willing participants—whether out of a desire to find a supportive partner and economic security or as a means to gain legal entry into another country. The tradeoff, however, is that they are dependent for their legal status on their grooms-to-be. In this case, demand is also driving supply. In Russia, for example, nearly 1,000 agencies offer intermediary services, with an estimated 10,000 to 15,000 Russian women emigrating every year on fiancée visas: According to the Department of Justice, 80,000 have entered the United States in the past ten years. In addition, mail-order bride businesses can act as facades to recruit and traffic women— including those that send Russian women to toil in the sex industries in Germany, Japan and the United States. Worried about the possibility of abuse, the US passed a law in 2005 authorizing consulates to share information with would-be brides regarding their husbands-to-be.

Private Labour and Public Needs

Domestic work is one of the largest sectors driving international female labour migration. As more North American, Western European and East Asian women have entered the workforce, fewer are available to attend to the elderly, children and the infirm. In the United States, for example, the proportion of working women with children under the age of six soared from 15 per cent in 1950 to upwards of 65 per cent today. Despite the rapid entry of women into the labour force, a corresponding shift that would have more men carry an equal share of household responsibility has not occurred.

Furthermore, a lack of family-friendly policies and childcare facilities makes hiring nannies and domestic workers essential for those who can afford it. Indeed, two-income households have become a necessity where costs of living are high. More prosperous families, declining social benefits (owing to welfare reform and privatization) and increases in the longevity and size of the elderly population are also adding to the demand. These factors have all spurred massive outflows of women from Asia, Latin America and the Caribbean, and now also increasingly from Africa. In Spain, for example, approximately 50 per cent of annual immigrant quotas are designated for domestic workers. Most Asian domestic workers head to the

Middle East, where prosperity is driving demand. Domestic workers also move within regions, from poorer countries to richer ones.

For millions of women and their families, the "global care chain" offers considerable benefits, albeit with some serious drawbacks: i.e., separation from children and other loved ones. Aside from salaries that are several times higher than what they receive at home, international domestic workers also gain personal and social benefits, including improved educational and health opportunities for their children, gifts, extra cash to send back home and travel with employer families. In the case of Muslim domestic workers in the United Arab Emirates, the opportunity to make the pilgrimage to Mecca can lead to the fulfilment of a lifetime dream.

Entertainment, Hospitality and the Sex Industry

Globalization has resulted in an explosion in the entertainment and sex industries. These are providing additional migration channels for women—albeit largely owing to few other alternatives. In 2004, United Kingdom records revealed that the second largest category of work permit applications from foreign women were for "entertainment and leisure" at 5,908—with another 4,627 applying for "hospitality, catering" and "other" occupations. In Canada, over 1,000 temporary work permits a year were granted to exotic dancers in the mid-1990s. In 2004, Japan admitted nearly 65,000 women on entertainment visas, the majority of whom were from the Philippines. These high numbers (coupled with concerns over trafficking) have prompted the Government to review requirements for entertainers.

The boundary between "entertainment" (singers, dancers, hostesses) and sex work is often blurred— especially for those women who have been coerced and/or abducted. For instance, in 2004, more than 1,000 Russian women were engaged in sex work in the Republic of Korea. Most had entered the country on entertainment or tourist visas but were then forced into prostitution by business owners and recruiters.

Sex work is a lucrative business. Throughout the 1990s, it accounted for more than 2 per cent of the GDP in four South-East Asian countries. Sex workers circulate in Asia and Europe, and also move from Latin America to Europe and North America, and from Eastern to Western Europe. Given the largely unregulated and underground nature of these industries, actual numbers are hard to come by and are likely higher than available estimates. Many workers also remain in the host country once their visas have expired. Some estimates pin the numbers of women working in the illegal sex trade in the European Union at 200,000 and 500,000. Many have been trafficked.

Socio-economic Impacts of Female Migration

The money that female migrants send back home can raise families and even entire communities out of poverty. Of the more than US$1 billion in remittances sent back to Sri Lanka in 1999, women contributed over 62 per cent of the total. Of the roughly US$6 billion remitted annually to the Philippines in the late 1990s, migrant women transferred one third. Because they typically receive less pay for equal work (or are employed in sectors that offer poor remuneration), the total women remit may be less in comparison to men. Available data, however, shows that women send a higher *proportion* of their earnings—regularly and consistently.

A 2000 study by the United Nations International Research and Training Institute for the Advancement of Women (INSTRAW) and the International Organization for Migration (IOM) shows that Bangladeshi women working in the Middle East send home 72 per cent of their earnings on average. The same study reveals that 56 per cent of female remittances were used for daily needs, health care or education—a pattern which reflects the spending priorities of migrant women elsewhere. This is largely because women are more inclined to invest in their children than men, and, in more traditional societies, they tend to lack control over financial decision-making, assets and property.

Men, on the other hand, tend to spend remittance income on consumer items, such as cars and television sets, and for investments, such as property and livestock. One study of Ghanaian migrant women in Toronto, however, revealed that many were planning to build homes in their country of origin (56 per cent had already begun the process). In the Dominican Republic, another survey found that 100 per cent of the women returning from Spain established their own businesses.

Remittances would have an even greater role in poverty reduction and development if women did not face wage, employment, credit and property discrimination and if they were not excluded from decisionmaking within the family and in hometown organizations.

Another deterrent for poorer women is that traditional banks tend to charge hefty user fees. Some institutions are working to lower transfer costs and are enabling women to retain control over their remittances and further their uses for productive activities and development. These include Fonkoze, the Haitian alternative bank whose clientele is 96 per cent women; ADOPEM in the Dominican Republic, an affiliate of the Women's World Banking Network; the Inter American Development Bank (IADB); and the Bangladeshi Ovhibashi Mohila Sramik Association (BOMSA), established by returning migrant women.

The international community has also been looking more closely at the issue of female migrant remittances in order to understand how best to maximize their contributions for socioeconomic development. This includes recent efforts by INSTRAW and UNFPA to strengthen research and policy dialogue.

Beyond financial remittances, the *social remittances* of migrant women (ideas, skills, attitudes, knowledge, etc.) can also boost socioeconomic development and promote human rights and gender equality. Migrant women who send money transmit a new definition of what it means to be female. This can affect how families and communities view women. Women abroad also play a role when it comes to promoting the rights of their counterparts back home. A good example of this is the vigorous lobbying undertaken by Afghan expatriate women to promote greater female participation in the new constitution of their home country. In Belgium, Congolese expatriates supported their countrywomen in the struggle for increased National Assembly representation in the firstever free elections in the Democratic Republic of the Congo.

Women living abroad often acquire attitudes, opinions and knowledge that can lead to enhanced family health in the home country. A World Bank report attributes improved child health and lower mortality rates to the health education that female migrants receive while living abroad. This was found to hold true for families in Guatemala, Mexico and Morocco. Furthermore, these health benefits are more likely to result when mothers migrate as opposed to fathers.

Collective remittances—those pooled by diaspora associations—are rarely aimed explicitly at improving the lives of women. One exception is the Netherlands Filipino Association Overseas. Members provide collective remittances to support poor women through microcredit programmes and the development of small enterprises. Another is an association of Mexican expatriates in the United States that sends funds to Michoacan State in

Mexico. The local Government uses these donations to train women to produce school uniforms that are then sold to the Chamber of Commerce for distribution throughout the country. In general, however, as research into Latin American migrant hometown associations in the United States demonstrates, migrant women are often excluded from decisionmaking both on the sending and receiving end. Men manage most of the associations in host and destination countries, while women take on secretarial, fundraising and event organizing roles.

As more women migrate abroad, increasing numbers are establishing their own migrant networks that are transferring skills and resources and are sparking transformations in traditional notions of appropriate gender roles. In Germany, selforganized immigrant women's groups have been instrumental in battling trafficking, fighting racism and advocating for the independent legal status of migrant spouses. Women's groups also successfully lobbied authorities to make forced marriage illegal among the country's 2.5 million Turkish immigrants. Through IOM's Migration for Development in Africa programme, Guinean women living overseas are assisting impoverished women back home to develop and establish microenterprises. Since 1993, African women living in France have formed a network of migrant associations that aims to facilitate integration into host societies and improve the quality of life in countries of origin.

Impact of Migration on Gender Roles and Equality

Migration can transform the traditional private and public roles of men and women. The relationship between migration and gender equality is, however, complex. While experiences vary, women who migrate alone (rather than as part of a family), who enter the country legally and work outside the home, are more likely to report a positive experience—especially if the move is permanent.

Where women migrate for family reunification, overzealous relatives may restrict social relations in an attempt to preserve cultural identity and "honour". This is particularly difficult for women and girls who have left behind an extended network of female relatives and friends on whom they can rely for emotional support. This kind of cultural isolation is more likely to occur among immigrant families and communities who feel marginalized and believe their cultural identity is being challenged by the dominant host society.

For many other migrant women, however, the migration experience is so positive that they may be reluctant to return home for fear of having to relinquish their newfound autonomy. Male migrants, on the other hand, are sometimes more likely to express the desire to return. Studies of migrants from the Dominican Republic and Mexico living in the United States illustrate the point. While work can hold the key to increased independence for women, their husbands may face downward mobility and wind up in lowerskill jobs. Women migrants were also found to be more likely to integrate faster, owing to contact with local institutions (such as schools and social services), and were more likely to become US citizens.

When a male head of household migrates abroad, some women gain a greater say in how household funds are used even though they are still dependent on remittances. In Kerala, India, for example, women who stayed behind reported that remittances from their husbands in the Gulf States raised their authority and status: 70 per cent had opened their own bank accounts, 40 per cent had their own income, and half held land or homes in their own names.

However, when remittances are meagre or dry up altogether, women compensate for lost income—usually through paid work or the establishment of a small business. Despite additional stress and responsibility, this, too, can lead to greater autonomy and status. During the 1980s and 1990s, as destination country economies contracted and remittance income dried up, African women took control of farming and contributed more to family income. However, when immigrant husbands abandon their wives altogether, the consequences can be dire—particularly where women are stigmatized for being alone, barred from owning property and land, or are unable to secure work.

Migration affects traditional male roles as well. A study of former Bangladeshi male migrants to Singapore revealed that, once home—and contrary to customary practice—many selected their own wives, and, in some cases, treated them in a more equitable manner based on overseas experience. When men are left behind, they, too, can adjust to and accept new roles. One study of migrant Indonesian females found that many reported that their husbands were more respectful and took greater responsibility for childcare. In the United States, husbands of Dominican migrants were more likely to help with household chores and spend more time at home rather than with friends. Nonetheless, for men who stay behind, the migration of their wives can also be an affront to traditional notions of male identity and authority.

Discriminatory Immigration Policies

The experiences of migrant women are as diverse as the backgrounds they come from and the communities to which they move. While migration has many benefits, it does not come without challenges.

Right from the start, discriminatory immigration policies can limit legal migration channels. This relegates many women to the most vulnerable labour sectors or as dependents of male migrants. In the worst cases, they may windup as trafficking victims. Most women migrants come from countries where discrimination against females is deeply embedded in the social and cultural fabric. This places many at a disadvantage which can in turn result in inadequate access to information regarding work opportunities in destination countries, costs, benefits and steps necessary to migrate legally and safely. Soliciting the aid of another person or smuggler may place a woman in considerable debt and danger.

During transit, female—and, in particular, unauthorized—migrants risk sexual harassment and abuse. They may be coerced into providing sexual favours in exchange for protection or permission to pass through frontiers. For example, researchers conducting a study of migrant women travelling alone through Central America en route to Mexico found that males perceived them to be "ready for anything". Male migrants often forced female migrants to have sex with border authorities in order to guarantee safe passage for the entire group. In 2005, Médecins Sans Frontières reported that security officers and fellow migrants were sexually abusing subSaharan.

African women and minors while they transited through Morocco to Spain. Women along the Moroccan-Algerian border are also vulnerable—particularly to smugglers and traffickers intent on sexually exploiting them. Unsafe abortions are not uncommon, and incidents of pregnant women being deposited and abandoned at the Moroccan-Algerian border were also registered. Anecdotal evidence suggests that as many as 50 per cent of female migrants making the trip from West Africa to Europe via Morocco are either pregnant or are travelling with small children. Many give birth unattended in the forest for fear of being deported should they seek medical services.

Upon arrival in the destination country, female migrants are doubly disadvantaged—both as migrants and as women—and sometimes triply so, when race, class or religion are factored in. Those suffering abuse and violence may have no idea of what their rights are, and may fear repercussions if they contact the police or seek support services. Women also have priority needs in the area of reproductive health and rights, but legal, cultural or language barriers mean that many have difficulty accessing information and services.

Sending and receiving country policies affect who will migrate and how. Sometimes discrimination is inadvertent, while in other situations, women may dominate in certain migration streams such as nursing and domestic work, but specific needs and rights may go ignored. Some policies result in the exclusion of female migrants altogether. Other policies—often well meaning and aimed at increasing employment opportunities—nonetheless ignore multiple work, family and community responsibilities. In the absence of childcare and extended family networks, these can prevent women from partaking in skills training or other educational opportunities open to migrants.

A country's particular labour needs directly affect to what degree men and women are likely to find work abroad and whether they can migrate legally. Traditionally, policies that invited migrants on a temporary basis to fill gaps in specific sectors tended to favour maledominated occupations. Since the 19th century discovery of gold and diamonds in South Africa, for example, male migrants have been in high demand. In South Africa, citizens of the 14 Southern African Development Community (SADC) countries are most likely to find legal work within the mining industry, where 99 per cent of employees are men. No equivalent employment sector that facilitates entry for women exists. By contrast, South African commercial farmers prefer female workers from neighbouring countries, but because crossborder migration is typically irregular, female labour migrants remain unprotected by existing laws. While industrialization in Asia has required labourers for construction, manufacturing and plantation work ("men's work"), women have been more likely to fill the demand for domestic and childcare support.

When destination countries prefer skilled candidates, implications for migrant women can cut both ways. Women of low socioeconomic and educational status can be at a serious disadvantage. They are more likely to wind up toiling in informal, irregular and seasonal jobs, with fewer possibilities to obtain work permits or citizenship entitlements. In France, for example, one study found that women constitute twothirds of those refused citizenship on the grounds of insufficient linguistic knowledge. Entry for skilled workers can also be based on criteria, such as proof of years of uninterrupted work, language or of income and educational level. These unintentionally discriminate against women. On the other hand, the demand for skilled labour can also open up opportunities for bettereducated women to migrate, as was the case during the 1980s when Australia shifted from a preference for manual labourers to that of professionals.

Governments sometimes restrict female migration in order to "protect" women. Such bans on female migrants have been in place, for example, in Bangladesh, the Islamic Republic of Iran, Nepal and Pakistan. Bangladesh government data show that less than 1 per cent of those emigrating between 1991 and 2003 were women. This was largely owing to greater restrictions and bureaucratic hurdles that made it more difficult for women to emigrate. These, needless to note, only increase the likelihood that women will resort to irregular methods. A case in point: According to the Asian Development Bank, the Gulf States and South-East Asia are home to considerable numbers of undocumented Bangladeshi women.

Government policies, however, have recently begun to change. In 2005, Bangladesh lifted the ban and, in the same year, the Nepalese Supreme Court ended the requirement of parental or spousal consent for a woman under the age of 35 to obtain a passport.

Labour laws tend to exclude certain sectors of the economy in which women migrants predominate—such as domestic work and the entertainment industry. This leaves many female migrant workers dependant on employers for legal status, basic needs such as housing and food, and the payment of due wages, which employers may arbitrarily withhold in order to ensure compliance. In addition, government efforts to curtail immigration and thus restrict it to temporary, shortterm contracts means that many women are unable to change employers. This can trap them into abusive situations, outside the public view, and, in many cases, beyond the purview of public policies.

Rights, terms of employment and working conditions vary according to the labour laws and immigration policies in each receiving country. In many countries, for example, the rights of domestic workers are neglected, and many spend years abroad before ever seeing their families. Host country regulations often prohibit lowskilled migrants from bringing family members with them. This is prompting calls for family-friendly policies that will support female migrant workers. Italy and Spain are among the very few countries that grant unskilled workers the possibility of family reunification— a privilege usually reserved for "skilled" migrants. They are also among the few countries that have actively furthered domestic worker rights, largely owing to the vigorous lobbying on the part of women's organizations.

Dependency Trap

Women who migrate under family reunification schemes usually enter as dependents and may enjoy only limited access to employment, health care and other social services. In countries that distinguish between the rights of migrants to work or to reside, women entering as dependents may only be able to work illegally. Dependent status can also result in "brain waste". This occurs when skilled female migrants remain unemployed or are able to find work only in occupations far below their qualifications. Furthermore, if the marriage founders, or if the relationship is abusive, migrant women may find themselves trapped by threats of deportation or the loss of custodial rights. Children also suffer from the absence of material and emotional support when fathers abandon the family or the marriage dissolves. Granting abused women migrants independent legal status, such as Sweden and the United States have done—rather than keeping it contingent on male relatives or husbands—helps protect their rights and frees them from violence.

Work and Wages

The proportion of immigrant women who are in the labour force varies by country, yet unemployment is generally higher for immigrant women. In many cases this is true in comparison to native men and women—as well as fellow male migrants. For example, in 17 OECD countries (for which data are reported), unemployment rates for foreign women are substantially higher than the rate for native women. Among immigrants from SADC countries living in South Africa, 38 per cent of female immigrants were unemployed as compared to 33 per cent of female natives, 30 per cent of male natives and 23 per cent of male migrants.

Where migrant women face high unemployment rates and discrimination, many are forced to take whatever work is available. This can contribute to host population perceptions that migrant women are "unskilled", though many may actually be better qualified than their work implies. In some cases, however, migrants may be offered the opportunity to move up the pay scale: In the United Arab Emirates (UAE), Filipina domestic workers are increasingly being employed as drivers—a job with higher salaries and greater benefits.

Relative to the status of women in their home countries, newcomers may earn higher wages. Compared to women in the receiving country, however, they are likely to be far worse off. Lower earnings can lead to impoverishment and can negatively impact families left behind owing to less remittance income. Data from the 2000 United States Census Bureau shows that 18.3 per cent of the foreignborn women live in poverty, compared to 13.2 per cent of the nativeborn women, and that 31 per cent of the femaleheaded migrant households are poor. Low wages can also affect family reunification for female migrants who are the sole sponsors of relatives. This is because many countries, such as Canada and the United States, require proof of sponsorship based on income and economic self-sufficiency.

Low wages can have dire implications for older migrant women—especially for those who are underemployed, undocumented, widows or working in jobs without benefits. Pension plans and other social programmes in receiving countries, such as Canada and the United States, are based on longterm paycheque contributions. In addition, a lifetime of irregular labour means many older migrants are without savings for retirement or health care. In many European countries, pension entitlements are based on years of work and residency. The increasing number of older migrants within the region is sparking particular concern for the needs of elderly immigrant women. In the Netherlands, more than 90 per cent of Moroccan women aged 55 years and above report never having worked. In Austria, immigrant non-EU women have the lowest earnings in the country. Among those 60 years and older, 19 per cent from the former Yugoslavia and 23 per cent from Turkey had no income of their own whatsoever.

Ethnicity and Racism

Ethnicity and class compound the problem of gender discrimination, stymie advancement and result in lower wages. For example, in the United Kingdom (which has long relied on immigrants to fill health-care jobs) harassment is widespread with black staff (mostly Caribbean women) largely concentrated in the lower grades. In the UAE, a college-educated domestic worker from the Philippines earns much more than her counterpart from India—regardless of the latter's skills. One European study found that when fellow nationals undertake domestic work—as opposed to foreigners—they tend to be treated as professionals. The United States provides one example of how domestic work is divided along ethnic and racial lines. During the 1950s and 1960s, African-American women dominated the occupation but by the end of the 1980s, their numbers had dropped dramatically throughout the country. Around that same time, foreign-born Latin American women stepped in to fill the breach—from 9 per cent to 68 per cent in Los Angeles alone.

Sexual and Reproductive Health

The health of any migrant is affected by gender, socio-cultural and ethnic background, type of occupation and legal status, as well as the degree to which he or she can cover costs and access services, transportation and health insurance. Prior exposure to relevant health education and services will also affect a migrant's capacity to make informed health decisions.

If a migrant cannot speak the language, she or he is more likely to encounter problems accessing health care. Low-paying and exploitative labour also has an impact, as does the degree to which the migrant and his or her community are integrated into the mainstream society. Discrimination and racism on the part of healthcare providers only adds to cultural and linguistic barriers.

Both the host country itself and immigrant women will benefit from improved access to reproductive health information and services—including pregnancy-related services and the prevention and treatment of HIV and other sexually transmitted infections. However, migrant women often come from countries where poor health is a fact of life. Many possess little information regarding health matters and tend to be poorer and less educated than their native counterparts. Health status may be further compromised by the stress of adjusting to a new country and/or violence and sexual exploitation.

Pregnancy-related problems among migrants have been a major problem throughout the EU, where studies have found that migrants receive inadequate or no antenatal care and exhibit higher rates of stillbirth and infant mortality. One United Kingdom study found that social exclusion and being non-white were among the main predictors of severe maternal morbidity. Other research in the country reveals that babies born of Asian women had lower birth weights and that perinatal and post-natal mortality rates were higher among Caribbean and Pakistani immigrants than in the general population. Hospital-based studies also show that African women delivering in France and Germany had higher rates of pregnancy complications and perinatal death than their native counterparts. Turkish immigrants in Germany also had higher rates of perinatal and neonatal mortality, and rates of maternal mortality tended to be higher overall among immigrant women. In Spain, premature births, low birth weight and delivery complications are especially common among African and Central and South American migrants.

Immigrant women often have a higher incidence of unplanned pregnancies owing to poor access and a lack of information regarding contraceptives and how to obtain them. Research in Latin America shows that migrant women report more unintended pregnancies, have lower contraceptive use and generally utilize reproductive health services less often than do non-immigrants. Throughout Western Europe the story is the same. In Germany, researchers attribute low contraceptive use to the fact that programmes are geared towards German speakers and that immigrants often come from countries where family planning information is simply not available. Sociocultural pressures may also prevent migrant women from accessing services for fear of being discovered by family members.

Higher abortion rates among immigrants reflect women's limited decisionmaking power and lack of access to quality family planning services. In Spain, requests for abortions tend to be twice as common among immigrant women—especially those from North and sub-Saharan Africa. In Norway, non-western women account for more than one quarter of all abortion requests—although they represent only 15 per cent of the population. In one Italian region, a study found that foreign-born women were three times more likely to undergo an induced abortion than local women.

Culturally Sensitive Care

Socio-cultural factors can influence migrant reproductive health status, including pregnancy and childbirth outcomes and access to family planning services. Women from more traditional backgrounds are often embarrassed when dealing with male medical personnel—a problem when it comes to accessing reproductive and obstetric healthcare services. In Denmark, studies show that poor communication between migrants and healthcare providers, coupled with insufficient use of trained interpreters, is a key cause of poor and delayed gynaecological care. In Sweden, one study found that young, single immigrant women with children were more likely to register late (more than 15 weeks) at prenatal care centres. The study concluded that training staff in transcultural skills and providing them with interpreters could result in improved care. In Sao Paulo, doctors report that maternal and infant mortality rates among Bolivian migrant women are far higher—the latter by 3 to 4 times—than among local women. Migrants often decline caesarean section—a lifesaver in the event of obstructed labour— because in some indigenous cultures it implies a loss of femininity that can prompt the husband to desert his spouse. In response, the Municipal Health Secretariat is working to refine its programme, including providing outreach in the Quechua and Aymara languages.

Nonetheless, despite increased risks and obstacles to accessing health care, exposure to new childbearing and female decisionmaking norms can be empowering. Indeed, in some cases, female migrants gain access to reproductive health information and services for the very first time.

Female Migrants and HIV

Data on HIV infection rates among international migrants are scarce. The alarming "feminization" of the pandemic, however, is well documented and speaks to what can transpire when the rights of women are neglected en masse.

Physiological, social and cultural factors mean that women and girls face particularly high risks of contracting HIV and other STIs throughout the migration process. Undocumented migrant women who become stranded in transit countries *en route* to their intended destination and are unable to work may be forced into "survival sex" in exchange for basic commodities or food. This increases the likelihood of infection.

Sexual violence makes them even more vulnerable. In one South African study, female migrant farm workers from Mozambique and Zimbabwe were found to be particularly susceptible to HIV infection owing to sexual violence. About 15 per cent of those surveyed reported having been raped or knowing someone who had been raped or sexually harassed while working on farms. Most were too fearful of losing their jobs to report violence. According to interviewees, male Zimbabweans were the main perpetrators.

The vulnerability of migrant women is borne out by some grim statistics. According to UNAIDS, in France, 69 per cent of all HIV diagnoses attributed to heterosexual contact during 2003 occurred among immigrants—65 per cent of whom were women. In Costa Rica, one service organization found that 40 per cent of the women treated for sexually transmitted infections were immigrants. In Sri Lanka, the Government reported that, for every one male migrant that tested positive in 2002, there were a corresponding seven females. Although the causes behind this gross disparity have not been established, researchers suggest that sexual abuse by employers and exploitation in so-called domestic worker "safe" houses could be factors. To minimize the risks of infection, the Government (with support from UNAIDS and WHO) has established HIV/AIDS awareness pre-departure orientation sessions aimed at migrant women.

Seasonal and circular migration, whereby individuals leave their homes and then return home, can also con-tribute to HIV transmission. One study undertaken in Senegal revealed that migrants have unprotected sex while abroad and then infect their wives upon return. Women without adequate support from migrant husbands also turn to sex work for survival while their spouses are abroad.

When male migrants become infected with HIV, remittances often dry up—either through job loss or because they have to spend more of their income on health care. According to UNAIDS, women may resort to transactional sex or will migrate themselves in order to make up for lower remittances and provide for family members. A country with one of the highest HIV prevalence rates in the world (33.5 per cent), Botswana is witnessing decreased remittances from husbands with AIDS-related illnesses. This leaves women—usually older—shouldering the care of orphaned children.

Violence against Women and Harmful Practices

Gender-based violence is the ultimate manifestation of unequal relations between men and women. Owing to their status as women and as foreigners (in addition to race and ethnicity), migrant women face disproportionate risks of physical abuse and violence at home, in the streets or in their places of work. So profound is the problem, that the UN Secretary-General now issues reports exclusively focused on the topic.

Gender-based violence is not only a violation of human rights, but also threatens health, productivity and social and economic integration into the host society. Some immigrants also come from cultures that maintain harmful practices such as female genital mutilation/cutting, forced marriages and so-called "honour killings".

While there is a notable dearth of data on violence against migrant women, smaller studies indicate a high incidence of abuses. In Mexico, a recent study revealed that 46 per cent of migrant women had suffered from some sort of violence, with 23 per cent reporting that customs officials were the main perpetrators; federal police followed next at 10 per cent; judiciary and municipal police at 10 per cent; and, finally, the armed forces at 6 per cent. According to the Sri Lanka Bureau for Employment, in 2001, over 1,600 women reported harassment in their workplaces overseas.

Domestic violence knows no boundaries. It permeates every society, group and income level worldwide: between 10 per cent of women in some countries, and 69 per cent in others, are the victims of domestic abuse. The strains of moving to a new environment, unemployment, inadequate wages and racism can lead to frustration that finds its outlet in the abuse of female partners.

One survey found that 31 per cent of abused Latin American female immigrants reported increased violence from their partners since moving to the United States and 9 per cent reported that abuse began after migration. Studies indicate that domestic violence among immigrant groups is markedly higher than the estimated 22.1 per cent lifetime rate in the general American population. Rates of sexual and physical abuse against immigrant women surveyed ranged from 30 to 50 per cent among Latin American, South Asian and Korean groups. A study of highly-educated middle-class South Asian women living in Boston revealed that nearly 35 per cent had experienced physical abuse and 19 per cent had experienced sexual abuse at the hands of their male partner. And a New York City health report cited that 51 per cent of female homicides by intimate partners occurred among foreign-born women, compared to 45 per cent among the native population. In Germany, a Government study found that 49 per cent of married Turkish women had experienced physical or sexual violence.

Migrant women who come from societies where domestic abuse is largely accepted as a "normal" aspect of gender relations are unlikely to seek help from police or access other services—especially if they fear deportation or retribution from their abusers. According to domestic violence data in Colombia, Nicaragua and Peru, migrant women are less likely to seek assistance from the police and health facilities compared to their native counterparts. And none of the women who reported abuse sought any medical attention whatsoever.

Similarly, a nationally representative survey in Canada found that immigrant and "visible minority" women (68 per cent of them immigrants) who reported abuse were less likely to seek services than the general population. Other factors, such as cultural, linguistic and social isolation, make it less likely that migrant women will seek assistance even where social protection and legal redress exist. This is especially the case when they are unaware of their rights. Research in the United States shows immigrant women tend to stay in abusive relationships longer than nativeborn Americans and suffer graver physical and emotional consequences as a result.

Women with children who migrate as dependents of their husbands are often unfairly forced to choose between their own personal safety and maintaining their legal status. The United States has amended legislation allowing migrant women who have suffered domestic violence to secure legal status irrespective of their partners. Sweden allows immigrant women who are victims of abuse by their Swedish partner to obtain a permanent residence permit. In 2003, 99 per cent of the requests for residence permits received from domestic violence victims were approved.

Azerbaijan, Belize, El Salvador, Indonesia and Jamaica report that they are training government officials, police officers, social workers, community leaders and other professionals to address more effectively the issue of violence against women migrant workers. NGOs in countries hosting large migrant populations have also been working to meet the diverse needs of women who suffer from domestic abuse. One example is the Vancouver-based organization, MOSAIC, which works with both men and women to prevent abuses and to address the mental, physical and psychological needs of female victims. The organization also offers small group sessions conducted in Hindi, Punjabi, Urdu and English to Indian and Pakistani migrant men to help them to take responsibility for, and end, their abusive behaviour.

Female Genital Mutilation/Cutting

Approximately 2 million women and girls every year are at risk of female genital mutilation/cutting (FGM/C)— a traditional practice that involves the partial, or total, removal of external genitalia. The practice has spread through migration, outward from 28 countries in Africa and others in Southern Asia and the Middle East to Europe, North and South America, Australia and New Zealand. In the United Kingdom alone, researchers estimate that approximately 3,000 to 4,000 girls are "cut" each year. An additional 86,000 firstgeneration immigrant women and girls have already undergone the procedure.

According to the 2000 United States census, 881,300 African migrants come from countries where FGM/C is widely practiced. This does not include refugees and asylumseekers (totalling an estimated 50,000 in 2000), many of whom came from Eritrea, Ethiopia, Somalia and Sudan, countries with some of the highest FGM/C prevalence in the world. Female genital mutilation/cutting is a human rights issue that can cause short and longterm physical and mental health problems, including higher risks of deliveryrelated complications and infant mortality.

Policymakers in countries receiving immigrants from FGM/C countries face the challenge of establishing culturally sensitive approaches designed to halt the practice. At least 11 industrialized countries have already passed legislation that prohibits FGM/C. Many organizations, such as the British Medical Association and the Danish Health System and Midwife Schools, are striving to ensure that health providers are well equipped to care for women who have undergone the practice. Belgium, Germany and Sweden have also established medical guidelines. NGOs are also working with immigrant women and their communities to support the right to bodily integrity. The United States-based Sauti Yetu Center for African Women is undertaking a comprehensive approach that includes cross-cultural training for service providers and the establishment of a centre to document the practice in Western countries.

Dis'Honourable' Crimes

Crimes committed in the name of "honour" and "passion" are socially sanctioned practices that allow a man to kill, rape or otherwise abuse a female relative or partner for suspected or actual "immoral" behaviour— i.e., behaviour socially defined as bringing "shame" to the family or challenging male authority.In 2000, in the first United Nations General Assembly resolutions specifically dedicated to the issue, countries from around the world reiterated that crimes committed in the name of honour and of passion are egregious human rights abuses and reaffirmed their commitment—as embodied in international human rights instruments—to end them. In 2003, the European Parliamentary Assembly adopted a resolution calling on all Member States to "amend their national asylum and immigration laws to ensure that women have the right to residence permits and/or asylum if threatened with so-called 'honour crimes'". It also calls on members to, among other things, enforce "legislation more effectively to penalize all crimes committed in the name of honour".

In the UK, police are re-examining past records of 117 murders to determine how many were committed in the name of honour. And Sweden maintains a system that includes working through the education sector, government authorities, immigrant orientation sessions and NGOs on issues around prevention and protection. County Administrative Board reports found that at least 200 girls in each of three counties had contacted social services, other authorities or NGOs to help them escape honour-related violence during 2001.

Governments, parliamentarians, civil society organizations, the media and the UN System are increasingly paying attention to the social, cultural, economic and political implications of the international migration of women. An increasing body of data and research— although still limited—is making it possible to grasp the magnitude and as yet little-understood potential of migrant women to contribute to social and economic development and gender equality. Migrant women face serious risks and obstacles that can have severe repercussions and, in the most extreme cases, threaten their very survival. Yet the migration experience need not be fraught with hazard when it has proven to be such a positive experience for so many millions. Risks and challenges can be averted through stronger measures aimed at empowering migrant women and protecting their human rights. Others are intrinsic to the migration experience itself and relate to greater social and cultural understanding and to shifting norms regarding male and female roles. But solutions can, and are, increasingly being sought within a human rights and culturally sensitive framework. Though largely incipient, insufficient in scope and reach, these efforts offer insights into how the migration process can be improved for the benefit of women, their children, their families and the global community at large.

Exploitative Terms of Work

A number of forces combine to render women migrant workers vulnerable to exploitative terms of work, especially in relation to pay, hours of work, and contracts. Restrictions on the right to cross borders for work, for example, create incentives for legal and illegal agents alike to take advantage of women migrant workers. Recruitment agencies often charge steep fees for placement and travel; when working irregularly or without government oversight, such agencies often charge fees that are close to impossible to repay, trapping women migrants into conditions akin to debt bondage.

Regardless of their means of entry, women migrants face myriad types of exploitation, and contract problems abound. Women who actually receive a contract may not understand the language in which it is written. They may find the contract they sign is later replaced by an inferior version stripped of worker protections, or they may be refused a copy entirely. In some countries, aliens or women who have contracts may face legal or economic barriers in accessing courts or other judicial institutions, and host country courts may deem the contracts unenforceable.

Women migrant workers face a range of abuses connected with compensation. Even when paid on time and according to the terms of any contract they may have been given, women migrant workers are often paid substandard wages. Employers may deduct dubious or blatantly unfair charges, including fees for health services that are never received, or fees for rent in situations of squalor. Payments may be delayed, improperly calculated, or withheld arbitrarily. In some places, employment agencies offer domestic employers the option of "returning" a migrant worker after a period of time often as long as three months in some places if their services are deemed unsatisfactory. During the trial period, the employee is rarely paid, and once they are "returned" they must begin a new probationary period, during which they will again likely not receive pay. This kind of cycle in which the employee is working without wages has reportedly lasted more than a year in some countries. Exorbitant fees for breaking contracts may be imposed.

Women domestic workers often work in completely unregulated conditions: in some countries, those in the domestic sector do not count as "employees" under legal definitions. In such circumstances, employers take advantage of the vulnerability of women migrant workers by forcing or coercing them to work long hours, often without breaks or leisure time.

Even when regulations do apply, discriminatory rules exempting domestic workers from normal hour limits, or setting long limits may exist. Exceptions to overtime and holiday pay rules also frequently apply to domestic workers. Further, women working as domestics rarely have days off even in places where rest days are regulated, domestic workers may be exempted or subject to special rules allowing a single or half day of leisure instead of the standard number applicable to other workers. An ILO study conducted in one country found that not one of the women working as domestics surveyed benefited from a regular day off. One domestic worker explains: "We are treated like strangers, we are not allowed to sit on the furniture. It does not matter for them if you have a profession or not, you are here, you are a maid." Another domestic worker adds: "When they talk about us they say words like: stupid, knows nothing, or maid. We are always inferior in their place." And finally: "I am treated as a lower person because I am poor. They order us in a way that hurts. They don't sympathise with us. We are vulnerable in their houses, because we are poor."

The ILO explains that a major cause of exploitation and ultimately forced labor is that labor standards are not applied or enforced, in either countries of destination or origin. These standards include respect for minimum working conditions and consent to working conditions. Worse still is the absence of worksite monitoring, particularly in such already marginal sectors as agriculture, domestic service and sex-work, which would contribute to identifying whether workers may be in situations of forced or compulsory labor.

States in which women migrants find employment may be required to adopt a wide variety of measures to ensure that women's rights to fair terms of work are fully respected, protected, and fulfilled. Based on the treaties and the guidance provided by the treaty monitoring committees, it is now clear that states may be required to adopt a range of measures to fulfill their obligations, including the following examples:

— Undertake comprehensive studies on the employment situation of women migrants.

— States that exempt domestic or non-national workers from labor protections should take steps to extend labor protections including working hours and minimum wage standards to these groups.

— Although some fair and non-discriminatory amendments might be needed to account for specific differences in workplaces, regulatory schemes concerning working conditions and terms of employment should be made applicable to workers in domestic service.

— In places where regulations already apply to non-national and domestic workers, states should ensure that enforcement measures are effective, that monitoring takes place regularly, and that fines are imposed or licenses revoked wherever necessary.

— States must take proactive steps to ensure that women migrant workers are not trapped in debt bondage, and to remedy the situation when it does arise.

Restrictions on the Freedom of Movement

Women migrants who work in the domestic sector are especially vulnerable to violations of their freedom of movement. Those who employ domestic workers often confiscate the worker's travel documents often making it impossible for the worker to leave the country even to return home without permission. Many domestic workers live within the home, or on the same property as the employing family; often, the family forbids the worker from leaving the premises alone and sometimes the worker will not be allowed to leave at all. For example, the ILO found that a travel agency in one country masquerading as an overseas employment firm asked women domestic workers to sign employment contracts stating explicitly that they were not permitted to leave the employer's premises. Seclusion is often extreme in the case of undocumented domestic workers. Such women are often "hidden" in the homes of their employers to avoid detection by the authorities.

Many women working as domestic helpers are locked in the home by their employers whenever they are left alone – sometimes for extended periods. In addition to the routine problems this causes, many women in such circumstances report being terrified that a fire or some other emergency would occur and they would be unable to escape.

The social exclusion created by the cloistering of migrant women in domestic service can take a heavy toll: many women do not have the opportunity to form friendships or create community ties. The resulting solitude exacerbates women's vulnerability to abuse, and deprives them of possible support when violations occur. It also can lead to depression and other psychological difficulties. Women who are deprived of contact with their families may suffer especially severely, to say nothing of the impact on the workers' family members, especially children.

One domestic worker told ILO researchers that she became ill during her employment as a domestic helper and could no longer work. Her contract stated that she was required to pay US $3,000 if she left her place of employment before the term of her employment had expired. When this was rejected as too little, the woman fabricated a mental illness to escape. Her employer's male relatives, as well as the local police, beat the woman before letting her return home.

In addition to fees charged by some agencies and employers when women migrants break their contracts, governments sometimes impose exit fees for time spent in the country illegally. In such instances, women are charged for each day they spent out of status. The actions needed to protect the rights of women migrant workers to freedom of movement will depend on the severity and prevalence of abuses in each state. Based on the treaties and the guidance provided by the treaty monitoring committees, it is now clear that states may be required to adopt a range of measures to fulfill their obligations, including the following examples:

— States should ensure that all employers, agencies, and migrant workers themselves, are aware that it is completely forbidden for identity documents and work or residence papers to be confiscated or destroyed, and failure to obey should be investigated and punished.

— Sending and host states should review domestic legislation and practice to ensure that women's right to freedom of movement is not subject to the approval of third persons, such as husbands, fathers, or other male relatives.

— Women should be allowed to freely obtain their own individual identity, work, and residence papers.

— Arbitrary restrictions on the ability of migrant workers legally in the country of employment to freedom of movement within that country should be removed.

— Restrictions on the right of all migrant workers to leave a country, and arbitrary limits on the ability to enter the home country and remain there, should be repealed or amended.

— Host country governments should take steps to end restrictions imposed by private employers especially severe restrictions like locking in the home.

Human Rights Framework to Protect the Rights of Migrant Women

Through provisions on equal rights in employment, just and favorable working conditions, and equal protection under the law, the major human rights conventions offer robust protections for women migrant workers against exploitative terms of work.

The *Convention on the Elimination of All Forms of Discrimination Against Women* (CEDAW) guarantees women equal rights in employment, including: the same employment opportunities as men, the free choice of profession, and the right to promotion.

The *International Covenant on Economic, Social and Cultural Rights* (ICESCR) recognises the right to fair wages – defined in the Covenant as wages that, at a minimum, provide a decent living for the worker and her family. This right must be extended to women and men without discrimination, and includes the specific right to equal pay for equal work.

The *International Convention on the Elimination of All Forms of Racial Discrimination* (CERD) prohibits discrimination on the basis of race, color, or national or ethnic origin in work, free choice of employment, and just and favorable working conditions.

Under the *International Convention on Civil and Political Rights* (ICCPR), all individuals including aliens and citizens are guaranteed equality before the law, which means that aliens may not be treated differently in court based on their alien status.

This guarantee of equality is amplified in the *International Convention on the Protection of the Rights of All Migrant Workers and their Families* (MWC), which clearly requires states to ensure that migrant workers benefit from the same terms of work as nationals, including remuneration, hours of work, overtime pay, weekly rest, and holidays with pay.

Article 11(1) of the Convention on the Elimination of All Forms of Discrimination against Women guarantees women equal rights in employment, including the right to the same employment opportunities as men and the application of the same criteria for selection in matters of employment.

Article 7(a) of the International Covenant on Economic, Social and Cultural Rights recognises the right to the enjoyment of just and favorable conditions of work, including remuneration which provides all workers, at a minimum, with fair wages and equal remuneration for work of equal value without distinction of any kind, in particular women being guaranteed conditions of work not inferior to those enjoyed by men, with equal pay for equal work; and a decent living for themselves and their families. Article 2 calls on states to ensure that the rights included in the Convention are exercised without discrimination of any kind as to race, color, sex, language, religion, political or other opinion, national or social origin, property, birth or other status. Article 3 requires states to ensure the equal right of men and women to the enjoyment of all economic, social and cultural rights in the Convention.

Article 14 of the International Covenant on Civil and Political Rights provides that all people shall be equal before the courts and tribunals. In its General Comment on the Position of Aliens under the Covenant the Human Rights Committee emphasised that this guarantee of equality before the courts and tribunals applies to aliens, who must not be treated differently from citizens on the basis of their status. Article 8 provides that no one shall be held in slavery, and that no one shall be held in servitude or required to perform forced or compulsory labor.Article 2 provides that states must respect and ensure to all individuals within its territory and subject to its jurisdiction the rights included in the Convention, without distinction of any kind, such as race, color, sex, language, religion, political or other opinion, national or social origin, property, birth or other status. Article 26 provides that all persons are equal before the law, and are entitled without any discrimination to equal protection of the law. The law should prohibit discrimination and guarantee to all persons equal and effective protection against discrimination on any ground, including sex, race, color, national or social origin, or other status.

Article 5(e)(i) of the International Convention on the Elimination of All Forms of Racial Discrimination guarantees the rights to non-discrimination on the basis of race, color, or national or ethnic origin in work, to free choice of employment, to just and favorable conditions of work, to protection against unemployment, to equal pay for equal work, to just and favorable remuneration.

Article 11 of the International Convention on the Protection of the Rights of All Migrant Workers and their Families provides that no migrant worker or member of his or her family shall be held in slavery or servitude, and that no migrant worker or member of his or her family shall be required to perform forced or compulsory labor. Article 25 provides that migrant workers shall enjoy treatment not less favorable than that which applies to nationals of the state of employment in respect of remuneration and other conditions of work, including overtime, hours of work, weekly rest, holidays with pay, safety, health, termination of the employment relationship and any other conditions of work covered under domestic law. The same Article also requires states to take all appropriate measures to ensure that migrant workers are not deprived of any rights concerning remuneration and other conditions of work on the basis of irregularities in their work or residence status. Under Article 25, employers may not be relieved from obligations toward their workers on the basis of irregularities. Article 54(2) provides that if a migrant worker claims that the terms of his or her work contract have been violated by his or her employer, he or she shall have the right to address his or her case to the competent authorities of the state of employment on the basis of equality with nationals of that state.

Empowerment: An Alternative Perspective

Without doubt, women migrant workers are more vulnerable to exploitation than male migrant workers or female nationals of host countries. The challenge for human rights advocates, however, is how to view this situation – should women migrant workers be cast as victims or as possible agents of change? Should the international community look at issues faced by women migrant workers through a victimization perspective, or through a perspective of empowerment? Clearly, this paper argues for the integration of concepts such as agency and empowerment in the discourse on women migrant workers.

A rights-based approach involves "a process of enabling and empowering those not enjoying their economic, social, and cultural rights to *claim* their rights." Legal, policy, social, and other institutions must respect human rights, and ensure appropriate and enabling enforcement and monitoring mechanisms to give legal effect to these rights. Countries that have a strong respect for human rights have achieved this respect through internal struggle from the bottom up, not the top down. An empowerment perspective will allow women migrant workers, quite simply, to stake a claim to their human rights.

Advocates might turn to South and East Asian organizations for examples of effective empowerment perspectives. Grassroots organizations and other non-governmental organizations (NGOs) are a potential force for dramatic change in women migrant workers' rights. First, migrant workers are marginalized and vulnerable because of their temporary status in the society of the host countries, and secondly because governments, left alone, often lack the political will to protect or empower migrant workers. South and East Asia has emerged as a leader in migrant activism.

In the Philippines, for example, MIGRANTE is one of the most successful of the country's migrant worker NGOs. The Philippines has initiated comprehensive measures to protect Filipino/a overseas workers, in particular, laws, rules, and regulations that provide worker protection even in countries where labor enforcement is nonexistent or lax. MIGRANTE is grassroots-based and is staffed by former migrant workers. The organization addresses the root causes of migration in the Philippines, while member organizations outside the country protect overseas workers.

An empowerment perspective entails not just the grassroots action of women migrant workers. For human rights to be claimed, there must be policies or mechanisms through which workers can claim their rights. For an in-depth look at such policies, the paper now turns to UNIFEM's Regional Programme on Empowering Migrant Workers in Asia.

A strong proponent of an empowerment, rights-based approach to women migrant worker issues is UNIFEM's Regional Programme on Empowering Migrant Workers in Asia (Regional Programme). The Regional Programme's participants include Indonesia, Nepal, the Philippines, Sri Lanka (all countries of origin for women migrant workers), and Jordan (a host country). The objectives of the Regional Programme include promoting gender responsive migration policies that help realize women's human rights; promoting sustained dialogue between home and host countries to empower women migrant workers; strengthening the capacity of women migrant workers and their organizations to access and claim their rights; and piloting innovative reintegration projects for women who return to their home countries.

An empowerment perspective in addressing women migrant issues has several components. First, there must be a shift from a victimization perspective to a rights-based perspective. Issues of migration, a woman's right to work, and the exercise of choice as fundamental human rights should inform the discussion on women migrant workers. The international community should not focus solely on the physical safety and integrity of women migrant workers, but should emphasize that workers' rights too are human rights.

Second, both host and home countries must recognize the contributions of women migrant workers. Host countries benefit from women migrant workers as a source of cheap labor, while home countries often rely on women migrant workers as a source of remittances. For the host country, particular attention should be paid to the women who perform domestic care work. Domestic care work and other informal sector work should be viewed as work, and women migrant workers should be viewed as workers with legal rights. Jordan, for example, recently has made a change in policy allowing domestic workers protection under its labor laws, and has acknowledged the importance of domestic workers in its economy.

An increased emphasis on the contributions of women migrant workers should also include recognition of the impact of remittances, the forwarding home of wages by migrant workers. Remittances are an extremely important aspect of migration. Remittances to home countries by migrant workers working in developed countries equaled \$100 billion in 1999; international development aid in the same year came to \$40.3 billion. In 2000, remittances accounted for more than ten percent of the gross domestic products (GDP) of Albania, Bosnia and Herzegovina, Cape Verde, El Salvador, Jamaica, Jordan, Nicaragua, Samoa, and Yemen. In addition to being an important addition to a country's GDP, remittances are a major source of foreign exchange earnings for home countries. For the families who receive the money, remittances can be used to import capital goods and provide investment funds, increase household income and savings, and purchase products and services.

The available data on remittances should be improved, and the data analyzed by sex, so as to better understand how women contribute to their home countries' economies. One study points to the impact of remittances sent by Filipina migrant workers. Over 95 percent of Filipina domestics in Malaysia send remittances to family members in the Philippines. In Sri Lanka, women migrant workers contributed over 62 percent of the more than \$1 billion total remittances in 1999, accounting for over half of the country's trade balance and 145 percent of gross foreign loans and grants. Other studies of young girls' migration from Latin America, the Philippines, and the South Pacific, indicate that migration of women may be a part of a household's survival strategy, as women are often seen as a reliable source of remittances.

Third, human rights advocates must work to strengthen the fulfillment of women migrant workers' rights in host countries. Many countries do not cover the work performed by women migrant workers in their labor laws. For example, the United States lacks an effective enforcement mechanism for labor violations against domestic care workers. The U.S. Department of Labor's Wage and Hour Division investigated only 231 cases involving domestic workers in private households from January 1, 1995 through October 1, 1999. According to calculations from the human rights organization Human Rights Watch (HRW), the Division investigated only 0.006 percent of employment relationships involving domestic care workers, while in 98 percent of cases investigated by HRW, domestic care workers reported unpaid wages in violation of U.S. law. Limited enforcement measures are scarce for invisible workers in many host countries. Access to effective remedies, however, is essential to the fulfillment of human rights.

Fourth, the international community can investigate alternatives to migration, promote community-based development, and enact anti-poverty programs. This strategy acknowledges the particular needs of migrant workers before migration or upon returning to their home countries. Such programs may include reintegration programs for women migrant workers who return to their home countries, but find few employment opportunities. Effective reintegration programs might allow women to secure economic opportunities in their home countries, eliminating the need to migrate again.

Using the Convention on Migrant Workers as a Model of Empowerment

Human rights related to migration and to migrant workers are long-established in many international human rights instruments. The right to freedom of movement is recognized in the Universal Declaration of Human Rights: "Everyone has the right to freedom of movement and residence within the borders of each state," and "everyone has the right to leave any country, including his own, and to return to his country." The right to work was the first of the specific rights recognized under the International Covenant on Economic, Social, and Cultural Rights. Article 6 of the ICESCR includes in its definition of the right to work "the right of everyone to the opportunity to gain his living by work." The right to unionize is enshrined in the main human rights instruments, but also in the International Labor Organization (ILO) Conventions 87 and 98. These ILO conventions are extensive elaborations on the preamble section of the ILO Constitution that deals with the freedom of association and the right to unionize. ILO Nos. 87 and 98 also enjoy widespread acceptance, with 121 and 137 ratifications, respectively. Despite the high numbers of ratifications, many workers throughout the world face serious problems in exercising their right to unionize, including violence against union members and leaders, as well as restrictions on the right to unionize for certain kinds of workers.

The ILO was the first international body to enact standards to protect specifically the rights of migrant workers. The ILO Migration for Employment Convention (Revised) (No. 97) of 1949 requires that States Parties treat legal migrant workers as they treat nationals. The Migrant Workers Convention (Supplementary Provisions) (No. 143) of 1975 requires States to respect the basic human rights of migrant workers, including taking steps to stop smuggling and

trafficking activities. The UN first became involved in 1978, when the first World Conference to Combat Racism and Racial Discrimination recommended the UN draft a convention on the rights of migrant workers. The UN General Assembly also requested a draft convention on the subject, and in 1980, the UN established a working group to draft a convention. By 1990, the Convention on Migrant Workers was complete.

The Convention on Migrant Workers seeks to protect migrant workers from exploitation and to provide the international community with universal standards of treatment of migrant workers. Although previous UN and ILO conventions deal with rights related to migrant workers, Convention drafters felt the rights of migrant workers should be emphasized and elaborated upon. The Convention on Migrant Workers is not the first convention to take the approach of consolidating the rights of one specific group of persons in a single instrument. The 1979 Convention of the Elimination of All Forms of Discrimination Against Women (CEDAW) and the 1989 Convention on the Rights of the Child also apply established international human rights norms to specified groups.

The Convention on Migrant Workers is innovative, however, in a number of ways. First, the Convention emphasizes the idea that migrant workers are entitled to enjoy their human rights regardless of their legal status. This idea, however, is perhaps best expressed as an ideal, as many of the provisions of the Convention apply only to workers whose immigration status is regularized. The hope of the drafters of the Convention is that irregular migration will be discouraged if the human rights of all migrant workers are more strongly recognized. The lowering of irregular immigration is perhaps the least understood aspect of the Convention by nations that are not willing to ratify the Convention; many such nations may fear that ratifying the Convention will increase the numbers of migrants in their midst, whether they be lawfully or unlawfully present. In fact, little support for the Convention on Migrant Workers exists among labor-receiving countries, which stands in sharp contrast to the other group-specific conventions, which enjoy wide support – and ratification – around the world.

Further, the Convention includes a groundbreaking definition of exactly who is a migrant worker. Under the Convention, "the term 'migrant worker' refers to a person who is to be engaged, is engaged, or has been engaged in a remunerated activity in a State of which he or she is not a national." Migrant worker categories specifically enumerated in the Convention include frontier workers, seasonal workers, seafarers, workers in offshore installations, itinerant workers, project-specific workers, and self-employed workers.

The Convention is the first international instrument to provide a comprehensive definition of a migrant worker based on "remunerated activity." Through this definition, the Convention drafters make a distinction between migrants and migrant workers, and note that not all migrants are migrant workers. Migrant workers are not just economic entities, however, but social entities as well. The Convention recognizes this by including members of the family in its provisions. Finally, the definition of migrant workers is broad, including those who are planning to become migrant workers, those who are actually working outside their home country, and those who have returned home from work abroad. Such a broad definition allows application of the Convention at any stage of migration for work, and takes into account the experiences of migrant workers in origin, transit, and destination countries.

Women Migrant Workers and the Convention

The Convention on Migrant Workers is significant for women, and not just because the Convention specifically covers women migrant workers. Article

1 states that the Convention is applicable “without distinction of any kind such as sex,” and Article 2(1) defines a migrant worker in gender-inclusive language as “a person who is to be engaged … in a State of which he or she is not a national.”

The Convention’s inclusive language, however, was not automatic. Only at the end of the drafting process did the Convention Working Group adopt the “he or she” terminology and apply it throughout the instrument. Some representatives in the Group argued that such terminology would create translation problems. The result is that, at least in the English language version of the Convention, women as well as men are specifically recognized as migrant workers.

The Convention is also significant for women migrant workers because it outlines specific measures that States Parties should undertake to promote migrant workers’ rights.

Perhaps these extensive measures explain why only 30 nations have ratified the Convention, and why only labor-sending countries have ratified it. This paper proposes that the Convention, with its numerous provisions related to migrant worker policy, can be an effective tool specifically for promoting the rights of women migrant workers. If viewed through an empowerment perspective, the Convention can inform advocates, policy makers, and workers themselves on workable strategies for fulfilling women migrant workers’ rights. This is the challenge faced by human rights practitioners: to take the human rights norms enunciated in international instruments, and put them to practical use in improving people’s day-to-day lives.

Protecting Women Migrant Workers’ Rights at Work

Women migrant workers face employment problems unique to them. Women migrant workers’ employment opportunities are more restricted than for men, and women typically bear the major responsibility for care of the family and for cultural maintenance. Therefore, measures to fulfill women migrant workers’ rights must improve the treatment of women migrant workers as workers, and must minimize the hurdles women migrant workers face in maintaining their family and cultural obligations.

The Convention on Migrant Workers offers a potential framework for protecting women migrant workers’ basic rights at work. If followed by national policy makers, the Convention’s framework might strengthen the laws affecting migrant women workers. Article 25 (1) states that migrant workers should not be remunerated less favorably for their work than are nationals. This Article can be applied to women migrant workers, so that women too are entitled to equality in treatment with nationals. Other conditions of work also covered by the Convention include overtime, hours of work, weekly rest, holidays with pay, safety, health, termination of the employment relationship, and any other conditions of work covered by national law and practice. The Convention also provides for equality in treatment with nationals in the areas of social security and medical care, although the Convention does not recognize an absolute right to these services. Access to social security and medical care would increase the economic security and well-being of women migrant workers, perhaps allowing them to escape the trap of economic inequality.

Although equality of treatment with nationals is integral to the Convention, the Convention provides no protection from unequal wages between men and women, nor from gender-based, occupational segregation. Furthermore, the Convention does not specify which nationals, men or women, it intends to reference. In other words, the Convention does not take into account disparate treatment between men and women workers that may occur in host countries. Although such treatment would be contrary to UN principles of non-discrimination, the issue of disparate treatment is not specifically addressed in the Convention on Migrant Workers.

The Convention also specifies a respect for the cultural identity of migrant workers, including not preventing workers from maintaining cultural ties with their home country. The Convention urges States, when crafting migration policies, to contemplate not just their labor needs and resources, but also to ensure the social, economic, cultural, and other needs of migrant workers and their families. If applied to women, these provisions might allow women to more effectively balance their employment with their cultural responsibilities. The provisions also might significantly improve the mental health of women migrant workers who are isolated from their families and communities.

The Convention does not, however, address the more practical question of work-family balance. The Convention does not address the fact that women are generally primary caregivers of their children. The Convention does not mention access to child care, or the need for women to move in and out of the labor force while raising their children.

Self-employed workers abroad are specifically recognized as migrant workers. The inclusion of self-employed workers in the definition of migrant worker recognizes the large number of migrant workers who operate small family businesses. However, advocates for women migrant workers might argue that self-employed workers include women in the informal economy, such as domestic workers and others who are typically excluded from nations' labor laws. This definition would apply to documented workers only. Despite this limitation, advocates may be able to extend labor laws to cover traditionally excluded women migrant workers by maintaining that such workers are self-employed, and thus specifically protected under the Convention on Migrant Workers.

Unionizing and Organizing Opportunities

Migrant workers have a right to information under the Convention. Migrant workers who are documented have a right to be informed of their rights under the Convention. The duty to inform is not limited to host countries, but applies to origin, transit, and destination countries. Moreover, States are directed to disseminate the information widely, through employers, trade unions, or other appropriate bodies or institutions, cooperating with other States if appropriate. The information must be provided to migrant workers free of charge and in a language the worker can understand. The Convention also covers access to information for undocumented migrant workers, though these provisions do not guarantee a right to information for undocumented workers. Rather, such workers may receive information from government agencies regarding migration and work-related laws and regulations, as well as information about country and employment conditions.

Promoting workers' access to information may be a powerful first step to fulfilling workers' rights to organize. Promotion of access to information is particularly beneficial for women migrant workers, who often labor in isolated jobs. A systemic outreach program on migrant worker rights, one that targets multiple sources, might succeed in informing women migrant workers of their rights. Furthermore, information campaigns based in home countries and disclosing exploitative employment practices abroad might discourage smuggling and trafficking.

Article 40 (1) of the Convention grants workers "the right to form associations and trade unions in the state of employment for the promotion and protection of their economic, social, cultural, and other interests." Far more than establishing the right to unionize, this article enables women in typically non-unionized work, such as domestic workers, to form organizations to secure their interests. This broad definition is significant for women migrant workers, who face obstacles to union participation, particularly in leadership positions. "Associations" protected under the Convention include trade unions as well as other groups to promote and protect their interests. A major barrier to realization of this right, however, is that Article 40 only applies to host countries that are States Parties to the Convention, and only applies to documented workers. As noted above, no major labor-receiving country has ratified the Convention.

Article 26 offers an alternative to Article 40. States Parties recognize the right of migrant workers and members of their families "to take part in meetings and activities of trade unions and of any other associations established in accordance with law, with a view to protecting their economic, social, cultural, and other interests, subject only to the rules of the organization concerned." Like Article 40, the definition of associations is sufficiently broad to include a variety of NGOs. Unlike Article 40, Article 26 does not apply only to host countries, but to all States Parties. Therefore, the right of women migrant workers to organize or join associations to protect their interests in home countries or transit countries is recognized. Furthermore, Article 26 applies to all workers, regardless of their legal status.

The Convention protects the rights of women migrant workers to form organizations geared towards societal change, whether in their home countries, transit countries, or host countries. NGOs such as MIGRANTE in the Philippines and UNIFEM's Regional Programme on Empowering Migrant Workers in Asia, discussed above, serve as powerful examples of the kinds of organizations women migrant workers and their advocates might form. The actual organizations formed, either by women migrant workers themselves or by their advocates, are limited only by the women's needs and goals.

Economic Opportunities

The standard of "equality of treatment with nationals" applies not just to migrant workers' rights at work, discussed above, but applies to access to economic opportunities as well. The Convention's Article 43 gives documented migrant workers equality of treatment with nationals in access to a number of educational and social services, including vocational training facilities and educational institutions. Through these opportunities, women migrant workers can improve their economic situations and countries can open new paths to women's development.

Unfortunately, the Convention has no specific provision for language instruction, so that women migrant workers can become competent in the local language. Without language skills, many women will be unable to take advantage of their right to access educational and employment programs. Language barriers also prevent women from reporting human rights abuses, or from accessing crucial services and programs.

Protecting the Families of Migrant Workers

The Convention on Migrant Workers is not limited to workers. The Convention recognizes family as the fundamental group unit of society. As such, family unification is a major goal of the Convention. States Parties are directed to "take appropriate measures to ensure the protection of the unity of the families of migrant workers." This provision benefits not just women who are "left behind" by their migrant worker husbands, but it benefits women migrant workers who wish for their husbands and children to join them. Furthermore, the Convention requires appropriate measures to be taken not just by host countries, but by all States Parties to the Convention. Home countries also have a role in family reunification.

Family unification may be particularly important when it is the mothers, rather than the fathers, who migrate for work. When women migrate for work, leaving their children behind, the children are more likely to suffer academically, have emotional problems, suffer from substance abuse, be forced into the labor force at an early age, and suffer physical or sexual abuse.

The Convention offers opportunities for economic advancement of family members who migrate with the worker. Even members of the family, including non-working spouses, have a right to access to education and vocational training under the Convention. Like Article 43, Article 45 provides for equality of treatment with nationals in access to educational and social services, including vocational training facilities and educational institutions. A major difference between Articles 43 and 45 is that family members do not have any right to access to co-ops and self-managed enterprises. The Convention nonetheless provides an important opportunity for family members to be less dependent on the migrant worker, and gives families more economic security overall.

References

Grace Chang, (2000). *Disposable Domestics: Immigrant Women Workers in the Global Economy*. South End Press.

Joan Fitzpatrick & Katrina R. Kelly, (1998). "Gendered Aspects of Migration: Law and the Female Migrant," 22 *Hastings Law Review* 47.

Gender Promotion Programme, (2003). *Preventing Discrimination, Exploitation and Abuse of Women Migrant Workers: An Information Guide: Why the Focus on Women International Migrant Workers.* International Labor Organization.

International Catholic Migration Commission (ICMC), (2004). *How to Strengthen Protection of Migrant Workers and Members of their Families with International Human Rights Treaties.* ICMC.

7

Women, Globalization and Human Rights

There is no clear-cut definition of the concept of globalisation. Instead the concept has been approached in different ways by different authors. A common understanding is that globalisation refers to the intensification of social and economic relations beyond state borders, with the consequence that local and global events are increasingly linked to and influenced by each other. The markets and the technology, particularly the information technology, have been identified as the main arenas of globalisation. This integration involves among other things a removal of barriers to trade and investment and an increasing movement of capital across national boundaries. The dominant policy trend today when it comes to economic integration includes trade liberalisation, privatisation of state functions, deregulation of various activities and the emergence of new powerful actors in the economic field. When analysing the impact of globalisation on various groups in society it is often the effect of these trends and policies which are addressed.

There is no unambiguous answer to the question how economic globalisation affects the lives of women worldwide. In order to be able to analyse the impact of globalisation on women one should be able to isolate the factors which are linked to the globalisation process and which causes changes in the position of women, thereby excluding possible other factors which also affect women's position but which are not directly linked to the globalisation process. Instead reference will be made to studies and research done by other researchers and experts.

Generally it has been submitted that globalisation affects women differently in different parts of the world and within different social groupings. Moreover, a common understanding is that the impact may include both positive and negative aspects. In fact empirical evidence shows a significant increase in women's share of industrial employment in developing countries such as Bangladesh, Malaysia, Indonesia, Thailand and the Philippines. However, at the same time these new employment opportunities might be coupled with inferior working conditions and low remuneration. For women living in countries at the margin of the globalisation process the employment opportunities are much more scarce forcing the majority of women into the informal sector often with poverty as the result.

Also in the developed world globalisation is often characterised as a two-edged sword. Dominant policies linked to globalisation have been fairly successful in facilitating economic growth and combating inflation in many rich countries. However, simultaneously this has caused "increasing income polarisation, persistently high levels of unemployment, and widespread social exclusion". In some studies the impact of globalisation on women has been linked to an increase in sexual exploitation of women in the form of trafficking for prostitution particularly in countries undergoing rapid economic transformation.

In sum, present globalisation trends and policies influence a number of human rights both civil and political as well as economic, social and cultural rights.The selection of rights has been determined by an interest to look into several areas of human rights protection rather than only one. Areas which have been identified as particularly relevant to women are employment, poverty and trafficking. All these areas are broad encapsulating a number of different rights.

The international human rights machinery subject to investigation includes particularly the human rights treaty bodies established to monitor the implementation of various human rights treaties. In addition, the treaty monitoring work done within some of the specialised agencies, particularly the International Labour Organisation (ILO), will be considered. Only brief references will be made to the work of the political branch of the United Nations, that is, the General Assembly, the Commission on Human Rights,the Commission on the Status of Women, and the Sub-Commission on the Promotion and Protection of Human Rights.

Different Actors

The globalisation development poses a number of challenges to the international protection of human rights. Not only are individual rights threatened, but also more profound questions linked to the role of the state in protecting human rights may be raised.

Traditionally the state is viewed as the main bearer of obligations when it comes to safeguarding internationally protected human rights. It has been argued that in the global economy other actors become more central to the protection or rather the violation of human rights. An increasing amount of research has been done in trying to establish to what extent, if at all, these kinds of actors are bound by international human rights law. Here only few remarks with respect to non-state actors will be made.

When it comes to international financial institutions, such as the World Bank (WB) and the International Monetary Fund (IMF), they have themselves been highly reluctant to accept that they would be bound by international human rights norms. This standpoint has recently been contested in an academic study that holds that the WB and the IMF are obliged to respect human rights in their own operations.

When it comes to the question concerning to what extent international organisations are legally bound by human rights norms, of particular interest to us is the position of the World Trade Organisation (WTO). Since WTO lacks a formal link to the UN, the possible relationship between WTO and human rights has to be determined on the basis of the Agreement establishing WTO and general rules governing international law. Academic scholars have argued that human rights law should supersede trade law, particularly in situations where the rights violated forms part of *jus cogens* or customary international law.

With respect to transnational corporations a legal responsibility under international human rights law has not so far been established. Transnational corporations are only indirectly affected by international human rights law through legislative and other measures which State Parties adopt in order to comply with their legal obligations under human rights treaties and other instruments. Instead of establishing direct legally binding rules on transnational corporations the approach internationally has so far been to advance voluntary actions.

With the increasing emphasis on new actors it is easy to neglect the role of the state which despite changes in the environment still is significant in the international legal arena. The state continues to bear the main responsibility for implementing human rights within their own jurisdiction.

The central role of the state in handling social consequences caused by neo-liberal economic policies has been recognised also by other actors on the global arena. In the World Development Report of 1997, the World Bank stresses that "the state is central to economic and social development, not as a direct provider of growth but as a partner, catalyst, and facilitator".

State Obligations

A lot has been said on the nature and scope of state obligations under international human rights law. Especially in the past the categorisation of obligations has often been determined on the basis of the perceived character of a specific right. For example, state obligations linked to civil and political rights have often been defined as negative and immediate, whereas obligations linked to economic, social and cultural rights have been described as positive and progressive. This distinction between obligations depending on the characterisation of rights has been highly criticised in scholarly writings as well as in the work of international human rights treaty bodies.

The most quoted categorisation of state obligations in current research and practice is the one developed by *Asbjern Eide* in his UN study on the Right to Adequate Food as a Human Right, that is, the obligations to respect, to protect and to fulfil. The Committee on Economic, Social and Cultural Rights has directly applied this categorisation in its general comments on the right to adequate food and on the right to the highest attainable standard of health. The categorisation finds support also in the context of civil and political rights, which in Article 2 explicitly states that "Each State party to the present Covenant undertakes to respect and to ensure to all individuals ... the rights recognised in the present Covenant".

The content of these obligations has been defined by Eide in the following manner:

i) "The *obligation to respect* requires the State to abstain from doing anything that violates the integrity of the individual or infringes on her or his freedom, including the freedom to use the material resources available to that individual in the way she or he finds best to satisfy basic needs.

ii) The *obligation to protect* requires from the State the measures necessary to prevent other individuals or groups from violating the integrity, freedom of action, or other human rights of the individual.

iii) The *obligation to fulfil* requires the State to take the measures necessary to ensure for each person within its jurisdiction opportunities to obtain satisfaction of those needs, recognised in the human rights instruments, which cannot be secured by personal efforts".

It is clear that the obligation to respect is of particular relevance to many civil and political rights such as the freedom of association, assembly and expression and that the obligations to protect and to fulfil are pivotal in connection with the realisation of many economic, social and cultural rights. However, this does not mean that the first obligation would not be relevant in conjunction with economic, social and cultural rights and the two last ones in conjunction with civil and political rights. The right to fair trial, a typical civil and political right, on the other hand, may require active measures by the state both in the form of establishing and maintaining a functional court system as well as providing legal assistance to individuals who lack own means.

Female Participation in Employment

Female participation in paid employment has increased as a consequence of the new policies and trends linked to globalisation in most parts of the world. This concerns especially work in the manufacturing, service and agricultural sectors. The number of female employees has been particularly high in export-oriented manufacturing industries set up in so-called export processing zones (EPZ).

Export processing zones have been defined as "industrial zones with special incentives set up to attract foreign investment, in which imported materials undergo some degree of processing before being exported again". The establishment of free trade areas is by no means a new phenomenon. However, the increase in EPZ during the 1980's and 1990's has commonly been attributed to the globalisation process. Whereas 24 developing countries had export processing zones in 1976, the figure in 1999 was 93 developing countries. The incentives usually offered to the investors include: financial benefits such as tax reductions and duty free imports and exports, infrastructure, favourable labour costs and strategic location or market access.

Despite some common features, the design of export processing zones may differ considerably between countries. For example with respect to wages, it has been shown in some countries that manufacturing industries within EPZ have offered better wages than industries outside the zones. In other instances, however, the high number of female workers in EPZ has clearly resulted in upholding a continuous low wage level, which in turn has safeguarded the competitiveness of the export sector.

Human Rights in the Field of Employment

There are a number of human rights that are relevant in the field of employment. In an effort to present an overview of these rights *Kristof Drzewicki* has introduced a division into four categories of rights: Employment-related rights; Employment-derivative rights;Equality of treatment and non-discrimination rights; and Instrumental rights.

Firstly, employment-related rights refer to the most fundamental labour rights and include: the freedom from slavery and similar practices; the freedom from forced and compulsory labour; the freedom to work; the right to free employment services; the right to employment; the right to protection of employment; and the right to protection against unemployment.

Secondly, employment-derivative rights refer to rights that become operational when a person has an employment, that is, rights which first and foremost deal with different aspects of the employment relationship.

Thirdly, the rights of equality of treatment and non–discrimination are relevant both as independent rights and in conjunction with the application of other rights.

Fourthly, instrumental rights refer to rights that are required in order to safeguard that other work-related rights can be fully exercised. The most pivotal rights in this category are the right to organise, the right to collective bargaining, the right to strike and the right to effective remedies.

In sum, the main work-related rights to be considered in this study are rights listed under the headings employment-derivative rights, equality and non-discrimination rights and instrumental rights.

Relevant Human Rights Instruments

It goes without saying that the most comprehensive international regulation in the employment field can be found among the 184 conventions and 192 recommendations adopted by the International Labour Organisation since its inception in 1919. The former conventions concern freedom of association, abolition of forced labour, equality, and elimination of child labour. For the purposes of this study especially the conventions relating to the freedom of association and equality will be considered. With respect to the basic human rights conventions reference could in this context be made to the ILO Convention No. 156 concerning Equal Opportunities and Equal Treatment for Men and Women Workers: Workers with Family Responsibilities. Moreover, there are a number of other conventions which address the question of female workers from different perspectives, particularly women in underground work and night work as well as the issue of maternity protection.

Whereas the fundamental human rights conventions adopted by the ILO have received a considerable number of ratifications, many of the conventions, which are of particular importance to women, have been ratified by only few states. Since conventions providing general human rights protection, such as the CCPR, the CESCR and the CEDAW, tend to be ratified by a bigger number of states than the ILO conventions in general, these conventions become important also in the field of labour rights. Article 8 on the prohibition of slavery, forced and compulsory labour falls outside the scope of this study. The CESCR deals more comprehensively with work-related rights, that is, the right to work (Article 6), rights in work (Article 7), trade union rights (Article 8), social security rights (Article 9) and maternity protection (Article 10).

Treaty–Monitoring Bodies

In the subsequent effort to elucidate state obligations with respect to selected work related rights, the focus will be on the international practice produced by the UN and ILO treaty monitoring bodies. It is evident that the most comprehensive material is to be found within the ILO system. The monitoring system under the ILO differs from the corresponding systems under the UN treaties and needs therefore some more elaboration at this stage. There are basically two supervisory procedures attached to the ILO conventions, one is based on the consideration of state reports and the other on the investigation of alleged violations of treaty provisions. For our purposes the reporting procedure is of particular relevance and thereby the material produced by the Committee of Experts on the Application of Conventions and Recommendations, which considers the reports and makes observations with respect to their content. The investigation procedures include an inter state complaint procedure, a so called representations procedure, which may be initiated by workers' or employers' organisations, and a complaint procedure in the field of freedom of association which may be initiated by one of the tripartite partners.

Already a preliminary study of the UN treaty practice indicates that the question of work-related rights has not yet been at the top of the agenda. For example, the Committee on Economic, Social and Cultural Rights has not addressed work-related rights in its general comments. The CEDAW Committee has adopted only one general recommendation in this field, that is, one focusing on equal remuneration in 1989. The Human Rights Committee has adopted general comments on equality and non-discrimination, but has so far not addressed comprehensively the question of freedom of association and thereby the right to join trade unions.

The limited availability of general comments and recommendations within the UN treaty system, requires a focus on the concluding observations adopted at the end of the consideration of state reports. Rather than going through all available state reports the focus will be on reports put forward by developing countries that have established export processing zones. One criterion used when singling out the states has been that they have ratified the UN human rights conventions and the main part of the ILO conventions.

Employment-Derivative Rights

As indicated above the main problems linked to women's work-related rights in the globalised economy seem to be found among the so-called employment-derivative rights. This concerns particularly the question of minimum wages and working conditions, including maternity protection.

Minimum Wages

Concerning the level of remuneration there are basically two sets of standards of relevance. In addition, the ILO Convention No. 131 concerning Minimum Wage Fixing, with Special Reference to Developing Countries provides that when determining the level of minimum wages attention shall be paid both to the needs of the workers and their families as well as to economic factors.

The question of minimum wages in international human rights law has basically two dimensions, one deals with the material content of the concept of minimum wages and the other with the procedure whereby the minimum wage is established and controlled. Here only the first dimension will be dealt with. It is evident that the minimum wage cannot be established *in abstracto* but will be dependent on the social and economic context of a particular country.

The Committee on Economic, Social and Cultural Rights has in connection with the consideration of state reports addressed the question of the level of the minimum wage, for example, in the case of Panama. The Committee expressed its concern "that the minimum wage was not sufficient to provide for the basic needs of the worker's family". Moreover, the fact that "about five minimum wages are needed to obtain the officially set basic food basket" was not in compliance with Article 7

(a) of the CESCR. It is of interest to note that the Committee in this case clearly adopted a normative stand indicating non-compliance with the Covenant.

Closely linked to the material content of minimum wages is the question of the inclusiveness of the right, that is, what categories of workers should be entitled to a minimum wage. Article 7 of the CESCR stipulates that fair wages should be provided for "all workers". The concept of workers has not been explicitly defined in the Covenant. It is unclear to what extent it covers other groups than wage earners, such us employers and self-employed. In the ILO Convention No. 131 it is regulated that the system of minimum wages shall cover "all groups of wage earners whose terms of employment are such that coverage would be appropriate". The Committee of Experts has in its general survey on minimum wages observed that Convention No. 131 "complements and strengthens the objective and obligation arising from the previous Conventions", thereby emphasising the need to protect wage earners who are not organised. In its general survey, the Committee of Experts regrets that only a limited number of Governments has listed in its first report the excluded groups.

No direct reference to the question of minimum wages in export processing zones has been found in the treaty practice of the CESCR or the ILO conventions. However, the application of labour legislation in EPZ in general has been dealt with. Thus, the Committee on Economic, Social and Cultural Rights has expressed its concern with respect to practices whereby labour standards have been withdrawn or modified with respect to free trade areas. The ILO Committee of Experts has considered this issue in connection with Bangladesh's state report on ILO Convention No. 87 concerning Freedom of Association and Protection of the Right to Organise. Of course, the right to form trade unions belongs to the fundamental rights and has therefore a stronger position in the ILO system than the issue of minimum wages. Consequently the Committee of Experts held in the case of Bangladesh that no restrictions are acceptable, not even temporarily.

The partial exclusion of EPZ from the national labour laws is further problematic from an equality perspective, since women tend to be in the majority among workers in free trade areas, in many instances up to 80 %. By leaving out the EPZ clearly more women than men are affected. This in turn raises the question of possible indirect discrimination on the basis of sex.

Working Conditions

The concept of working conditions is here used as an umbrella concept for working hours, employment contracts and benefits. The problems often raised in connection with export processing zones include both long working hours, short term labour contracts and, as a consequence thereof, insecure labour contracts and reduced benefits.

Within the ILO system there are over 20 general conventions which deal with safe and healthy working conditions and around the same number of conventions in the field of working hours and holidays. It has not been possible within the scope of this study to examine these conventions comprehensively. This could be partly due to the fact that many of the developing countries with extensive EPZ have not ratified the relevant conventions.

In connection with the consideration of state reports, the Committee on Economic, Social and Cultural Rights has with respect to working hours expressed concern about "excessive overtime work in the Export Processing Zones". It is of particular interest to note that the Committee has in this context raised the topic of the position of women, by noting that it is seriously concerned about "the situation of those persons working in the "maquillas" many of whom are women".

Also the Committee on the Elimination of Discrimination against Women has expressed concern about the situation of women in export processing zones. The Committee notes that "while the percentage of women employed in free-trade zones is laudable, because it gives them a financial footing, women workers suffer considerable discrimination in income and benefits".

Maternity / Family Protection

The combination of family life and participation in employment outside the home is an equation which many women worldwide struggle with daily. The problems faced in this regard by women working in export processing zones are often particularly severe. International human rights law provides a fairly broad protection of women's reproductive rights.

The application of these rights in the context of EPZ has been addressed in connection with several state reports. The Committee on Economic, Social and Cultural Rights expresses deep concern, in conjunction with the consideration of the Mexican report, regarding women's situation in so-called *maquiladoras*. The Committee does not provide insights into what human rights are at stake when such practices are carried out. It seems that at least Article 7 on just and favourable conditions of work is threatened.

However, these practices may also be addressed under other human rights, such as the right to privacy.

The ILO Committee of Experts has addressed these kinds of practices under the right to non-discrimination provided for in ILO Convention No. 111 concerning Discrimination in Respect of Employment and Occupation. The Committee exemplifies discriminatory practices against female workers in export processing zones by referring to the practice whereby "women are required to provide urine samples and, during the probationary period, provide proof to the enterprise of the continuation of their menstrual cycles". In both these cases the Committee confirms that these practices constitute discrimination on the basis of sex.

The non-discrimination approach is also dominant in the CEDAW. Without necessarily referring to free-trade areas the CEDAW Committee has addressed questions of maternity protection in conjunction with a number of state reports. For example in the case of Panama the lack of "effective protection with respect to maternity leave and breastfeeding breaks" is pointed out. In the case of Mauritius, the Committee raised questions concerning the rule enshrined in the labour law and the export-processing zone act, whereby women are entitled to maternity leave for only three pregnancies.

All these incidences of violations of women's reproductive rights are characterised by the fact that the perpetrator of the violation is a private employer, often a foreign employer operating in the country. This means that the first level of state obligations, that is, the obligation to respect is not at stake, but instead the obligation to protect is relevant. In an effort to exemplify what these obligations may entail reference can be made to the observations made by the ILO Committee of Experts in considering Mexico's report under Convention No. 111.

As shown above, the application, or rather lack of application, of employment-derivative rights in export processing zones has been addressed by all treaty monitoring bodies dealt with in this study. With the exception of the ILO system, the content of work-related rights is still to a large extent undefined. However, the monitoring bodies have adopted a strong gender specific approach particularly in conjunction with the realisation of reproductive rights in export processing zones.

Equality of Treatment and Non–Discrimination Rights

The equality of treatment and the non-discrimination rights are, as noted earlier, central to the protection of women's human rights. In the context of economic, social and cultural rights it is generally argued that the right not to be discriminated against belongs to one of the immediate state obligations as opposed to obligations which may be progressively realised on the basis of available resources. In this sense the non–discrimination rights under the CESCR resembles the corresponding provisions of the CCPR and the ILO Convention No. 111. With respect to the CEDAW the operative article of the Convention provides that "State parties ...agree to pursue by all appropriate means and without delay a policy of eliminating discrimination against women" In other words, the state party has an immediate obligation to initiate the work to identify the appropriate means.

Furthermore, the right to non-discrimination, particularly in the interpretation of treaty-monitoring bodies, contains discriminatory practices committed by both public and private actors. With respect to CEDAW, this is clearly spelt out in the text of the Convention. Article 1 of the Convention stipulates that the term "discrimination against women" shall mean any infringements on women's enjoyment of "human rights and fundamental freedoms in the political, economic, social, cultural, civil or any other field".

The Human Rights Committee has with respect to Article 26 of the CCPR submitted that the provision "prohibits discrimination in law or in fact in any field regulated and protected by public authorities". Furthermore, the Committee has requested state parties to provide information on discriminatory practices carried out “by public authorities, by the community, or by private persons or bodies”. The CESCR Committee has adopted a similar approach in their consideration of state reports. The same goes for the ILO Convention No. 111 concerning Discrimination in Respect of Employment and Occupation.

Even if the right to non-discrimination in general terms provides a broad protection against discrimination, the application of the right on gender relations is often afflicted with difficulties. The reason for this is to be found in the traditional way of understanding discriminatory practices. Thus, the application of the right to non-discrimination on the basis of sex often requires a comparison between two similarly situated individuals, a woman and a man. If it is found that the woman and the man are similarly situated they are to be treated alike, if not, they should be treated different from each other. Discrimination occurs when similarly situated individuals are treated differently or vice versa. From women’s point of view the problem is that the male easily becomes the norm against whom the situation of women is compared. In areas where no male comparator exists the right to non-discrimination easily becomes obsolete.

The interpretation of international human rights treaty monitoring bodies, particularly those operating under the ILO and CEDAW, have clearly defined distinctions made on the basis of maternity or pregnancy as discrimination on the basis of sex, or in the case of CEDAW, discrimination against women. The CEDAW Committee has further defined gender-based violence, including sexual harassment in the work place, as discrimination against women.

Another aspect of discrimination, which is of particular relevance in the field of employment, is the situation where gender neutral distinctions are made which have gender specific effects. Such distinctions are only indirectly discriminating against women. This question is particularly pertinent in conjunction with the application of the principle of equal pay for equal work or work of equal value. The term pay or remuneration should here be interpreted as including both the salary and other benefits paid directly or indirectly by the employer. With respect to the ILO practice, the general survey on equal remuneration confirms this interpretation. This means that when an employer pays better work-related benefits for example to full time employees or employees with permanent labour contracts women might be victims of indirect discrimination in case they are in the majority, as often is the case, among the part-time workers or workers with temporary working contracts. The Committee on Economic, Social and Cultural Rights has partly addressed this question in the case of Korea, where the Committee questions the Korean distinction between "regular" and "irregular workers" and the provision of lower wages, pension benefits, unemployment and health benefits to the so-called irregular workers. In this context the Committee notes that "the proportion of irregular workers in the general labour force has grown to half, the great majority of them women".

Even if the treaty-monitoring bodies still need to clarify the content of the human right to non-discrimination, it is clear on the basis of available treaty practice that the monitoring bodies have tried to go beyond a formal approach to discrimination. As an example, increasing references to indirect discrimination has been made in connection with the consideration of state reports.

It appears that the implementation of women's rights to non-discrimination and equality in export processing zones has not yet been broadly addressed in treaty practice. The main exception in this regard is the practice of the CEDAW Committee which is based on the non-discriminatory approach embedded in the Convention.

Instrumental Rights

Instrumental rights refer to rights which are required in order to fully exercise other work-related rights. There are basically two rights which become highly important in the context of export processing zones. The first concerns the establishment and operation of trade unions advancing the rights of the workers in the free trade areas, and the second, the availability of mechanisms for protecting the rights, including effective remedies.

The right to establish and join trade unions is perhaps the most fundamental right within the ILO system. In fact it is today considered that every member of the ILO has an obligation to respect trade union rights irrespective of whether they have ratified the conventions which deal with the rights or not. Even if trade union rights are protected also under the CCPR and the CESCR, it is clear that the ILO system provides the paramount protection in this field.

It has already been noted in an earlier section that the restriction on trade union rights in export processing zones has been scrutinised by the

ILO Committee of Experts. This was done repeatedly in the case of Bangladesh which, ever since 1980, has denied the right to organise of workers in EPZ with the motivation that these temporary measures are "necessitated by the national situation, the level of development and the specific circumstances within Bangladesh". Moreover, the Committee observes that the national legislation which provides for the exemption of the zones from the enjoyment of the trade union rights "cannot be considered a 'temporary measure', in view of the fact that it was adopted in1980". The Committee on Economic, Social and Cultural Rights has discussed this in connection with the state report of Panama.

Even in cases where trade union rights are not formally restricted with respect to EPZ, the factual exercise of these rights might be limited due to informal restrictions put up by employers and ignorance among the workers of their rights. It has been shown in a number of studies that this often is the case in female dominated work places in EPZ where the majority of the workers are young and lack previous work experience.

The Human Rights Committee has raised this question in conjunction with the consideration of the state report of Mauritius. The Committee recommends that the Government will consider "whether workers in export processing zones (who include a majority of women) need additional legal protection to ensure their full enjoyment of their rights guaranteed by Article 22 of the Covenant". With respect to the report of the Dominican Republic, the Committee on Economic, Social and Cultural Rights has expressed concern that "workers in the free trade zones are allegedly discouraged from joining or forming trade unions and that the regulations concerning the right to strike in the Labour Code are not complied with by the employers". However, the treaty monitoring bodies do not seem to have addressed a possible obligation to promote trade unionisation, which could be important in order to reach the workers in EPZ.

This brings us to the second aspect of the instrumental rights, that is, the question of the existence of legal and other remedies in order to protect the rights. The CCPR explicitly stipulates that anyone whose rights are violated under the Covenant shall have access to an effective remedy. The CEDAW, on the other hand, provides that states parties undertake "to establish legal protection of the rights of women on an equal basis with men and to ensure through competent national tribunals and other public institutions the effective protection of women against any act of discrimination".

Even if the CESCR lacks an explicit reference to effective remedies, the Committee on Economic, Social and Cultural Rights has, in its General Comment No. 9 on domestic application of the Covenant, addressed the issue. The Committee states "the Covenant norms must be recognised within the domestic legal order, appropriate means of redress, or remedies, must be available to any aggrieved individual or group, and appropriate means of ensuring governmental accountability must be put in place". A part from judicial remedies, also administrative remedies may be utilised. However, the Committee observes that "there are some obligations, such as those concerning non–discrimination, in relation to which the provision of some form of judicial remedy would seem indispensable in order to satisfy the requirement of the Covenant".

In the case of work-related rights, where the alleged human rights violator is a private enterprise, the question of a functioning system of control and supervision of the application of labour standards becomes imperative. The Committee submits in connection with Guatemala's state report that "despite the Government's stated policy of undertaking further commitments to strengthen the labour inspectorate and introduce changes in the monitoring and enforcement of labour standards, including through the proposals on economic policy and labour legislation contained in recently signed agreements, the possibilities for ensuring effective implementation of the new proposals continue to give grounds for concern to the Committee".

With respect to the ILO system, the Convention No. 81 concerning Labour Inspection in Industry and Commerce has been singled out by the Governing Body of the ILO as one of the four so-called priority international labour standards. The Convention, which has been ratified by 128 states, regulates in considerable detail the function, organisation and operation of the labour inspectorate. The Committee of Experts has regularly addressed the problems linked to the insufficient number of inspectors and their inadequate means to carry out the tasks under the Convention effectively. In the case of Sri Lanka, the Committee has explicitly addressed the topic of labour inspection in export processing zones, by requesting information on the activities of the labour inspectorate in EPZ.

Feminization of Poverty

Statistical surveys have shown that the present globalisation trends have contributed to widening the gap between rich and poor both in comparisons between developed and developing countries as well as between different population groups within a single country. Furthermore, whereas the richest 20 % of all countries count for 68-86 % of the world's gross domestic product, exports of goods and services, and foreign direct investment, the poorest 20 % count for only 1 %. Not only has the gap between rich and poor countries grown, but the Human Development Index, which is applied in the Human Development Report, has for the first time since 1990 dropped for as many as 30 countries by the end of the decade. This indicates a growth in absolute poverty.

It is not possible in this study to comprehensively analyse how this development has influenced the lives of men and women living in poor countries. Only a few examples will be given. Firstly, many poor countries, which have opened up their markets for the global economy, have faced an increase in production costs, a growing competition on the local market and an overemphasis on export production at the expense of the production for the local market by local producers. Secondly, poor countries, which are dependent on borrowing money from international lending institutions, are usually required to implement structural adjustments programmes aimed at improving the country's overall economic performance.

Thirdly, it has been argued that the globalisation trends have contributed to the "feminisation of poverty". In some instances this concept has been used to describe the increase in the share of poverty among women. However, a commonly held view is that women and men experience poverty in different ways. The feminisation of poverty could from this perspective be used to highlight the greater hardships that women living in poverty usually face compared to men. This brings us to the definition of poverty. In earlier approaches, poverty was often seen as the lack of material commodities or of resources to acquire them. Today poverty is generally viewed in a broader perspective also referring to the capabilities required for achieving well-being.

The concept of poverty is not included in the international conventions on human rights. In the preamble of the Universal Declaration of Human Rights, reference is made to the "freedom from want" and in Article 28 to the entitlement of everyone "to a social and international order in which the rights and freedoms set forth in this Declaration can be fully realised".During the 1990s an increasing recognition of the link between poverty and human rights can be observed in the work of the United Nations. The Commission on Human Rights and the Sub-Commission have both increasingly emphasised a human rights-based approach to poverty. A number of special rapporteurs and independent experts have studied poverty-related issues, *inter alia*, structural adjustment, extreme poverty, income distribution, globalisation. The discussion both within academic circles and the United Nations is still very much in the beginning and there is no common understanding of poverty as a human rights issue.

The Committee on Economic, Social and Cultural Rights has in a statement on poverty outlined the normative dimensions of poverty eradication. It seems meaningful for our purpose to briefly depict the outcome of the Committee's deliberations. Furthermore, the Committee regrets that "human rights dimensions of poverty eradication policies rarely receive the attention they deserve", because, according to the Committee, "a human rights approach to poverty can reinforce anti-poverty strategies and make them more effective".

In defining poverty, the Committee adopts a broad understanding of the concept. Of interest is to note that the Committee advocates for a definition which strongly emphasises the indivisibility and interdependent nature of human rights. In other words, poverty reduction cannot successfully be implemented only by fulfilling basic needs through the provision of material resources, but requires that the poor are equipped with political and civil capabilities as well.

In the context of the Covenant on Economic, Social and Cultural Rights, the Committee identifies rights which are directly linked to the eradication of poverty. In addition, the Committee identifies non-discrimination, equality, participation and accountability as essential elements of a successful anti-poverty strategy. All these elements constitute central dimensions of a normative human rights framework. The rights to non-discrimination and equality address above all the rights of individuals and groups who are vulnerable, marginal, disadvantaged or socially excluded and are consequently of outmost relevance from a gender perspective. Participation refers to the right to take part in the conduct of public affairs at various societal levels. Most directly this concerns the right to take part in the formulation, implementation and monitoring of development undertakings aimed at improving the position of those affected. These remedies may be judicial, quasi-judicial, administrative or political.

The Committee on Economic, Social and Cultural Rights has not in detail elaborated the civil and political rights which are of direct relevance to the discussion on poverty and human rights. It has been argued in a recent discussion paper submitted by academic human rights experts to the High Commissioner for Human Rights that the rights to information, association, fair trial, liberty and security of persons as well as the prohibition against cruel, inhuman and degrading treatment should be included in a human rights based poverty reduction strategy.

Economic, Social and Cultural Rights

The poverty-related rights identified by the Committee on Economic, Social and Cultural Rights are the right to work, an adequate standard of living, housing, food, health and education. In order to guide the states parties in their implementation of these rights, the Committee has adopted general comments with respect to the right to adequate housing, plans of action for primary education, the right to adequate food, the right to education, and the right to the highest attainable standard of health. It is not possible within the ramifications of this study to analyse in depth the material content of these rights.

In accordance with Article 2 of the CESCR, "Each State Party ... undertakes to take steps, individually and through international assistance and cooperation, especially economic and technical, to the maximum of its available resources, with a view to achieving progressively the full realisation of the rights recognised in the present Covenant".In other words, the CESCR pays attention to the financial and other resources available and therefore accepts that the level to be attained and the timetable to be pursued may vary depending on each country's economic situation.

Even though a certain period of time is acceptable under the CESCR, it has been repeatedly stressed by the Committee on Economic, Social and Cultural Rights that there are elements of the various rights which require immediate realisation. Moreover, states parties are obliged immediately to "take steps" to implement the rights. As an example, in connection with the right to adequate housing, the Committee has established that the adoption of a national housing strategy and the implementation of an effective monitoring system require immediate action.

In its general comment on the nature of state parties' obligations, the Committee on Economic, Social and Cultural Rights has introduced the concept minimum core obligation, which covers a minimum level of obligations which have to be realised immediately. The Committee argues that without such a minimum core obligation the Covenant would be largely deprived of its *raison d'être*. In 1990 the Committee held that "in order for a state party to be able to attribute its failure to meet at least its minimum core obligations to a lack of available resources it must demonstrate that every effort has been made to use all resources that are at its disposition in an effort to satisfy, as a matter of priority, those minimum obligations". In the general comment on the right to the highest attainable standard of health it is stated that "a state party cannot, under any circumstances whatsoever, justify its non-compliance with the core obligations ...which are non-derogable".

Furthermore, the Committee has in its practice developed a restrictive stand on so-called retrogressive measures, that is, measures which lower an already attained level of human rights protection. A state party which adopts such measures deliberately has the burden of proving that "they have been introduced after the most careful consideration of all alternatives and that they are fully justified by reference to the totality of the rights provided for in the Covenant and in the context of the full use of the state party's maximum available resources". In connection with the general comment on the right to the highest attainable standard of health, the Committee further observes that "the adoption of any retrogressive measures incompatible with the core obligations under the right to health ... constitutes a violation of the right to health".

In order to exemplify what has been understood by minimum core obligations, it might be useful to briefly list some of them:

Right to adequate food:

i) The availability of food in a quantity and quality sufficient to satisfy the dietary needs of individuals, free from adverse substances, and acceptable within a given culture;

ii) The accessibility of such food in ways that are sustainable and that do not interfere with the enjoyment of other human rights.

Right to education:

i) To ensure the right of access to public educational institutions and programmes on a non-discriminatory basis;

ii) To ensure that education conforms to the objectives set out in article 13, paragraph 1;

iii) To provide primary education for all in accordance with article 13, paragraph 2(a);

iv) To adopt and implement a national educational strategy which includes provisions for secondary, higher and fundamental education;

v) To ensure free choice of education without interference from the state or third parties, subject to "conformity with minimum educational standards".

Right to the highest attainable standard of health:

i) To ensure the right of access to health facilities, goods and services on an non-discriminatory basis, especially for vulnerable and marginalised groups;

ii) To ensure access to the minimum essential food which is nutritionally adequate and safe, to ensure freedom from hunger to everyone;

iii) To ensure access to basic shelter, housing and sanitation, and an adequate supply of safe and potable water;

iv) To provide essential drugs, as from time to time defined under the WHO Action Programme on Essential Drugs;

v) To ensure equitable distribution of all health facilities, goods and services;

vi) To adopt and implement a national public health strategy and plan of action, on the basis of epidemological evidence, addressing the health concerns of the whole population; the strategy and plan of action shall be devised, and periodically reviewed, on the basis of a participatory and transparent process.

These minimum core obligations have in the poverty statement by the Committee on Economic, Social and Cultural Rights been defined as "an international minimum threshold that all development policies should be designed to respect".

Non–Discrimination and Equality

As indicated in the list of the minimum core obligation of the various economic, social and cultural rights, special attention is put on the right to non-discrimination and the realisation of the rights of vulnerable and marginalised groups. The strong emphasis on the realisation of the rights of disadvanteged groups clearly indicates that the implementation of the rights to non-discrimination and equal treatment require positive action on the part of the state. In fact the Committee on Economic, Social and Cultural Rights submits that "states parties must give due priority to those social groups living in unfavourable conditions by giving them particular consideration". When it comes to improving the position of women living in poverty it is evident that a formal right to equality with men to land, financial resources, services etc. will not guarantee that their position really improves. Instead also special measures are required.

With the exception of few provisions, the CESCR is gender neutral, thereby guaranteeing the same rights to both women and men. This is the case despite the fact that in some instances the text of the treaty reflects a stereotyped view on gender roles, which dominated at the time of the drafting of the treaty. The Committee on Economic, Social and Cultural Rights has observed that "the phrase cannot be read today as implying any limitations upon the applicability of the rights to individuals or to female-headed households or other such groups".

It is clear that many of the human rights problems faced by women living in poverty are not new problems, which can solely be attributed to globalisation trends. Instead discrimination and inequality, as an example, are often deeply rooted in the culture and in the customs of many developing countries. Particularly customary law is, as a rule, based on disparate gender roles within the family and society rather than on the idea of equality between men and women. Whereas customary norms at least to some extent provided protection to women in the traditional societies, they do not adequately address the current problems and needs of women in developing countries.This means that today discriminatory norms and practices, embedded either in statutory or customary law, can be detrimental to a woman's possibility to provide effective means of subsistence for herself, her children and family. This is particularly the case with regard to discriminatory practices in connection with property and ownership rights, which are essential for women's access to economic resources.

Even if women in international human rights law are viewed as a disadvantaged group, it should be kept in mind that there are huge differences between different groups of women. In this regard, special attention should be paid to the provision on rural women, which is included in the CEDAW.

i) To participate in the elaboration and implementation of development planningat all levels;

ii) To have access to adequate health care facilities, including information, counselling and services in family planning;

iii) To benefit directly from social security programmes;

iv) To obtain all types of training and education, formal and informal, including that relating to functional literacy, as well as, *inter alia*, the benefit of all community and extension services, in order to increase their technical proficiency;

v) To organise self-help groups and co-operatives in order to obtain equal access to economic opportunities through employment or self-employment;

vi) To participate in all community activities;

vii) To have access to agricultural credit and loans, marketing facilities, appropriate technology and equal treatment in land and agrarian reform as well as in land resettlement schemes;

viii) To enjoy adequate living conditions, particularly in relation to housing, sanitation, electricity and water supply, transport and communication".

This provision is highly interesting from a legal perspective. Not only are all appropriate measures required to eliminate discrimination against rural women, but these women shall, additionally, be ensured rights enumerated in (a)-(h). Whereas states parties under CEDAW generally are obliged to ensure rights "on equal terms with men", the equality phrase is less prominent in Article 14. The term "on a basis of equality of men and women" belongs to the first part of the sentence and is not repeated in the second part. The wording of the provision seems to indicate that a comparison with the corresponding rights of men is not necessary, but that the rural women are entitled to these rights *per se*.

The CEDAW Committee has not so far provided clear guidance on this point. Furthermore, at the time of drafting, it appears that the implication of the formulation of Article 14 (2) was not analysed in depth. Hence, the phrase "that they participate in and benefit from rural development and, in particular, shall ensure to such women the right", which divides paragraph

2 into two parts, was inserted in the end of the preparatory work by a working group which made final corrections in the draft before it was submitted for consideration by the Third Committee.

Participation

The concept of (popular) participation forms an integral part of any current discussion on development. It is generally held that a successful development undertaking requires the effective participation by those affected during every stage of the development process. In the past the concept of participation was often equated with the "mobilisation of people to undertake social and economic development projects", whereas today the emphasis, at least in theory, is on "the process of empowerment of the deprived and the excluded".

A cursory glance at the key human rights provisions shows that the main form of participation regulated in human rights law is the right to take part in the election of representatives to national decision-making bodies, that is, parliaments. Even if this form of participation is important also to women, it may be argued that in an effort to eradicate poverty other forms of participation become even more central.

At the outset it may be observed that there are fairly few provisions in legally binding instruments which regulate other participatory rights than electoral rights. The Human Rights Committee observes in its general comment that the phrase "conduct of public affairs" should be interpreted broadly, thereby including "the exercise of legislative, executive and administrative powers" as well as "all aspects of public administration, and the formulation and implementation of policy at international, national, regional and local levels". The CESCR contains an indirect reference to participatory rights by the stipulation that "education shall enable all persons to participate effectively in a free society". In other words, in order for this to take place some form of mechanisms for effective participation are required.

The participation of women is more comprehensively regulated in the CEDAW, that is, in Article 7 and, with respect to rural women, in Article 14. In addition to the same areas listed by the Human Rights Committee, the CEDAW Committee continues by stating that Article 7 also covers "many aspects of civil society, including public boards and local councils and the activities of organisations such as political parties, trade unions, professional or industry associations, women's organisations, community-based organisations and other organisations concerned with public and political life".

Characteristic of both Articles 25 of the CCPR and 7 of the CEDAW is that they do not require that the state parties establish certain forms of participation, but leaves this to the discretion of the respective state. Thus, the Human Rights Committee submits that "the allocation of powers and the means by which individual citizens exercise the right to participate in the conduct of public affairs protected by Article 25 should be established by the constitution and other laws". From a strictly legal perspective it seems that the only mode of participation which is explicitly required by Articles 7 and 25 is the participation in national decision-making through freely chosen representatives. However, it has been argued that a state obligation to promote additional forms of participation can be deduced from the above mentioned provisions.

This interpretation would be in line with Article 14 of the CEDAW which, as has been observed earlier, seems to contain a broader obligation on the part of the state to provide opportunities for rural women "to participate in the elaboration and implementation of development planning at all levels" and "to participate in all community activities". No further elaboration on how to organise rural women's participation in development is provided.

It seems evident that the mode of participation will vary not only depending on the political and administrative system of each state party but also on the societal level of application. At the local or village level, direct forms of participation, such as general meetings and interviews with members of the village can be appropriate means of participation. In this context representative decision-making and/or an administrative machinery might be more suitable.

Concerning the question of institutional mechanisms for integrating a gender perspective into policy- and decision-making, the CEDAW Committee has already in 1988 adopted a General Recommendation entitled effective national machinery and publicity. The Committee recommends that states parties "establish and/or strengthen effective national machinery, institutions and procedures, at a high level of Government, and with adequate resources, commitment and authority".

Feminization of Labor

The International Labor Organization estimates that there are between 80 and 100 million migrant workers in the world today. Women account for about half of these workers, and in some countries they make up more than half of all migrant workers. Indeed, many analysts— most notably the ILO— speak of the increasing feminization of migration. This feminization results from a number of worldwide forces in which gender roles and sex discrimination are intertwined with globalization. Trends contributing to this include: the growing demand for labor in fields dominated by women the lower cost of production when labor-intensive tasks are shifted to women migrant workers; and the sex-stereotyping of large business enterprises and governments that may see women as cheap, temporary, or supplemental laborers whose "docile" nature makes them easily exploitable.

Other forces are more regional. Women's widespread participation in the wage labor market in the North, when combined with global income disparities in the South and persisting demands article for Northern women to retain responsibility for household and child rearing tasks, has led to a dynamic in which Northern women's reproductive labor is transferred to women migrants working as domestics, whose reproductive labor is in turn shifted to family members or poor women at home. Other changes include short-term labor shortages in sectors dominated by women, and the increasing participation of women in the labor market in newly industrialized countries.

From the perspective of women seeking work, a wide variety of factors combine to make border-crossing an attractive, acceptable, or—in desperate circumstances—the only viable option. In countries where structural adjustment policies and privatization have been imposed, broad cuts to the public sector often have a disproportionate impact on women, who make up a sizable proportion, therefore, within the context of women's position within global labor markets and the intimate family setting." of the lower-level public sector jobs in many countries. Unemployment and cuts in social services may send such women abroad in search of new opportunities.

Most job opportunities for women migrants are in unregulated sectors, including domestic work, informal/"off the books" industries or services, and criminalized sectors, including the sex industry. This means that even women who cross borders legally may find themselves in unregulated—and often irregular—work situations. In addition, the majority of opportunities that offer legal channels of migration are in male-dominated sectors such as agriculture and construction work, putting women at a great disadvantage.

In sum, globalization has ushered in increasing "pull" and "push" factors for women's migration for labor at the same time as it has resulted in decreasing regulation of the labor market, growth in the informal sector, and the emergence of new forms of exploitation, many of which are gendered. In the midst of these trends, many governments are tightening migration controls while simultaneously allowing private employers and recruiting agencies to operate unchecked by regulation or inspection. For women in many parts of the world, these trends spell increased vulnerability to exploitation and abuse, while simultaneously presenting opportunities for empowerment.

Women's Vulnerability and Role of the State

Although the human rights system is in many ways limited by the single-variable framework described in the introduction, the system is also flexible enough to allow for alternative interpretive methodologies. Through intersectionality, human rights law can effectively be used by advocates to respond to the myriad aspects of women migrant workers' experience as multiply situated individuals. Further, human rights law can support carefully crafted responses to discrimination and exploitation that do not reinscribe women as "victims" in need of "protection." Since states have obligations under treaty law to end discrimination and exploitation carried out by "private" actors, governments' efforts to end abusive practices should reach employers and recruitment agencies.

Intersectionality and International Human Rights

Intersectionality should be situated within a family of analytical frameworks designed to explore how individuals' experiences and identities interact with forms of authority and discipline, including the law. Developed by scholars from around the world, the larger family of critical methodologies in which intersectionality finds its home includes such well-established schools of critique as subaltern studies, post colonialism, and a range of feminist inquiries in both the global North and South concerned with issues of identity and difference.

Briefly, intersectionality is an approach to combating discrimination in which the various forms of subordination that people face are taken into consideration as they act together. Instead of conceiving of a Filipina domestic worker, as separately or consecutively disadvantaged by gender and racial discrimination in the United States, intersectionality calls attention to the ways in which race and gender interact to create specific forms of discrimination and oppression. A Filipina migrant woman's experience of racism in the U.S. will be different than the racism experienced by a Filipino migrant man in the same location, and her experience of gender discrimination will differ from that of a native born American woman of any race; these differences are seen as crucially important by those using intersectional analysis, since they may require different remedial and preventive actions.

The version of intersectionality most familiar to North American legal audiences was formulated in the 1990s by critical race feminists. This American strand of intersectionality has since blended with other forms of intersectional analysis, and has been used and recrafted by scholars, advocates, and jurists in both North America and abroad. The concept of "multiple forms of discrimination" has even entered the language of U.N. documents. One of the most important instances is in the Declaration adopted at the United Nations World Conference Against Racism, Racial Discrimination, Xenophobia and Related Intolerance, which recognizes that those suffering racial discrimination often "suffer multiple or aggravated forms of discrimination based on other related grounds such as sex, language, religion, political or other opinion, social origin, property, birth or other status."

Some scholars have pointed out that when combined with various strands of critical race and anti-essentialist theory, intersectionality allows analysts to move beyond debates over the ontological "essence" of the myriad identity categories used by individuals, communities, and states, enabling analysis of identities instead as fluid and changeable. This transcendence could be especially valuable when examining identities that cross borders, since the conditions that construct and impact on those identities are likely to vary a great deal in different settings.

In recent years, a number of scholars have applied intersectionality analysis to international human rights norms and processes. In the course of her discussion, Crooms notes the ways in which the human rights system—built on treaties that address different forms of discrimination and different groupings of substantive rights—seems to resist intersectionality on an institutional level, while making space for it at a theoretical Level through the concept of indivisibility, which holds that all rights are equally important.

If applied holistically and robustly, Crooms concludes, human rights law can respond effectively to women's intersectional experiences of racism, sexism, and other forms of discrimination.

Similarly, Kimberle Crenshaw—a pioneer of intersectional analysis in relation to U.S. domestic law—has explored the ways in which "neither the gender aspects of racial discrimination nor the racial aspects of gender discrimination are fully comprehended within human rights discourses." Crenshaw recommends a number of specific steps that should be taken by the human rights community to implement intersectionality. The majority of her recommendations are institutional or procedural, ranging from improved disaggregation by gender and race of all statistics used in human rights monitoring to the appointment of a Special Rapporteur to develop greater awareness about the conditions of women of color and the convening of joint meetings by the CERD and CEDAW monitoring committees.

Building on this work, Johanna Bond has recently called for renewed attention to intersectionality in the international arena, and has identified specifically the need for both a "theoretical shift" toward using intersectionality, and institutional reforms aimed at encouraging intersectional analyses by the treaty bodies and other U.N. human rights mechanisms. When it comes to concrete proposals, Bond's focus is heavily on institutional reforms, with suggestions ranging from the drafting of General Recommendations and Comments that would promote intersectionality to the appointment by treaty committees of cross-treaty liaisons and the development of joint reports by the Special Rapporteurs on Violence Against Women and the Special Rapporteur on Racism and Xenophobia. She also points to the need for more scholarship that applies—rather than theorizing—intersectionality to human rights problems.

Although necessary, rooting an analysis of human rights violations in women's lived experiences is fraught with danger. As Ratna Kapur has explained, this kind of focus can lead to "victimization rhetoric," in which women—usually from the global South—are presented as nothing other than the sum of their vulnerability, abuse, and victimhood.Kapur explains that there are three main problems with this kind of approach:

i) It relies on gender essentialism, or "overgeneralized claims about women,"

ii) "It is a position based on cultural essentialism" in which "women in the Third World are portrayed as victims of their culture, which reinforces stereotyped and racist representations of that culture and privileges the culture of the West," and

iii) The rhetoric of victimization "has invited protectionist, and even conservative, responses from states" to violations of women's human rights.

Women migrant workers face abuses at the hands of government officials, as well as private individuals, companies, and other "non-state actors." This is true all along a migrant's trajectory of movement, as well as in her chosen place of work. For this reason, it is important to acknowledge the ways in which the human rights framework has evolved to respond to abuses that are carried out by agents other than the state.

Against a general backdrop in which human rights obligations were assumed to function as a check on state actions, a number of developments have emerged in the last several decades that can be said to have dramatically altered that orientation forever. First, as scholars of economic and social rights are quick to point out, human rights law was never really designed only to halt the abuses of the state. Through the development of the economic, social and cultural (ESC) rights regime, it has become clear that the state is not necessarily required to *provide* the goods needed to fulfill ESC rights. Private individuals and groups may provide food, water, shelter and work to people in various countries. The state, however, is recognized as obligated to ensure that (a) conditions are such that even the most marginalized and poor can access their subsistence rights in some way—whether through access to private schemes or through direct provision of goods by the state, and (b) when entrusting basic rights protections to the private sector, the state must regulate and monitor actions that could impinge on the rights of its people.

The second major development that clarified the affirmative duties of the state in the "private" sphere was the achievement, through the work of feminists in many parts of the world, of acceptance that abuses such as domestic violence, even when carried out in the most sacrosanct of spaces, constitute human rights violations. This means that the state is required to take steps to prevent such abuses, to punish them when they occur, and to provide remedies to those who have been injured.

This broad set of positive and negative obligations for both private and public conduct has been abbreviated in the human rights field into the three-part requirement that states must respect, protect, and fulfill rights. States must *respect* rights by ensuring that the state and its instrumentalities do not violate rights; *protect* rights by preventing violations by non-state actors and investigating, punishing, and redressing violations when they do occur; and *fulfill* rights by creating enabling conditions for all individuals to enjoy their full rights. In sum, then, in relation to both civil and political rights and economic, social and cultural rights, the state must ensure that conditions are such that all people enjoy all of their rights.

One additional note is necessary here: human rights norms and interpretive methodologies have not yet been adequately well developed to respond sufficiently to the varying capacities of different states in the context of global economic inequality. This is a glaring gap in human rights law, since it means that states in poor Southern countries technically have similar responsibilities to fulfill individuals' rights to adequate food and shelter, for example, as those in the North, even when Southern states' governments may be encumbered by debt and lack of infrastructure or resources. Work is being done to rectify this deficiency, through stronger application of the rule that states are bound only to the extent of their capability and by emphasizing the obligation to pursue international assistance and cooperation.

References

Johnsson, AB (1989). "The International Protection of Women Refugees: A Summary of Principal Problems and Issues." *International Journal of Refugee Law*, 221.

Peters, Julie and Andrea Wolper, eds. (1995). *Women's Rights, Human Rights.* Routledge, NY.

Romany, Celina (1993). "Women as Aliens: A Feminists Critique of the Public Private Distinction in International Human Rights Law." *Harvard Human Rights Journal*, 87(105).

Stark, Barbara (1991). "Nurturing Rights: An Essay on Women, Peace, and International Human Rights." *Michigan Journal of International Law*, 13:144.

Wali, Sima (1995). "Human Rights for Refugee and Displaced Women." In Peters and Wolper, eds. *Women's Rights, Human Rights.*

8

Convention on the Elimination of All Forms of Discrimination Against Women

The Universal Declaration of Human Rights, adopted in 1948, enshrines "the equal rights of men and women", and addressed both the equality and equity issues. In 1979 the United Nations General Assembly adopted the Convention on the Elimination of All Forms of Discrimination against Women (CEDAW). Described as an international bill of rights for women, it came into force on 3 September 1981. The seven UN member states that have not ratified the convention are Iran, Nauru, Palau, Somalia, Sudan, Tonga, and the United States. Niue and the Vatican City have also not signed it. The United States has signed, but not yet ratified.

The fulltext of the the Convention is goven below:

The States Parties to the present Convention,

Noting that the Charter of the United Nations reaffirms faith in fundamental human rights, in the dignity and worth of the human person and in the equal rights of men and women,

Noting that the Universal Declaration of Human Rights affirms the principle of the inadmissibility of discrimination and proclaims that all human beings are born free and equal in dignity and rights and that everyone is entitled to all the rights and freedoms set forth therein, without distinction of any kind, including distinction based on sex,

Noting that the States Parties to the International Covenants on Human Rights have the obligation to ensure the equal rights of men and women to enjoy all economic, social, cultural, civil and political rights,

Considering the international conventions concluded under the auspices of the United Nations and the specialized agencies promoting equality of rights of men and women,

Noting also the resolutions, declarations and recommendations adopted by the United Nations and the specialized agencies promoting equality of rights of men and women,

Concerned, however, that despite these various instruments extensive discrimination against women continues to exist,

Recalling that discrimination against women violates the principles of equality of rights and respect for human dignity, is an obstacle to the participation of women, on equal terms with men, in the political, social, economic and cultural life of their countries, hampers the growth of the prosperity of society and the family and makes more difficult the full development of the potentialities of women in the service of their countries and of humanity,

Concerned that in situations of poverty women have the least access to food, health, education, training and opportunities for employment and other needs,

Convinced that the establishment of the new international economic order based on equity and justice will contribute significantly towards the promotion of equality between men and women,

Emphasizing that the eradication of apartheid, all forms of racism, racial discrimination, colonialism, neo–colonialism, aggression, foreign occupation and domination and interference in the internal affairs of States is essential to the full enjoyment of the rights of men and women,

Affirming that the strengthening of international peace and security, the relaxation of international tension, mutual cooperation among all States irrespective of their social and economic systems, general and complete disarmament, in particular nuclear disarmament under strict and effective international control, the affirmation of the principles of justice, equality and mutual benefit in relations among countries and the realization of the right of peoples under alien and colonial domination and foreign occupation to self-determination and independence, as well as respect for national sovereignty and territorial integrity, will promote social progress and development and as a consequence will contribute to the attainment of full equality between men and women,

Convinced that the full and complete development of a country, the welfare of the world and the cause of peace require the maximum participation of women on equal terms with men in all fields,

Bearing in mind the great contribution of women to the welfare of the family and to the development of society, so far not fully recognized, the social significance of maternity and the role of both parents in the family and in the upbringing of children, and aware that the role of women in procreation should not be a basis for discrimination but that the upbringing of children requires a sharing of responsibility between men and women and society as a whole,

Aware that a change in the traditional role of men as well as the role of women in society and in the family is needed to achieve full equality between men and women,

Determined to implement the principles set forth in the Declaration on the Elimination of Discrimination against Women and, for that purpose, to adopt the measures required for the elimination of such discrimination in all its forms and manifestations,

Have agreed on the following:

Part I

Article 1

For the purposes of the present Convention, the term "discrimination against women" shall mean any distinction, exclusion or restriction made on the basis of sex which has the effect or purpose of impairing or nullifying the recognition, enjoyment or exercise by women, irrespective of their marital status, on a basis of equality of men and women, of human rights and fundamental freedoms in the political, economic, social, cultural, civil or any other field.

Article 2

States Parties condemn discrimination against women in all its forms, agree to pursue by all appropriate means and without delay a policy of eliminating discrimination against women and, to this end, undertake:

1) To embody the principle of the equality of men and women in their national constitutions or other appropriate legislation if not yet incorporated therein and to ensure, through law and other appropriate means, the practical realization of this principle;
2) To adopt appropriate legislative and other measures, including sanctions where appropriate, prohibiting all discrimination against women;
3) To establish legal protection of the rights of women on an equal basis with men and to ensure through competent national tribunals and other public institutions the effective protection of women against any act of discrimination;
4) To refrain from engaging in any act or practice of discrimination against women and to ensure that public authorities and institutions shall act in conformity with this obligation;
5) To take all appropriate measures to eliminate discrimination against women by any person, organization or enterprise;
6) To take all appropriate measures, including legislation, to modify or abolish existing laws, regulations, customs and practices which constitute discrimination against women;
7) To repeal all national penal provisions which constitute discrimination against women.

Article 3

States Parties shall take in all fields, in particular in the political, social, economic and cultural fields, all appropriate measures, including legislation, to en sure the full development and advancement of women, for the purpose of guaranteeing them the exercise and enjoyment of human rights and fundamental freedoms on a basis of equality with men.

Article 4

1) Adoption by States Parties of temporary special measures aimed at accelerating de facto equality between men and women shall not be considered discrimination as defined in the present Convention, but shall in no way entail as a consequence the maintenance of unequal or separate standards; these measures shall be discontinued when the objectives of equality of opportunity and treatment have been achieved.

2) Adoption by States Parties of special measures, including those measures contained in the present Convention, aimed at protecting maternity shall not be considered discriminatory.

Article 5

States Parties shall take all appropriate measures:

1) To modify the social and cultural patterns of conduct of men and women, with a view to achieving the elimination of prejudices and customary and all other practices which are based on the idea of the inferiority or the superiority of either of the sexes or on stereotyped roles for men and women;

2) To ensure that family education includes a proper understanding of maternity as a social function and the recognition of the common responsibility of men and women in the upbringing and development of their children, it being understood that the interest of the children is the primordial consideration in all cases.

Article 6

States Parties shall take all appropriate measures, including legislation, to suppress all forms of traffic in women and exploitation of prostitution of women.

PART II

Article 7

States Parties shall take all appropriate measures to eliminate discrimination against women in the political and public life of the country and, in particular, shall ensure to women, on equal terms with men, the right:

1) To vote in all elections and public referenda and to be eligible for election to all publicly elected bodies;

2) To participate in the formulation of government policy and the implementation thereof and to hold public office and perform all public functions at all levels of government;

3) To participate in non-governmental organizations and associations concerned with the public and political life of the country.

Article 8

States Parties shall take all appropriate measures to ensure to women, on equal terms with men and without any discrimination, the opportunity to represent their Governments at the international level and to participate in the work of international organizations.

Article 9

1) States Parties shall grant women equal rights with men to acquire, change or retain their nationality. They shall ensure in particular that neither marriage to an alien nor change of nationality by the husband during marriage shall automatically change the nationality of the wife, render her stateless or force upon her the nationality of the husband.
2) States Parties shall grant women equal rights with men with respect to the nationality of their children.

Part III

Article 10

States Parties shall take all appropriate measures to eliminate discrimination against women in order to ensure to them equal rights with men in the field of education and in particular to ensure, on a basis of equality of men and women:

1) The same conditions for career and vocational guidance, for access to studies and for the achievement of diplomas in educational establishments of all categories in rural as well as in urban areas; this equality shall be ensured in preschool, general, technical, professional and higher technical education, as well as in all types of vocational training;
2) Access to the same curricula, the same examinations, teaching staff with qualifications of the same standard and school premises and equipment of the same quality;
3) The elimination of any stereotyped concept of the roles of men and women at all levels and in all forms of education by encouraging coeducation and other types of education which will help to achieve this aim and, in particular, by the revision of textbooks and school programmes and the adaptation of teaching methods;
4) The same opportunities to benefit from scholarships and other study grants;
5) The same opportunities for access to programmes of continuing education, including adult and functional literacy programmes,

particularly those aimed at reducing, at the earliest possible time, any gap in education existing between men and women;

6) The reduction of female student dropout rates and the organization of programmes for girls and women who have left school prematurely;

7) The same Opportunities to participate actively in sports and physical education;

8) Access to specific educational information to help to ensure the health and well-being of families, including information and advice on family planning.

Article 11

1) States Parties shall take all appropriate measures to eliminate discrimination against women in the field of employment in order to ensure, on a basis of equality of men and women, the same rights, in particular:

    (a) The right to work as an inalienable right of all human beings;

    (b) The right to the same employment opportunities, including the application of the same criteria for selection in matters of employment;

    (c) The right to free choice of profession and employment, the right to promotion, job security and all benefits and conditions of service and the right to receive vocational training and retraining, including apprenticeships, advanced vocational training and recurrent training;

    (d) The right to equal remuneration, including benefits, and to equal treatment in respect of work of equal value, as well as equality of treatment in the evaluation of the quality of work;

    (e) The right to social security, particularly in cases of retirement, unemployment, sickness, invalidity and old age and other incapacity to work, as well as the right to paid leave;

    (f) The right to protection of health and to safety in working conditions, including the safeguarding of the function of reproduction.

2) In order to prevent discrimination against women on the grounds of marriage or maternity and toensure their effective right to work, States Parties shall take appropriate measures:

(a) To prohibit, subject to the imposition of sanctions, dismissal on the grounds of pregnancy or of maternity leave and discrimination in dismissals on the basis of marital status;

(b) To introduce maternity leave with pay or with comparable social benefits without loss of former employment, seniority or social allowances;

(c) To encourage the provision of the necessary supporting social services to enable parents to combine family obligations with work responsibilities and participation in public life, in particular through promoting the establishment and development of a network of child-care facilities;

(d) To provide special protection to women during pregnancy in types of work proved to be harmful to them.

3) Protective legislation relating to matters covered in this article shall be reviewed periodically in thelight of scientific and technological knowledge and shall be revised, repealed or extended as necessary.

Article 12

1) States Parties shall take all appropriate measures to eliminate discrimination against women in the field of health care in order to ensure, on a basis of equality of men and women, access to health care services, including those related to family planning.

2) Not with standing the provisions of paragraph I of this article, States Parties shall ensure to women appropriate services in connection with pregnancy, confinement and the postnatal period, granting free services where necessary, as well as adequate nutrition during pregnancy and lactation.

Article 13

States Parties shall take all appropriate measures to eliminate discrimination against women in other areas of economic and social life in order to ensure, on a basis of equality of men and women, the same rights, in particular:

1) The right to family benefits;

2) The right to bank loans, mortgages and other forms of financial credit;

3) The right to participate in recreational activities, sports and all aspects of cultural life.

Article 14

1) States Parties shall take into account the particular problems faced by rural women and the significant roles which rural women play in the economic survival of their families, including their work in the non-monetized sectors of the economy, and shall take all appropriate measures to ensure the application of the provisions of the present Convention to women in rural areas.

2) States Parties shall take all appropriate measures to eliminate discrimination against women in rural areas in order to ensure, on a basis of equality of men and women, that they participate in and benefit from rural development and, in particular, shall ensure to such women the right:

   a) To participate in the elaboration and implementation of development planning at all levels;

   b) To have access to adequate health care facilities, including information, counselling and services in family planning;

   c) To benefit directly from social security programmes;

   d) To obtain all types of training and education, formal and non-formal, including that relating to functional literacy, as well as, inter alia, the benefit of all community and extension services, in order to increase their technical proficiency;

   e) To organize self-help groups and co–operatives in order to obtain equal access to economic opportunities through employment or self employment;

   f) To participate in all community activities;

   g) To have access to agricultural credit and loans, marketing facilities, appropriate technology and equal treatment in land and agrarian reform as well as in land resettlement schemes;

   h) To enjoy adequate living conditions, particularly in relation to housing, sanitation, electricity and water supply, transport and communications.

Part IV

Article 15

1) States Parties shall accord to women equality with men before the law.

2) States Parties shall accord to women, in civil matters, a legal capacity identical to that of men and the same opportunities to exercise that capacity. In particular, they shall give women equal rights to conclude contracts and to administer property and shall treat them equally in all stages of procedure in courts and tribunals.

3) States Parties agree that all contracts and all other private instruments of any kind with a legal effect which is directed at restricting the legal capacity of women shall be deemed null and void.

4) States Parties shall accord to men and women the same rights with regard to the law relating to the movement of persons and the freedom to choose their residence and domicile.

Article 16

1) States Parties shall take all appropriate measures to eliminate discrimination against women in all matters relating to marriage and family relations and in particular shall ensure, on a basis of equality of men and women:

    a) The same right to enter into marriage;

    b) The same right freely to choose a spouse and to enter into marriage only with their free and full consent;

    c) The same rights and responsibilities during marriage and at its dissolution;

    d) The same rights and responsibilities as parents, irrespective of their marital status, in matters relating to their children; in all cases the interests of the children shall be paramount;

    e) The same rights to decide freely and responsibly on the number and spacing of their children and to have access to the information, education and means to enable them to exercise these rights;

    f) The same rights and responsibilities with regard to guardianship, wardship, trusteeship and adoption of children, or similar institutions where these concepts exist in national legislation; in all cases the interests of the children shall be paramount;

    g) The same personal rights as husband and wife, including the right to choose a family name, a profession and an occupation;

h) The same rights for both spouses in respect of the ownership, acquisition, management, administration, enjoyment and disposition of property, whether free of charge or for a valuable consideration.

2) The betrothal and the marriage of a child shall have no legal effect, and all necessary action, including legislation, shall be taken to specify a minimum age for marriage and to make the registration of marriages in an official registry compulsory.

PART V

Article 17

1) For the purpose of considering the progress made in the implementation of the present Convention, there shall be established a Committee on the Elimination of Discrimination against Women (hereinafter referred to as the Committee) consisting, at the time of entry into force of the Convention, of eighteen and, after ratification of or accession to the Convention by the thirty–fifth State Party, of twenty–three experts of high moral standing and competence in the field covered by the Convention. The experts shall be elected by States Parties from among their nationals and shall serve in their personal capacity, consideration being given to equitable geographical distribution and to the representation of the different forms of civilization as well as the principal legal systems.

2) The members of the Committee shall be elected by secret ballot from a list of persons nominated by States Parties. Each State Party may nominate one person from among its own nationals.

3) The initial election shall be held six months after the date of the entry into force of the present Convention. At least three months before the date of each election the Secretary–General of the United Nations shall address a letter to the States Parties inviting them to submit their nominations within two months. The Secretary–General shall prepare a list in alphabetical order of all persons thus nominated, indicating the States Parties which have nominated them, and shall submit it to the States Parties.

4) Elections of the members of the Committee shall be held at a meeting of States Parties convened by the Secretary-General at United Nations

Headquarters. At that meeting, for which two thirds of the States Parties shall constitute a quorum, the persons elected to the Committee shall be those nominees who obtain the largest number of votes and an absolute majority of the votes of the representatives of States Parties present and voting.

5) The members of the Committee shall be elected for a term of four years. However, the terms of nine of the members elected at the first election shall expire at the end of two years; immediately after the first election the names of these nine members shall be chosen by lot by the Chairman of the Committee.

6) The election of the five additional members of the Committee shall be held in accordance with the provisions of paragraphs 2, 3 and 4 of this article, following the thirty-fifth ratification or accession. The terms of two of the additional members elected on this occasion shall expire at the end of two years, the names of these two members having been chosen by lot by the Chairman of the Committee.

7) For the filling of casual vacancies, the State Party whose expert has ceased to function as a member of the Committee shall appoint another expert from among its nationals, subject to the approval of the Committee.

8) The members of the Committee shall, with the approval of the General Assembly, receive emoluments from United Nations resources on such terms and conditions as the Assembly may decide, having regard to the importance of the Committee's responsibilities.

9) The Secretary-General of the United Nations shall provide the necessary staff and facilities for the effective performance of the functions of the Committee under the present Convention.

Article 18

1) States Parties undertake to submit to the Secretary–General of the United Nations, for consideration by the Committee, a report on the legislative, judicial, administrative or other measures which they have adopted to give effect to the provisions of the present Convention and on the progress made in this respect:

   a) Within one year after the entry into force for the State concerned;

b) Thereafter at least every four years and further whenever the Committee so requests.

2. Reports may indicate factors and difficulties affecting the degree of fulfilment of obligations under the present Convention.

Article 19

1) The Committee shall adopt its own rules of procedure.

2) The Committee shall elect its officers for a term of two years.

Article 20

1) The Committee shall normally meet for a period of not more than two weeks annually in order to consider the reports submitted in accordance with article 18 of the present Convention.

2) The meetings of the Committee shall normally be held at United Nations Headquarters or at any other convenient place as determined by the Committee.

Article 21

1) The Committee shall, through the Economic and Social Council, report annually to the General Assembly of the United Nations on its activities and may make suggestions and general recommendations based on the examination of reports and information received from the States Parties. Such suggestions and general recommendations shall be included in the report of the Committee together with comments, if any, from States Parties.

2) The Secretary-General of the United Nations shall transmit the reports of the Committee to the Commission on the Status of Women for its information.

Article 22

The specialized agencies shall be entitled to be represented at the consideration of the implementation of such provisions of the present Convention as fall within the scope of their activities. The Committee may invite the specialized agencies to submit reports on the implementation of the Convention in areas falling within the scope of their activities.

Part VI

Article 23

Nothing in the present Convention shall affect any provisions that are more conducive to the achievement of equality between men and women which may be contained:

1) In the legislation of a State Party; or
2) In any other international convention, treaty or agreement in force for that State.

Article 24

States Parties undertake to adopt all necessary measures at the national level aimed at achieving the full realization of the rights recognized in the present Convention.

Article 25

1) The present Convention shall be open for signature by all States.
2) The Secretary-General of the United Nations is designated as the depositary of the present Convention.
3) The present Convention is subject to ratification. Instruments of ratification shall be deposited with the Secretary-General of the United Nations.
4) The present Convention shall be open to accession by all States. Accession shall be effected by the deposit of an instrument of accession with the Secretary-General of the United Nations.

Article 26

1) A request for the revision of the present Convention may be made at any time by any State Party by means of a notification in writing addressed to the Secretary-General of the United Nations.
2) The General Assembly of the United Nations shall decide upon the steps, if any, to be taken in respect of such a request.

Article 27

1) The present Convention shall enter into force on the thirtieth day after the date of deposit with the Secretary General of the United Nations of the twentieth instrument of ratification or accession.

2) For each State ratifying the present Convention or acceding to it after the deposit of the twentieth instrument of ratification or accession, the Convention shall enter into force on the thirtieth day after the date of the deposit of its own instrument of ratification or accession.

Article 28

1) The Secretary General of the United Nations shall receive and circulate to all States the text of reservations made by States at the time of ratification or accession.
2) A reservation incompatible with the object and purpose of the present Convention shall not be permitted.
3) Reservations may be withdrawn at any time by notification to this effect addressed to the Secretary–General of the United Nations, who shall then inform all States thereof. Such notification shall take effect on the date on which it is received.

Article 29

1) Any dispute between two or more States Parties concerning the interpretation or application of the present Convention which is not settled by negotiation shall, at the request of one of them, be submitted to arbitration. If within six months from the date of the request for arbitration the parties are unable to agree on the organization of the arbitration, any one of those parties may refer the dispute to the International Court of Justice by request in conformity with the Statute of the Court.
2) Each State Party may at the time of signature or ratification of the present Convention or accession thereto declare that it does not consider itself bound by paragraph I of this article. The other States Parties shall not be bound by that paragraph with respect to any State Party which has made such a reservation.
3) Any State Party which has made a reservation in accordance with paragraph 2 of this article may at any time withdraw that reservation by notification to the Secretary–General of the United Nations.

Article 30

The present Convention, the Arabic, Chinese, English, French, Russian and Spanish texts of which are equally authentic, shall be deposited with the Secretary General of the United Nations. In witness where of the undersigned, duly authorized, have signed the present Convention.

Bibliography

Agarwal, Bina. 1994. "Gender and Command over Property: A Critical Gap in Economic Analysis and Policy in South Asia." *World Development* 22(10): 1455-1478.

Allendorf, Keera. 2007. Do Women's Land Rights Promote Empowerment and Child Health in Nepal? *World Development* 35(11): 1975-1988.

Amnesty International (1991). *Women in the Frontline: Human Rights Violations Against Women.* Amnesty International, NY.

Besley, T., and M. Ghatak. 2009. "Property Rights and Economic Development," in *Handbook of Development Economics,* ed. By D. Rodrik, and M. Rosenzweig. North Holland.

Blundell, Sue (1995). *Women in ancient Greece*, Volume 2.. Harvard University Press. p. 224.

Bunch, Charlotte (1995). "The Global Campaign for Women's Human Rights: Where Next After Vienna?" *St. John's Law Review*, 69(1-2):171-178.

Chang, Das (1987). "Violence against Women in the family: a national and international perspective." *International Journal of Comparative & Applied Criminal Justice*, 11:153-7.

Charo, R. Alta (1995). "Women's Health and Human Rights: The Promotion and Protection of Women's Health Through International Human Rights Law." *Journal of Law, Medicine & Ethics* v23, n2 (Summer, 1995):195-198.

Cook, Rebecca (1995). "International Human Rights and Women's Reproductive Health." *Studies in Family Planning*, 24,73.

DuBois, Ellen Carol. (1997). *Harriot Stanton Blatch and the Winning of Woman Suffrage* (New Haven and London: Yale University Press.

Elder, Betty G. (1986). "The Rights of Women: Their Status in International Law." *Crime and Social Justice*; 1986, 25, 1-39.

Freeman, Marsha A.(1994). "Women, law, and land at the local level: claiming women's human rights in domestic legal systems." *Human Rights Quarterly* v16, n3 (August, 1994):559-575.

Gender Promotion Programme, (2003). *Preventing Discrimination, Exploitation and Abuse of Women Migrant Workers: An Information Guide: Why the Focus on Women International Migrant Workers.* International Labor Organization.

Gerhard, Ute (2001). *Debating women's equality: toward a feminist theory of law from a European perspective*. Rutgers University Press. p. 33.

Grace Chang, (2000). *Disposable Domestics: Immigrant Women Workers in the Global Economy*. South End Press.

International Catholic Migration Commission (ICMC), (2004). *How to Strengthen Protection of Migrant Workers and Members of their Families with International Human Rights Treaties*. ICMC.

Joan Fitzpatrick & Katrina R. Kelly, (1998). "Gendered Aspects of Migration: Law and the Female Migrant," 22 *Hastings Law Review* 47.

Johnsson, AB (1989). "The International Protection of Women Refugees: A Summary of Principal Problems and Issues." *International Journal of Refugee Law*, 221.

Lauren, Paul Gordon (2003). *The evolution of international human rights: visions seen*. University of Pennsylvania Press. pp. 29 & 30.

Lederman, Joanne; Chow, Esther Ngan ling (1996). *Gender-Based Violence and International Human Rights: Women Claim Their Humanity*. American Sociological Association Paper, Washington, DC.

Lloyd, Trevor, (1971). *Suffragettes International: The Worldwide Campaign for Women's Rights* New York: American Heritage Press,

Lowry, D. (1997) 'White woman's' country: Ethel Tawse Jollie and the Making of White Rhodesia, Journal of Southern African Studies, 23(2), pp. 259–281.

Mackenzie, Midge, (1975), *Shoulder to Shoulder: A Documentary*. New York: Alfred A. Knopf,

Macklin, Ruth (1993). "Women's health: an ethical perspective." (Proceedings of the Third International Conference on Health Law and Ethics) *Journal of Law, Medicine & Ethics* v21, n1 (Spring, 1993):23-29.

Nelson, Toni (1996). "Violence against women." *World Watch* v9, n4 (July-August, 1996):33.

O'Neill, Onora (1990). "Justice, gender and international boundaries." *British Journal of Political Science* v20, n4 (Oct, 1990):439.

Panda, Pradeep and Bina Agarwal. 2005. *Marital violence, human development and women's property status in India*. World Development 33(5): 823-850.

Peters, Julie and Andrea Wolper, eds. (1995). *Women's Rights, Human Rights*. Routledge, NY.

Pomeroy, Sarah B. (2002). *Spartan Women*. Oxford: Oxford University Press.

Raeburn, Antonia. (1973). *Militant Suffragettes*. London: New English Library.

Romany, Celina (1993). "Women as Aliens: A Feminists Critique of the Public Private Distinction in International Human Rights Law." *Harvard Human Rights Journal*, 87(105).

Stairs, Felicite & Lori Pope (1990). "No Place Like Home: Assaulted Migrant Women's Claims to Refugee Status." *Journal of Law and Social Policy*, 148.

Stark, Barbara (1991). "Nurturing Rights: An Essay on Women, Peace, and International Human Rights." *Michigan Journal of International Law*, 13:144.

Steinzor, Nadia. 2003. "Women's Property and Inheritance Rights: Improving Lives in a Changing Time." Development Alternatives, Inc.

Stevens, Doris, edited by Carol O'Hare, (1920). *Jailed for Freedom: American Women Win the Vote* Troutdale, OR: NewSage Press.

Sullivan, Donna (1994). "Women's Human Rights and the 1993 World Conference on Human Rights." *American University Journal of International Law and Policy*, 152.

Taylor, Allyn (1992). "Making the World Health Organization Work: A Legal Framework for Universal Access to the Conditions for Health." *American Journal of Law and Medicine*, 301, 305.

Teson, Fernando (1993). "Feminism and International Law: A Reply." *Virginia Journal of International Law*, 647-84.

Thomas, Dorothy (1995). "Women's Human Rights: From Visibility to Accountability." *St. John's Law Review*, 69(1-2):217-230.

United Nations *Convention on the Elimination of All Forms of Discrimination against Women*: Introduction.

Van Bueren, Geraldine (1995). "The international protection of family members' rights as the 21st century approaches." *Human Rights Quarterly* v17, n4 (Nov, 1995):732-765.

Wali, Sima (1995). "Human Rights for Refugee and Displaced Women." In Peters and Wolper, eds. *Women's Rights, Human Rights*.

Warren, Priscilla (1994). "Women are Human: Gender-Based Persecution is a Human Rights Violation Against Women." *Hastings Women's Law Journal*, 5:2.

Walters, Margaret, (2005). *Feminism: A very short introduction*. Oxford.

Wheeler, Marjorie Spruill, ed., (1995). *One Woman, One Vote: Rediscovering the Woman Suffrage Movement*, Troutdale, OR: NewSage Press.

Wright, Shelley (1992). "Economic Rights and Social Justice: A Feminist Analysis of Some Human Rights Conventions." *Australian Yearbook of International Law*, 12,242.